Moving On From Community Care

The treatment, care and support
of older people in England

Lorna Easterbrook

BOOKS

D0227120

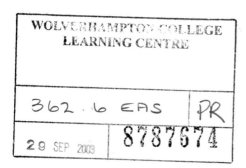
© 2003 Age Concern England
Published by Age Concern England
1268 London Road
London SW16 4ER

First published 2003

Editors Sue Henning and Richenda Milton-Thompson
Production Vinnette Marshall
Designed and typesetting GreenGate Publishing Services
Printed and bound in Great Britain by Bell & Bain Ltd, Glasgow

A catalogue record for this book is available from the British Library

ISBN 0-86242-348-1

Bulk orders
Age Concern England is pleased to offer customised edition of all its titles to UK
companies, institutions or other organisations wishing to make a bulk purchase. For
further information, please contact the Publishing Department at the address on this
page. Tel: 020 8765 7200. Fax: 020 8765 7211. Email: books@ace.org.uk

Contents

Dedication

This book is dedicated, with much affection and thanks, to the late Evelyn McEwen, Director of Information and Policy at Age Concern England, 1988–1999.

About the author

Lorna Easterbrook began working with and for older people as a theatre stage manager taking productions into old people's homes, long-stay hospital wards and community settings. She spent ten years working in the voluntary sector – for a Care and Repair Home Improvement Agency, Age Concern England, and the King's Fund where she was Fellow in Community Care. Since 2000, she has worked as an independent consultant on service development, policy analysis and research into older people's health, housing and social care services with local social services departments, NHS organisations, universities and charities. She is the author and co-author of several publications, and Editor of the quarterly journal, *Working With Older People* (Pavilion).

Aside from her stint training in the theatre (Welsh College of Music and Drama), Lorna has degrees in Archaeology and Prehistory (University of Sheffield) and Social Policy and Planning (London School of Economics).

Acknowledgements

A number of people have been involved in the production of this book, whether with layout, editing, comments or general support. Thanks must go to staff at Age Concern England – particularly to Vinnette Marshall and Donna Pearce, who helped with typing early drafts and with diagrams; to Sue Henning for early involvement in the editing process; and to Christine Watts for assistance with library matters. Helena Herklots, Head of Policy at Age Concern, played an important role, as did four of Age Concern's Policy Officers – Stephen Boyo, Stephen Lowe, Pauline Thompson and Michaela Willmott – in helping to confirm the accuracy of the contents. Tracey Rhoose and Sarah Mitchell very kindly acted as external reviewers; and the important later editorial stages were greatly assisted by the skills and experience of Richenda Milton-Thompson.

Despite this tremendous input, ultimate responsibility for factual accuracy and for any opinions expressed in the book lies with me.

It is sometimes easy to forget that there are others who support authors in more personal ways, although such authors may find they receive less generous birthday presents as a result. Although these acknowledgements tend to be of interest only to the author and those directly concerned, nonetheless it is important that they also be thanked. A large number of friends provided huge support, asking about the progress of the book well beyond the stage when they would have been forgiven for being bored by the whole process. *They know who they are.* Essential, emergency, housekeeping services were provided by my mum, Brenda, during a particularly fraught fortnight of changed deadlines, writing crises and a house move. Unfortunately for other authors in similar situations, this is not something she is willing to repeat.

The one dissenting view was expressed by the cat, whose failure to comprehend why I was hunched over a computer instead of paying him any attention manifested itself by his leaving wet paw prints over several piles of papers (fortunately, all belonging to me) – meaning that, in one household at least, there are some pieces of legislation whose name really is mud.

I hope this book is helpful, is easy to read and understand, and provides some clarity in an ever-changing policy and practice world. My very best wishes go to all of those who experience – in whatever way – the treatment, care and support of older people, now and in the future.

Lorna Easterbrook
August 2002

Foreword

The community care reforms of the 1990s brought about major changes in the ways health, housing and social services organisations provided services for different client groups. As the largest group who receive health and social care, older people were particularly affected by these reforms. At the heart of community care were concerns to support older people living in their own homes for as long as possible, and to ensure that those who could not remain at home received appropriate, good quality care.

Reading *Moving on from Community Care*, it is clear how much has changed even in the last decade. Not least is the extent to which older people's voices, describing what they need, are increasingly being heard and responded to through measures to promote good health, and maintain independence.

The National Service Framework for Older People reflects the concerns of many different individuals and organisations, to continue to improve services for older people. It sets out a comprehensive ten-year strategy for specialised and general services, in order to ensure that older people and their families and friends are always treated fairly, and with respect.

All of those who work with older people want to make sure that, as far as possible, older people remain healthy and well; but that, when health is affected, the highest quality of standards from both staff and services is received. One of the major aspects to ensuring improvements continue to be made is for older people, and those working with and caring for them, to be fully informed of new developments, requirements, expectations and rights. Without this knowledge, it can become easy for poor practices and experiences to continue unchallenged. *Moving on from Community Care* provides a clear account of what has been changing and why. It helps to explain, simply but carefully, the sometimes-complex policy areas and initiatives that are intended to ensure further improvement, and will necessitate some more change. I believe it will be as welcomed by those who are new to the topic, as it will by more experienced staff, academics, politicians and, perhaps most importantly, older people; and will be a central reference tool for all who are involved in securing high quality, integrated health, housing and social care services for older people.

Professor Ian Philp
National Director for Older People, Department of Health
October 2002

Introduction

On April 1, 1993, under the NHS and Community Care Act 1990, the community care reforms came into effect. The Act brought about a wide range of changes, including the establishment of General Practice (GP) fundholding services and new complaints systems for local authorities. It established local units to register and inspect independent sector residential and nursing homes, created additional rights for individuals to gain access to social care services, changed the system of state funding for residential care, and introduced different relationships between health and social services bodies.

A decade later, many of these changes have been replaced. Primary Care Groups and Primary Care Trusts have superseded GP fundholding practices; the purchaser/provider split has been replaced with new funding partnerships and revised commissioning arrangements; health and local authority inspection units for care homes have been abolished, and their place taken by a nationally based Care Standards Commission. Other elements – such as rights to assessment, funding and services, and systems of paying for care – have also undergone significant change. In short, the community care reforms have been reformed.

These changes in health, housing and social care services have, for the most part, taken place under the two Labour Governments elected since 1997. Many more changes are expected through the early years of the 21st century. This is not a matter simply of new legislation – although the amount and extent of legislative change should not be underestimated. Nor is it only a question of the speed of reform or what appears, at times, to be an ever-developing agenda for reform. These changes have been rapid, complex, multi-layered, constant, ongoing and – in the context of *The NHS Plan*, published in 2000 – will not be completed until 2010.

In the book, we make the distinction between previous governments (those that are no longer in power), central government (the wider machinery of Whitehall) and the Government (the enacting body comprising members of the Cabinet and Ministers of State) that is current at the time of writing. The aim here is to make the timing of policy changes clearer to the reader.

Other changes have also taken place since 1993. In particular, many important legal actions have given rise to case law that has appreciably affected our understanding of the powers and duties of local authorities and the NHS to provide services.

One of the singular attractions of the NHS and Community Care Act 1990 was that it brought together under one Act of Parliament seemingly disparate pieces of legislation, developed over many years, which affected the health and well-being of many people in the UK – including some of the most ill and vulnerable. Since 1993, however, this one Act has become many, including six new Acts introduced in just three years (1999–2001), outlining key changes to the systems of health, housing and social care of older people.

The key Acts of Parliament implemented since 1993 are:

- Carers (Recognition and Services) Act 1995;
- Disability Discrimination Act 1995;
- Community Care (Direct Payments) Act 1996;
- Human Rights Act 1998;
- Health Act 1999;
- Local Government Act 1999;
- Care Standards Act 2000;
- Local Government Act 2000;
- Carers and Disabled Children Act 2000;
- Health and Social Care Act 2001;
- NHS Reform and Health Care Professions Act 2002.

This book aims to bring these changes together in one place. It is intended primarily as a resource for staff and managers working with older people in health, housing and social care services across the statutory, private and voluntary sectors. It should also be helpful to older people, their families and friends, and to policy makers, academics, researchers, journalists and anyone with an interest in this subject. It is intended as a response to those involved at the heart of these changes, as users or patients, providers, commissioners, or inspectors, who wonder how we got from where we were, to where we are now – and who also sometimes wonder how much of where we were still remains. It succeeds the Age Concern publication, *The Community Care Handbook*, by Barbara Meredith (first published in 1993) that helped thousands across the UK towards a better understanding of the community care reforms of the 1990s.

The devolving of government within the UK is leading to increased differences between the systems of, and legislation relevant to, Scotland, Wales, England and Northern Ireland. **This book explains the changes as they relate to England.** It also considers the policy aspects to these changes, and so draws attention to some of the differences in the systems developing across the UK.

Age Concern England has long held the view that old age is not, in itself, an illness. Aspects of the health and well-being of older people are experienced just as readily by the rest of the population. A person does not have to be elderly to suffer from migraines or dental problems, for example. And people of all ages must sometimes undergo the stress of moving to live in another house. So, while this book explains the changing nature of systems and services run by the NHS, social services authorities, and housing bodies, it concentrates in detail on particular aspects most relevant to older people in need of ongoing (sometimes called continuing) treatment, care and support. In short, it seeks to do two things.

- **First:** it gives an overview of the wide range of recent changes within the NHS and local government.
- **Secondly:** having set out this overview, it explains, in some detail, a number of the most important aspects of this system for older people with ongoing care needs: getting access to services; knowing what help is available, and from whom; the standards and quality of services; paying for services; and how organisations should be communicating with users and carers.

It is not unheard of for such a book to be considered out of date almost before the print is dry. Inevitably, new announcements will be made shortly after publication. While much change has taken place, there is much more still to come. Some shape needs to be given to this evolving system, especially for those caught in its middle. In the context of *The NHS Plan* and the Government's longer-term agenda, this book therefore appears halfway between the 1993 community care reforms and the full changes of *The NHS Plan*, expected by 2010.

Readers need to be aware of the 'cut-off' date, beyond which new proposals could not be included. This book explains *actual* changes up to August 2002, and includes *anticipated* changes subsequent to that date. It also suggests ways to find out about and follow new developments and announcements.

The book can be read straight through, or dipped into for reference, using the contents pages, index and cross-referencing throughout the text to find areas of key interest. The appendices at the end include a glossary of some of the terms used, a list of commonly used abbreviations, and a list of useful organisations.

1 How did we get here?
A brief history

This chapter sets out the key changes in the provision of health, housing and social care services for older people. It gives background information to help the reader understand the community care reforms of the 1990s, and the changes that have taken place since. The more recent history of some specific changes is explored in greater detail in later chapters.

Wartime evacuation

That children were evacuated from London during the early 1940s is well known. Fewer people are aware, however, that some of London's older population were also evacuated during the Second World War. Robin Means and Randall Smith's book, *From Poor Law to Community Care* (1998), gives a detailed account of the evacuation of older people, which in part prompted the formation of the Old People's Welfare Committee (now Age Concern England). The emergence of the charity is not the key issue here, however. Rather, it is the opportunity to consider the concerns that were being raised at the time. In the early 1940s, these 'chronic sick' older evacuees, placed in Emergency Medical Service (EMS) hospitals, were often regarded as 'blocking' available beds. Controversy existed over whether they needed medical or surgical treatment (and so should remain in the EMS hospitals), or could be transferred to residential institutions under the Poor Law acts – and thus be disqualified from receiving non-contributory old age pensions.

This is an extremely pared-down explanation of a highly complex situation during some of the worst of the Second World War bombing campaigns on London. It is included here as a salutary reminder that some of the themes facing today's providers (and receivers) of community care services – and the impact on individuals' finances if they move into care homes – have a long and resonant past. This certainly includes 'bed-blocking', arguably a rather demeaning term.

It is also, perhaps rather sadly, a situation not without some irony. At least some of those older wartime evacuees will have been the grandparents – possibly the parents – of those who saw active service in the Second World War, and who are now seeking and receiving treatment, care and support in their own old age. It may also serve as something of a cautionary note to those working-age adults who confidently express the belief that things will be very different when they are old, but without necessarily explaining how this will be achieved.

Welfare services after the Second World War

Despite the apparent familiarity of these wartime themes, an enormous amount of change has taken place since that time. Some of the biggest changes came about with the establishment of the National Health Service in July 1948 (under the National Health Service Act 1946), and the implementation of the National Assistance Act 1948. The latter conferred on local authorities (sometimes called local councils) responsibilities to run services such as residential homes, and to administer a means-test for such places. It also signalled the formal end of the Poor Law, although many local authority residential homes (often still called 'Part III' homes, as they were established under Part III of the National Assistance Act 1948) were provided in former workhouse premises. They were not alone in this regard – much of the newly formed NHS's long-stay geriatric provision was in hospital premises formerly occupied by older, poor, chronically sick patients under Poor Law provisions.

These post-war developments created one of the central issues that still concerns many current policymakers, practitioners and users – the divide between the NHS, which is 'free at the point of use' (although with implications for state benefits for long-stay patients, described more fully in Chapter 6), and local authority residential services, for which individuals must pay a charge.

Other developments were brought about by the National Health Service Act 1946 and the National Assistance Act 1948. For example, the National Health Service Act 1946 gave local authorities powers to provide home help services and the ability to fund local voluntary services. Until 1974, local authorities also employed district (or community) nurses, although they had little responsibility to provide or fund care or support for people living at home, other than these nursing services. It was not until the 1974 local government reorganisation that the responsibility for district nursing services passed to the NHS, which was by then also being restructured. Importantly, local councils had not charged people for the district nursing services they received, making the transfer of the service to the 'free at the point of use' NHS relatively easy in respect of this element of policy.

Institutional care

By the 1960s, concerns were being raised about the effects on people of receiving care in large institutions. In 1962, Peter Townsend's study of local authority, private and voluntary residential homes found that many of the older residents did not need care, only 'housekeeping' support such as cooking, laundry and bed-making. Many of those needing 'housekeeping' were older men. Amongst this group, it was individuals without a spouse (whether never married, widowed or divorced), or who had only male children, or no children, or whose daughter did not live nearby, who were most likely to be living in a home.

Concerns were also raised about the quality of care in long-stay settings. In 1969, an investigation into Ely Hospital was the first of several to expose often-appalling practices in the care of people with mental health problems and learning disabilities. Increasingly during this time, government and other agencies were highlighting the need to find ways for people to be cared for in more homely environments, if not in their own homes.

Services for disabled people, and social services departments

Two important legislative changes were given Royal Assent in 1970. The first was the Local Authority Social Services Act 1970, which created social services departments (sometimes called 'social services authorities', or simply 'social services'), and under which much formal government guidance to local authorities continues to be issued. The idea of arranging social services to provide effective family services arose originally from concerns about welfare for children, explored in what became known as the Seebohm Report, published in 1968 (*Report of the Committee on Local Authority and Allied Personal Social Services*, 1968). This report set out the aim of creating a single point of help in each local authority for anyone with social care needs – social services departments.

The second legislative change, the Chronically Sick and Disabled Persons Act 1970 (CSDP), gave new rights to people with disabilities to receive services, and new responsibilities to local authorities, such as finding out the needs of their local population. This Act continues to form the basis of much service provision and decisions about services for people with disabilities.

Section 2 of the Act was particularly important, as it set out a range of services that local authorities had responsibilities to provide for individuals with disabilities or chronic sickness:

- practical assistance within the home;
- assistance with adaptations to the home;
- disability aids and equipment;
- meals at home, or elsewhere;
- provision of (or assistance in getting) a telephone, or any special equipment needed to use a telephone;

- provision of, or assistance in, taking advantage of educational or recreational facilities both inside and outside the home, including provision of (or assistance with) transport to and from these facilities;
- holidays.

The rights of people with disabilities to access support services were further enhanced by the Disabled Persons (Services, Consultation and Representation) Act 1986 (often called the Disabled Persons Act 1986). For example, it created a *duty* (a legal requirement, see Box 1.1) on local authorities to consider the needs of a disabled person for services under section 2 of the CSDP Act 1970, as detailed above.

Box 1.1 Duties and powers

In this book – and in other material, including government guidance and legislation – attention is often drawn to the **'powers'** and **'duties'** of statutory (or public) bodies, such as local authorities (or 'local councils') and the NHS. There are differences between these two terms.

A **'duty'** means that an organisation (usually a statutory or public body, such as the NHS or a local council) is bound by law to do something – such as provide a service, or assess someone's needs.

A **'power'** means the law leaves it up to the public body whether or not to do something. However, this does not mean that an organisation can always refuse to exercise that power – that is, always refuse to do the action that the power allows. Case law has established that organisations must act reasonably when deciding whether to exercise their powers. Refusing to do so at all times, and in all circumstances, would be considered unreasonable by the courts.

Private markets, state responses

During the 1980s, one of the more singular features in the care of older people was the enormous growth in the numbers of residential and nursing homes, particularly those run by the private sector, which, until that point, had been a minority provider of these services (see Tables 1.1 and 1.2). Although the post-war welfare settlement effectively divided much of the existing long-stay settings between the NHS and local authorities, the voluntary sector – particularly charities, churches and other religious organisations – continued to run and develop residential and nursing homes.

Box 1.2 Use of terms – residential and nursing homes

The **'private sector'** consists of individual proprietors and organisations that own and run services for a profit. Some of the larger private organisations that run care homes have been 'floated' on the Stock Market.

The **'voluntary sector'** is a term covering a range of organisations set up on a 'not-for-profit' basis. This includes registered charities, as well as housing associations and many religious organisations.

Together, the private and voluntary sectors are often referred to as the **'independent sector'**.

For many years, there has been a differentiation in the terms used to describe care homes that provided nursing care (**nursing homes**) from those that do not (**residential homes**) – and those that offered both residential care and nursing places have been known as **'dual registered homes'**. Collectively, these different types of home have often been called **'care homes'**.

Under the Care Standards Act 2000, which came into effect in April 2002, all types of home are called **'care homes'**. Homes that provide nursing care are called **'care homes with nursing'**. Over time, these terms will become more commonly used; in the meantime, this book refers to 'residential homes' and 'nursing homes' where a difference needs to be drawn, and uses 'care homes' as an umbrella term for both residential and nursing homes.

Tables 1.1 and 1.2 illustrate the phenomenal growth in residential and nursing homes, particularly in the private sector. Places in local authority residential homes grew by 28,400 between 1970 and their peak in 1985. However, places in private sector residential homes increased by 61,600 in the same period. Overall, between 1970 and 2000, places in private sector residential homes grew by an astonishing 161,300. In contrast, local authority residential home places nearly halved over the same period of time. Voluntary sector residential home places also increased, but by a more modest 14,400 places over 30 years (Laing and Buisson, 2001).

TABLE 1.1 CHANGES IN THE NUMBER OF RESIDENTIAL HOME PLACES *

Type of home	1970	1975	1985	1993	2000	Change between 1970–2000
Local authority	108,700	128,300	137,100	94,600	60,000	Decrease of 48,700 places
Private sector	23,700	23,700	85,300	165,800	185,000	Increase of 161,300 places
Voluntary sector	40,100	41,000	45,100	52,400	54,500	Increase of 14,400 places

* Figures include places for younger adults with physical disabilities, as well as older people

TABLE 1.2 CHANGES IN NUMBERS OF PLACES IN LONG-STAY NURSING HOMES AND HOSPITALS

Type of facility	1970	1975	1985	1993	2000	Change between 1970–2000
Private sector nursing homes				172,100	186,800	Overall increases in
	20,300**	24,000**	38,000**			both sectors
Voluntary sector nursing homes				15,800	18,000	of 184,500 places
NHS long-stay geriatric hospitals	52,000	49,000	46,300	37,800	21,000	Decrease of 31,000 places
NHS long-stay psycho-geriatric hospitals	23,000	Not recorded	Not recorded	22,200	11,700	Decrease of 11,300 places

** These figures not recorded separately
Source: Laing and Buisson, 2001

Nursing home provision also changed radically. Separate figures for private and voluntary sector homes pre-1985 are not recorded: nonetheless, between 1985 and 2000, the overall numbers of independent (private and voluntary) sector nursing home places grew by 166,800. By 2000, 91 per cent of places were provided by the private sector. Again, in contrast, NHS long-stay provision fell, from a total of 75,000 places in 1970, to 32,700 in 2000. (The NHS, however, now funds an increasing number of continuing care beds in private nursing homes – an issue which will be explored in later chapters.) More recent changes to the numbers of homes, and places in homes, are discussed in Chapter 3.

Why the expansion in homes?

There are arguably three main reasons why the numbers of private sector residential and nursing home places expanded so rapidly during the 1980s.

STATE FUNDING FOR RESIDENTS

One of the reasons why the number of private sector residential and nursing homes grew was related to funding. State funds became far more available to support those independent sector residents whose own resources had largely been exhausted meeting the costs of their care in the home.

The National Assistance Act 1948 gave local social security officials the power to fund board and lodging for people living in private and voluntary sector residential homes. In practice, this power was seldom used. Changes to the social security system in 1980, and campaigns by charities and others directed at ensuring this power was used more, meant that, for the first time, Supplementary Benefit (or Income Support, now called the Minimum Income Guarantee – MIG – for older people) was paid at special, higher rates to people living in private or voluntary sector residential or nursing homes. As with all such means-tested benefits, people were eligible on the basis of their income and capital (or savings). Their need for such care was not considered.

Until 1985, the actual amounts paid in each area were decided by local offices of the then Department of Health and Social Security (subsequently divided into two government departments). The amounts paid varied, depending on the local rates charged by the homes, among other factors. In 1985, as a result of concerns that this system of local rates was open to abuse, national limits were set for different client groups and categories of care. Again, individual residents received this state funding towards the cost of their care in private and voluntary sector homes solely on the basis of a means-test of their finances. No assessment was made of their care needs. Importantly, this state financial support was not available to pay towards the costs of care for people living in local authority Part III homes (see page 2).

GREATER DEMAND FOR A CHOICE OF LONG-STAY FACILITIES

A second reason concerned the choices available to older people at that time in terms of the state's long-term care facilities. Demographic change and need for services are discussed later in this chapter. However, there was a significant increase in the numbers of older people during the 1970s and 1980s. This took place against a background of widespread economic recession and uncertainty, and at a time when public sector spending was being restricted. Large numbers of older people were therefore presenting at hospitals and elsewhere with a range of needs that, increasingly, neither the NHS nor local authorities were able to meet. In addition, many of the long-stay NHS geriatric hospital wards had become rundown. Local authorities faced significant reductions in their capital spending allowances and programmes, which affected the refurbishment of their existing Part III homes, as well as their potential for building new Part III residential homes.

In contrast, the quality of some of the private and voluntary sector homes was much higher than this state provision. Some individuals, or their families, felt that they would prefer to pay privately for better quality care, rather than receive substandard care 'free at the point of use' in an NHS long-stay bed. Even the then not uncommon practice, of having unrelated older people sharing two- or three-bedded rooms in private and voluntary sector homes, may have seemed preferable to sharing open hospital wards with many other older patients.

At the same time, while the state was increasing funding for private and voluntary sector homes through the higher rates of Income Support described above, it was not making similar funds available to the NHS and local authorities to pay for their long-stay facilities. In some areas, therefore, local councils and the NHS felt they were left with little option but to close their long-stay wards, hospitals and homes. Not only were alternative long-term care services increasingly available through the growing numbers of private and voluntary sector homes, but the costs of this care did not have to come from NHS and council budgets – and older people could still receive the care they needed.

LACK OF FUNDING FOR CARE AT HOME

The third reason is that none of this additional social security funding was available to pay for care services to support people living in their own homes. There was little or no incentive for any of the organisations involved – NHS, local authority, or the private or voluntary sector – to invest in care services for people at home. Once older people's needs were more than could be met through the local provision of a few services – typically meals-on-wheels, 'housekeeping' home help services, some district nursing support and attendance at day care centres – most were being directed to move into residential or nursing homes run by the private and voluntary sectors. One study found that, between 1989 and 1993, the most common factors leading to older people living in such homes were the need for chiropody services, continence problems, and depression (Bowling and Grundy, 1997).

OUTCOMES

Whatever the order of events, there was an enormous growth in the numbers of older people entering private and voluntary sector residential and nursing homes; a massive increase in the social security bill to meet the costs of this care in the private and voluntary sectors; and a system of funding care which became increasingly skewed towards non-state provided, residential care solutions.

The turning points

Three reports in the 1980s signalled significant turning points in the provision and funding of care: the Audit Commission Report, the Wagner Report, and the Griffiths' Report.

The Audit Commission Report, 1986

The Audit Commission Report, *Making a Reality of Community Care*, explored what was happening for people with care needs, in terms of service provision and the cost of funding care. It found that the Supplementary Benefit system (outlined on page 9) was making it 'too easy' for people to enter residential and nursing homes. As a consequence, this was discouraging the development of services to help people stay in their own homes, which the Audit Commission believed would cost less in many cases than places in residential care.

The Wagner Report, 1988

In 1988, a Committee chaired by Gillian Wagner published *Residential Care: A positive choice*. This report examined the quality of care in residential and nursing homes, as well as making recommendations for local authorities in the overall planning of residential and other services. The Committee believed that individuals' *care* needs should be thought about and responded to separately from their needs for *accommodation*. They felt that older people (and others) should not have to move just because their care needs had changed. The report recommended a statutory duty be placed on local authorities requiring them to offer a reasonable package of services if individuals wanted to remain at home, and it was reasonable to do so. It also drew attention to the positive role of residential care, but called for the rights of individual residents as citizens to be central to the care provided. Residents should be given a contract with the home; there should be a formal complaints procedure; and residents should have a right to privacy. Staff should be adequately trained, and all homes (including local authority homes) should be inspected.

The Griffiths Report, 1988

Arguably the most influential of the three, the Griffiths Report, *Community Care: Agenda for Action*, was the precursor of the White Paper (*Caring for People*, 1989) and subsequent community care legislation. It set out the views of its author, Sir Roy Griffiths, for the organisation and funding of community care services.

The report's proposals were wide-ranging. Griffiths believed that people should be helped to stay in their own homes, or in as near a domestic environment as possible, for as long as possible. This would, he felt, leave residential, nursing home and hospital care reserved for those whose needs could only be met in those surroundings. A Minister of State with clear responsibility for community care should be established, and central government money specifically reserved (or ring-fenced) for local authorities to spend on community care. This should include some money from the social security budget currently meeting the costs of the special Income Support rates for those in homes.

The money for community care was to be managed by local authority social services departments. They should enable people to live at home for as long as possible, but not necessarily by directly providing community care services. Griffiths recommended developing a new 'community carer' post, a worker who straddled both health and social care services, and could help break down some of the barriers. Local authority social services departments would have to draw up plans to show how they were to co-operate with health and housing departments. Individual service users, and their carers, should receive services according to their needs and their wishes. Griffiths believed that local authorities should take the lead in this role because, as democratically elected bodies, they were closest to service users.

The 1990s – the community care reforms

In 1989, the White Paper, *Caring for People*, was published, setting out six key objectives for community care reform:

- To promote the development of domiciliary, day and respite services to enable people to live in their own homes, wherever feasible and sensible.
- To ensure that service providers make practical support for carers a high priority.
- To make proper assessment of need and good case management the cornerstone of high quality care. Packages of care should then be designed in line with individual needs and preferences.
- To promote the development of a flourishing independent sector alongside good quality public services.
- To clarify the responsibilities of agencies and so make it easier to hold them to account for their performance.
- To secure better value for taxpayers' money by introducing a new funding structure for social care.

Aspects of the NHS were also being identified for major reorganisation and change. The two elements were combined under the NHS and Community Care Act 1990, with the community care reforms implemented in full from 1 April 1993.

The NHS and Community Care Act 1990

Although at the time of implementation greatest attention was paid to the community care aspects of the reforms, the changes to the NHS also had an impact on long-term provision for older people, and other user and carer groups. Chief amongst these was the development of GP fundholding practices and NHS Trusts. These introduced fundamental change, by creating a distinction between those parts of the NHS which commissioned (or purchased) services for patients, and those which directly provided NHS services – in short, what became known as the 'purchaser/provider split'.

NHS Trusts were one of the provider 'arms' in this new arrangement. They were formed, in general, from existing distinctive services. For example, individual local hospitals acquired NHS Trust status, as did many community health services, such as district nursing and health visitor services. Many of these organisations continue to use 'NHS Trust' in their name.

GP fundholding practices, and the subsequently restructured Health Authorities, formed the major purchasers of NHS services. GP practices that successfully applied to become fundholders were given access to, and control of, sums of money to purchase a range of services such as hospital treatments on behalf of their patients. Health Authorities retained responsibility for purchasing (or commissioning) some services (for example, NHS continuing health care services which are explored in more detail in later chapters), as well as some specialist services. They also retained responsibility for NHS dentistry, and purchased treatments and services for patients of non-fundholding general practices.

On setting up, GP fundholding practices were given a lump sum to spend on their premises. Some patients first discovered their GP practice had gained fundholding status when the surgery reception areas were refurbished. Fundholding practices began to employ practice managers, and some started to offer a wider range of services, including minor surgery. The release of funds to spend on patients meant fundholders could make contractual arrangements to pay for their patients' care directly with hospitals and, in many cases, were able to ensure patients received hospital treatment more quickly than through the health authority arrangements. However, not all GP practices wished to become fundholders. Some preferred the health authority to continue to fund treatments as before; others became fundholders at much later stages. This led to early concerns that a 'two-tier' NHS was developing.

The 'purchaser/provider split' introduced through these changes was not unique to the NHS. In the community care sections of the reforms, social services departments' responsibilities for community care were also extended, including increasing their powers (and duties) to purchase care services from the private and voluntary sectors. However, the split was not entire, as local authorities continued to be able to provide their own community care services directly. This blending of direct local authority service provision (sometimes called 'in-house services'), and contracted-for services from the private and voluntary sector, was regarded as creating a 'mixed economy of care'.

Other major changes included the establishment of local authority units to inspect and register residential homes (see Chapter 4), and the establishment of local authority complaints procedures (Chapter 7). Individuals were given new rights to assessments of their care needs by local authority social services departments (Chapter 5). Perhaps most importantly, the major responsibility for administering state funding for means-tested places in residential and nursing homes passed from the then Department of Social Security (DSS) to local authority social services departments (Chapter 6). Social services had administered a means-test for places in their own 'Part III' residential homes since the National Assistance Act 1948. For the first time, they also had the responsibility to administer state funding to people first moving to live in private or voluntary sector residential *and* nursing homes on or after 1 April

1993. Social services' responsibilities to administer state support also involved contributing towards the cost of care in homes, although individual residents continued to be able to apply for some benefits from the DSS (now the Department for Work and Pensions – DWP).

Those already living in independent sector homes prior to 1 April 1993 came under the system of higher levels of Income Support, even if they were not yet claiming these benefits. This became known as the system of 'preserved rights' to Income Support. In effect, on 1 April 1993, two systems of state funding were established, with the expectation that the numbers of those under the 'preserved rights' system would naturally – and quite quickly – diminish over the following decade.

Implementing community care: 1993–1997

It would be fair to describe the first few months following implementation of the reforms as a time of relief for many in the statutory sector. Concerns about the readiness of social services departments, housing authorities and the NHS to implement 'community care' had been widespread for some time. There had been uncertainty about the implications for older people and other service users after 1 April 1993. Certainly, some older people's decisions to move to private or voluntary sector residential homes seemed to be 'speeded up'. It is likely that a number of older people moved into these homes prior to 31 March 1993 solely because the system of higher levels of Income Support (which continued under the name 'preserved rights' to Income Support) was a known quantity, whereas the new funding arrangements, supported by social services, were untested.

However, a number of issues soon arose following implementation of the reforms.

LEGAL CASES

The first concerned the understanding of the new legislative framework. Many of the key elements of the NHS and Community Care Act 1990 used phrases and words such as 'may' or 'appear to need' – terms that many felt could only be more clearly defined through case law. Not surprisingly, therefore, a number of legal cases were brought on behalf of service users (including several brought by older people). Many of these cases had a significant impact on the system of treatment, care and support for older people in terms of our understanding of how the system should work. They are referred to, where appropriate, throughout subsequent chapters.

'RATIONING' OF CARE

A second issue concerned what is often referred to as 'rationing' of care. Although the government of the day introduced a quite complex formula of additional funds (to reflect local authorities' additional responsibilities) as ring-fenced Special Transitional Grants (STGs), original plans on how these grants would be phased over a three-year period were changed shortly after implementation of the reforms. Some local authorities found that, having initially matched the anticipated level of need for services in their area to their budget (as expected to do so by the Audit Commission and other bodies), budget amounts were unexpectedly reduced. In these areas, local authorities responded by tightening their eligibility criteria for providing or funding community care services. This led to a number of significant court cases (see Chapter 5).

Perhaps more importantly, it led to concerns that local authorities were 'rationing', sometimes withdrawing, care services from individual users. In some areas, older people found they had lengthy waits to receive care assessments, services or funding. In other areas, local authorities set up panels that met weekly to decide which of the people assessed as needing care would receive services, and which would have to wait. At its most extreme, and in exceptional cases, funding for places in residential and nursing homes became, quite literally, a case of 'dead man's shoes' – local authorities having to wait for a resident to die to release the funds to pay for a new user's care. In some parts of the country, concerns remain about the lack of availability of, and restricted access to, services for older people. This is explored in later chapters.

LOCAL VARIATIONS

Equally importantly, local criteria for social care services varied around the country. This reflected such factors as the distribution of STG funds favouring some local authorities over others. In some areas, services provided or purchased by social services departments were more widely available than in others, leading to further concerns that 'rationing' was creating a 'lottery of care'. The help received by older people appeared to depend on whereabouts in the country they lived.

Other concerns were also linked to local variations. For example, as early as 1994, the then government was considering whether it should make any changes to the system of regulating residential and nursing homes. This was due largely to variations in the standards expected of homes by different local inspection and registration units, run by health authorities (for nursing homes) and local authorities (for residential homes). Concerns about the lack of national quality standards for care services, and the lack of national eligibility criteria to determine who should receive support from social services departments, were commonly voiced by older users, carers, charities and campaigning groups, independent sector providers, and even politicians.

GAPS BETWEEN ORGANISATIONS

A fourth issue to emerge early on concerned the apparent 'gap' between health and social services and, in some cases, housing authorities. This manifested itself in a number of ways. One example relates to the discharge of older patients from NHS hospitals. A key concern of many hospitals was to discharge older patients as quickly as possible, in order to meet targets such as length of time other people were waiting for operations and other treatments. Their contract, as the NHS provider 'arm', with NHS commissioners locally, often extended no further than the actual hospital treatment. However, NHS Trust hospitals also had a responsibility to follow hospital discharge guidance current at that time. This stressed the importance of appropriate discharge, including making sure any services needed after hospital treatment had been arranged. These tended not to be services the hospital would provide. Social services departments and housing authorities, which usually did have this latter responsibility, were often working to different time-frames from their NHS colleagues – especially in the provision of housing adaptations to people's own homes, for which waits of several months were not uncommon. The net result for some older people was either to be discharged home before any necessary support services or adaptations were in place or, conversely, the decision made relatively quickly that they should move to live permanently in a residential or nursing home following hospital treatment because alternatives could not be arranged fast enough. This led to some older people being rushed into making life-changing decisions; and further compounded concerns raised previously, by Sir Roy Griffiths and others in the 1980s, that some admissions to care homes were being made unnecessarily early.

Another potential problem emerging during 1996 and 1997 related to eligibility criteria set by social services departments for community care services, and those criteria set by the NHS – from 1996 – for continuing care services (see Chapter 5). In some areas, there were concerns that, although these two criteria had to be agreed between the relevant bodies, there were gaps between the ending of social services' responsibilities, and the beginning of the NHS's responsibilities. This led to instances where both bodies refused to take responsibility for funding or providing the care needed by some older people, each firmly believing the other held the legitimate responsibility.

FUNDING CARE IN HOMES

Many of these disputes between the NHS and social services departments centred on the funding of places in residential and nursing homes (a matter which arguably is still unresolved). Concerns about the system of paying for care included both the impact of the national, mandatory means-test for residential and nursing home care on older people's finances, and the long-term sustainability of what was fundamentally a tax-based system in the context of an ageing UK population.

As far as the means-test for care home places (established under the National Assistance Act 1948) was concerned, many older people were horrified to discover that the value of their flat or house would be included in certain circumstances. There was a period of significant media interest during the mid-1990s, with stories of older people selling their homes to pay for care in residential or nursing homes. Disappointingly, perhaps, there was less coverage explaining the wide variety of circumstances when the value of property would be ignored (see Chapter 6). Increased home ownership (including the Right To Buy council housing initiative from the 1980s), the rise in property prices, and a growing awareness of the role of housing as a source of inheritance, furthered these concerns.

Inquiries into the system of paying for care

During the mid-1990s, both the Joseph Rowntree Foundation (1997) and the House of Commons Health Select Committee (1996) held inquiries into the funding of older people's long-term care needs. Importantly, both concluded that there was no 'demographic time bomb' – an unfortunate and largely inaccurate description that is sometimes still applied to the natural ageing of two sizeable post-war 'baby boomer' generations. The consensus was that the costs of funding older people's care could be met by the state. However, the Rowntree Inquiry specifically recommended a new system to do so – national social care insurance. It also suggested a radical change to the system in terms of the elements of care for which older people (and others) should be expected to pay from their own resources. Central to its report was the proposal to separate the costs of accommodation and meals, which should be subject to a means-test, from the costs of health and social care, which should be free to users. The Health Select Committee called for the nursing element of care in nursing homes to be free to otherwise means-tested residents.

Both reports contained significant recommendations. The Health Select Committee called for national eligibility criteria for NHS continuing health care services, and for the formal regulation of

Long Term Care Insurance policies through the Financial Services Act 1986 or through other means. Both reports concluded that the system pushed people into residential care because of perverse incentives created by mandatory means-testing. There was a strong feeling, reported by both inquiries, that a contract between the state and the people had been broken. The NHS was seen as relinquishing its responsibility for care and making people rely on their own financial resources, while the system unfairly penalised those who had worked and saved, or who were home owners. Complexities and inconsistencies in the system (arising from the piecemeal way it had developed over many years) were also causes for concern.

Other significant reports

The reports of the two inquiries outlined above were not the only significant publications during the 1990s. Three reports from the Audit Commission were particularly pertinent. *United They Stand* (1995) set out the shortcomings of hospital treatment for older people with fractured neck of femur. Delays in treatment resulted in older patients being unable to return home, and entering care homes instead. *The Coming of Age* (1997) reported the Audit Commission's findings into care services for older people. This report concluded that many older people were locked into a 'vicious circle' of care. Reduced numbers of hospital beds and shorter lengths of stay in hospital, together with a lack of rehabilitative and convalescence opportunities, meant older people were increasingly needing more expensive and intensive levels of long-term care. A third report, *Home Alone* (2000), considered the role of housing in community care services, and found many issues that needed tackling, including financial and legal matters, if the housing needs of vulnerable people were to be better met.

Around the same time, the Health Advisory Service 2000 (HAS 2000, 1998) published *Not Because They are Old*, examining conditions for older patients in acute hospital wards in general hospitals. HAS 2000 found significant problems with the quality and availability of food and drink, and a lack of help from staff in relation to feeding. Staff themselves were under considerable pressure from heavy workloads. There were problems with preserving patients' dignity – some arising from poor physical environments on the wards, but others from poor staff attitudes. Although there were good examples of innovation with regard to planning for patients' discharge from hospital, there were also major problems with this in some areas. The study also found that outcomes for older patients, in terms of their care, were much better on specialist wards for older people than they were on general wards. It concluded that better education and training were needed for staff – irrespective of where they worked – about the specific needs of older people, as part of addressing both the poor image and profile of older patients and the skills of those providing services for them. A comprehensive range of rehabilitation and recuperation services, spanning hospital and community settings, should be made available for older people. The report also called for a National Service Framework for Older People, to set key indicators of quality care and service provision.

Other Acts of Parliament

Aside from the NHS and Community Care Act 1990, three other important Acts of Parliament were passed between 1993 and 1997.

DISABILITY DISCRIMINATION ACT 1995

This was implemented in stages – with some parts still to be enacted in full. It set out a number of requirements for businesses, public facilities and employers not to discriminate against people with mental or physical disabilities. Chief among the issues covered by this Act were those governing access to buildings and services. This includes the NHS, social services and housing authorities. By October 1999, service providers had to have taken reasonable steps to change policies, practices or procedures that made it impossible, or unreasonably difficult, for people with disabilities to use a service. This includes providing auxiliary aids or services. From 2004, providers will have to take reasonable steps to remove or alter physical features that impede people's use of services (*Implementing Section 21 of the Disability Discrimination Act 1995 across the NHS*, HSC 1999/156).

CARERS (RECOGNITION AND SERVICES) ACT 1995

The Carers (Recognition and Services) Act 1995 gave carers a new right to ask for their care needs to be assessed by the local authority. However, this assessment had to be carried out at the same time as the cared-for person's care needs were assessed. Local authorities could decide to respond to carers' assessed needs by providing services to support them in their caring role, but were not obliged to do so. (See also Chapters 3 and 5.)

COMMUNITY CARE (DIRECT PAYMENTS) ACT 1996

This was implemented in 1997 but its provisions were not extended to include older people until 2000. It gave local authorities new powers to issue payments to service users instead of, or as well as, community care services. Users then spend the money to provide themselves with the assistance they have been assessed as needing. (See Chapter 3 for more information about this system.)

1997: New Government, new legislation

Some of the reports outlined above were published during the early months of the Labour Government, elected in May 1997 following 18 years of Conservative administration. Their election heralded a raft of Green and White Papers, and subsequent legislation, under a common aim to modernise the NHS and local government. This overarching theme has continued since Labour's re-election to office in June 2001.

Box 1.3 Key Green and White Papers under New Labour

- *The New NHS: modern, dependable* (1997)
- *Modernising Social Services: promoting independence, improving protection, raising standards* (1998)
- *Modern Local Government: in touch with the people* (1998)
- *Saving Lives: our healthier nation* (1999)
- *Modernising Government* (1999)

- *Quality and Choice: a decent home for all* (The Housing Green Paper, 2000)
- *Reforming the Mental Health Act* (2000)
- *The NHS Plan* (2000)
- *Strong Local Leadership – quality public services* (2001)
- *Delivering the NHS Plan* (2002)

A significant amount of new legislation relevant to the systems of treatment, care and support for older people has also been enacted, key elements of which are set out in Box 1.4.

Box 1.4 Key elements of relevant legislation passed by New Labour

Health Act 1999

- Introduction of Primary Care Trusts (PCTs), repeal of GP fundholders
- Establishment of Commission for Health Improvement (CHI)
- Establishment of new co-operation and partnership funding options for health and social services

Local Government Act 1999

- Introduction of Best Value regime for reviewing all local authority services

Care Standards Act 2000

- New regulatory regime for voluntary, private and local authority residential homes
- New regulatory regime for private and voluntary sector nursing homes
- New requirement for domiciliary care agencies to be regulated
- New regulatory regime for nurses' agencies
- Formation of the General Social Care Council (GSCC)

Local Government Act 2000

- New powers for local authorities to promote the economic, social and environmental well-being of their areas
- New arrangements for elected councillors to fulfil their executive responsibilities (e.g. elected mayor, cabinet)

- Formation of Overview and Scrutiny Committees (OCS)

Carers and Disabled Children Act 2000

- Extension of rights of carers to have an assessment of their own needs for care
- Local councils given the opportunity for direct provision of services to meet carers' needs
- Extension of direct payments system to carers
- Local authorities given the wherewithall to provide 'vouchers' for carers for respite services

Health and Social Care Act 2001

- Extension of the powers of Overview and Scrutiny Committees (OSC)
- Establishment of independent advocacy services
- Creation of a duty on the NHS to involve the public and their representatives in planning, developing and deciding about health services
- Establishment of Care Trusts
- Abolition of the pre-1993 'preserved rights' system of funding care in homes
- Responsibility for funding the nursing element of means-tested care in nursing homes given to the NHS
- Introduction of other changes to means-tested places in homes

NHS Reform and Health Care Professions Act 2002

- Creation of 28 Strategic Health Authorities by merging the previous 95 health authorities in England
- Extension of CHI's powers to inspect NHS services and report 'failing' services to the Secretary of State for Health
- Establishment of Patients Forums in NHS Trusts and PCTs
- Establishment of the Commission for Patient and Public Involvement in Health (CPPIH)
- Establishment of the Council for the Regulation of Health Care Professionals
- Abolition of Community Health Councils (CHCs) in England (but not Wales), and the Association of Community Health Councils in England and Wales (ACHCEW)

In its first term of office, the New Labour government also passed the Human Rights Act 1998. This provides for the UK to incorporate into law the European Convention on Human Rights. Several of the Articles to this law are particularly pertinent to older people who need treatment, care or support. These include rights to privacy and dignity, to the peaceful possession of property, and to family life. Several cases concerning service users have since been brought before the courts, citing elements of the Human Rights Act 1998 as part of their petition, including a case concerning the provision of long-term NHS continuing health care, *R v North and East Devon Health Authority ex parte Coughlan.* (This is explored in more detail in Chapter 6.)

One of the Government's main 1997 election manifesto commitments was to establish a Royal Commission into the future funding of long-term care for older people. This first Royal Commission inquiry for nearly 20 years reported its findings in 1999, and is discussed in detail in Chapter 6.

However, one of the most important reports, in terms of overall changes to many of the systems of care from the NHS and social services, is *The NHS Plan* (DH, 2000). This includes the Government's response to the Royal Commission's recommendations, and its proposals to change long-term care services and funding for older people.

The NHS Plan

The NHS Plan is probably the single most important document in terms of outlining recent and future change for both the NHS and social services (despite its title, a number of its proposals directly affect social services). It sets out, in some detail, the Government's vision to create a health service designed around the patient. To achieve this, it expects changes for health care professionals, for patients, in the relationship between health and social services, and between the NHS and the private sector. It also expects changes specific to older people. *The NHS Plan* sets out the core principles on which the NHS is based.

Box 1.5 Core principles of the NHS

1 The NHS will provide a universal service for all, based on clinical need, not ability to pay
2 The NHS will provide a comprehensive range of services
3 The NHS will shape its services around the needs and preferences of individual patients, their families and carers
4 The NHS will respond to the different needs of different populations
5 The NHS will work continuously to improve quality services and to minimise errors
6 The NHS will support and value its staff
7 Public funds for healthcare will be devoted solely to NHS patients
8 The NHS will work together with others to ensure a seamless service for patients
9 The NHS will help keep people healthy and work to reduce health inequalities
10 The NHS will respect the confidentiality of individual patients and provide open access to information about services, treatment and performance

The NHS Plan sets out a comprehensive programme of change, and of targets, to be met over the decade from 2000. Some have already been translated into legislation, through the Health and Social Care Act 2001, and the NHS Reform and Health Care Professions Act 2002. These include:

- the establishment of Care Trusts;
- the development of an NHS-wide Patient Advice and Liaison Services (PALS);
- a requirement that every local NHS organisation and care home publish an annual account of the views received from patients, in a Patient Prospectus;

- a Patients' Forum to be established in every NHS Trust and Primary Care Trust (PCT);
- changes to the system of means-tested care in residential and nursing homes.

Key proposals in *The NHS Plan* that are relevant to older people with ongoing care needs are set out in Box 1.6.

Box 1.6 Key proposals affecting older people, from *The NHS Plan*

Changes in the relationship between health and social services

- Best Value system to be used jointly by the Commission for Health Improvement, Audit Commission and the Social Services Inspectorate, to check joint health and social services working practices, especially those regarding:
  - reducing delays in discharging older hospital patients
  - reducing preventable emergency hospital admission and re-admission of people aged over 75
  - assessing the speed at which older people's needs for care are assessed
- Creation of a National Performance Fund from April 2002, to reward health and social services' joint working arrangements
- Further integration of health and social services through Care Trusts, able to commission (purchase) and provide primary and community health services, as well as social care for older people and others

Changes for all patients

- Copies of letters between clinicians about an individual patient's care given to the patient as of right
- 'Smart cards' to allow patients easier access to their individual health records (subject to the necessary technical arrangements and new infrastructure for computerised patient records)
- By 2005, patients to be able to pre-book the date and time of every hospital appointment and planned admission

---

- New patient advocacy service from 2002
- All health services to ask patients and carers for their views on services they receive
- All local NHS organisations and care homes required to publish a Patient Prospectus

Changes between the NHS and private sector

- New arrangements for co-operative working (the Concordat), with national guidelines to the NHS on commissioning services
- Involving patients and voluntary sector organisations in the development of local health planning
- Development of locally agreed protocols for referral, admission and discharge in and out of NHS and private and voluntary sector facilities (including hospitals and homes)

Changes to waiting for treatment

- By 2004, callers to NHS Direct referred directly to out-of-hours health care where necessary
- By 2004, patients to see a GP within 48 hours
- By 2004, widespread 'bed-blocking' to be ended
- New standards to be introduced to ensure every NHS hospital patient has a discharge plan, including an assessment of their care needs, developed from the start of their hospital admission
- By 2004, no patient to wait more than four hours in Accident and Emergency hospital wards from arrival to admission, transfer or discharge
- By the end of 2005, the maximum wait for inpatient treatment to be cut from 18 months to six months, with plans to reduce this to three months by the end of 2008

Clinical priorities

- Cancer
- Coronary heart disease (CHD)
- Mental health

(These clinical priorities apply to all patients, regardless of age)

Source: *The NHS Plan* (DH, 2000)

The NHS Plan also sets out a number of key changes for health and social services provision for older people. This includes the Government's response to the Royal Commission's inquiry into the future funding of long-term care for older people, which is discussed in more detail in Chapter 6. The main changes are:

• automatic invitations for breast screening extended to all women aged 65–70;
• a Single Assessment Process for health and social services to use in the first instance to identify individuals' needs for treatment, care and support (initially from April 2002, subsequently rescheduled for June 2002);
• development of a personal care plan, agreed with the individual older person and held by them;
• piloting Care Direct services to provide information and advice on health, social care, housing, pensions and benefits by telephone and online advice services, drop-in centres and outreach services;
• additional £900 million investment by 2003/2004 in new intermediate care and related services (such as community equipment services);
• the NHS to take on the responsibility to fund the nursing element of care of means-tested places in nursing homes;
• payments of the state benefit, the Residential Allowance, to individual residents in independent sector homes to cease – the resources transferred instead to local authorities to be spent on further services to promote older people's independence.

National Beds Inquiry

The NHS Plan drew on the National Beds Inquiry, conducted during 1999 and early 2000 (HSC 2000/004, *Shaping the future NHS: long-term planning for hospitals and related services*). This considered the future of hospital beds, and other health and social services, over the next 10–20 years. It concluded that the trend of reduction in hospital bed numbers over the last decade or more could not keep pace with people's changing needs, and additional activities and new services within the NHS. It found that two-thirds of hospital beds were occupied by patients aged 65 or over. This suggested the need for radical change in services, moving towards proactive, ongoing care. Change would be needed at every level. Patients must be empowered and given the right information for self-care. Primary care services must be extended and access improved. Intermediate services must be introduced for older patients, bridging the gap between home and hospital and promoting rehabilitation and preventative care. The Inquiry concluded that, within the context of the NHS, there was a need to move away from managing single healthcare institutions, towards managing clinical conditions that spanned the range of services needed by patients.

The Wanless Report

In 2001, HM Treasury commissioned a separate inquiry to review how technological, demographic and medical trends are likely to affect the Health Service over the next 20 years. The inquiry, chaired by Derek Wanless, published an interim report later the same year, and a full report in April 2002. *Securing our Future Health: Taking a Long term View* built upon *The NHS Plan* by assessing the likely impact of key issues such as the ageing of the UK's population. It also considered some aspects of social care.

It made a number of recommendations. These include extending National Service Frameworks to other areas of the NHS (see Chapter 3). Alongside a range of suggestions for involving patients in health care services, it also suggested there may be an argument for charging a cost to patients who fail to keep health appointments. Perhaps most controversially, the report recommended that the Government should consider using financial incentives to help reduce what it described as the problem of bed blocking.

Although the report concluded there was no evidence that financing methods other than funding the NHS through taxation would improve services, it posed further questions as to whether increasing the range of non-clinical services that could be charged for would be one way of raising funds in order to meet anticipated increased expectations from patients. For example, NHS hospital car parking services have long been the province of separate, profit-making organisations. *The NHS Plan* included proposals for the NHS to contract with private organisations to provide bedside telephones and televisions at a charge to patients. In addition, the report suggested that the current policy of offering exemption on prescription charges to some groups of people was illogical, and should be re-examined. Finally, the report recommended that a further review of both health and social care be carried out in five years' time.

Delivering the NHS Plan

Delivering the NHS Plan (DH, 2002) is a very good example of the speed at which new reform continues to be identified. Also published in April 2002, this White Paper sets out a range of ways that the reforms identified in *The NHS Plan* will be implemented. It also suggests a number of new changes. Key amongst these are proposals to make local authorities financially responsible for meeting the costs of NHS hospital care for those patients who have been identified as ready for discharge, but are waiting for action from the local authority. This reflects the suggestion in the Wanless Report, and would require new legislation. (See Chapter 3.)

It also proposes to develop new bodies to inspect and regulate health and social care services provided by the NHS, local authorities, and the independent sector. This would affect a number of existing organisations, including the Commission for Health Improvement (CHI) and the National Care Standards Commission (NCSC) – with the latter's remit to regulate residential and domiciliary care services only commencing in April 2002. (See Chapter 4.)

Who are the users and carers?

Within all of these developments and changes, it is important not to lose sight of the people for whom the services are provided. However, it is equally important to recognise who is *actually* receiving services. The reform of organisations, funding systems and services are not the only changes to have been taking place over the last decade. The group of older people receiving ongoing health, housing and social care support has also changed; in some regards, this change has been significant.

Later chapters discuss how changes in community care have resulted in fewer older people each receiving more intensive help at home. This is one of the major changes resulting from the community care reforms. By 2000, the total numbers of households receiving home care or home help services had fallen by a fifth compared with 1992 (the year before the community care reforms). Between 1996 and 2002, the average number of hours of home care provided to each household each week increased by 45 per cent (*Community Care Statistics 2001: home care services,* DH, 2002).

The likelihood that an older person will move to live in a long-stay setting (whether a hospital or home) has reduced slightly in recent years. For example, in 1997, 5.1 per cent of people aged 75–84 lived in long-stay settings, but by 2000 it was 4.8 per cent. Similarly, for those aged 85 and over (the section of the population at greatest risk of living in a home or long-stay hospital), the proportion in long-term care fell from 22.4 per cent to 20.9 per cent (Laing and Buisson, 1998, 2001). This may, at least in part, reflect the shift in policy since 1993 towards supporting more older people to stay in their own homes for longer. In this respect alone, some reduction in the use of care homes would be expected.

The overall likelihood of a person needing services provided or funded by local authorities rises with age. This is partly accounted for by the fact that certain diseases that may lead some people to need support are considerably more common in the older age groups. One such example is dementia, which is much more likely to occur among people aged 80 plus. It is also partly as a result of the expectation that community care services would be targeted on those 'most in need'. Most authorities have interpreted this as meaning those with the greatest frailties, disabilities and illnesses.

Increasing amounts of state support are therefore being provided to the older, frailer part of the retired population. Anecdotally, at least, there is evidence that those receiving support from the state are most likely to be in their 80s or older.

In contrast, more family (unpaid, or informal) care is received by those aged under 85 (Rowlands, 1998). Although the biggest group of family carers consists of adult daughters aged between 45–64, it is often the spouse or partner of an older person who provides the most intensive support – particularly once care needs rise to 20 hours or more each week (Rowlands, 1998).

Overall, and since 1993, the state has been paying greatest attention to those who are frailest and with multiple disabilities. This tends to equate with much older age. This approach has lead to a number of consequences. Firstly, it is reported (at least anecdotally) that older people are now first moving to live in care homes at older ages and with greater frailties than was the case before the community care reforms. Secondly, older people also appear to be staying at home for longer with higher levels of need. These two consequences have implications for the services concerned, in terms of staff skill mix and numbers required, for example; for funding decisions (especially the divide between NHS and social services provision, explored in Chapter 6); and for the planning and delivery of community-based services, especially health services such as GPs, clinics and outpatient services. A third consequence has been the concern that older people with 'low level' needs are increasingly missing out on state-funded or state-provided support. There has been a focus, in recent years, on services that maintain or improve people's independence (see Chapter 3). However, many of these are short, time-limited responses, such as intermediate care services. Arguably, since 1993 a gap has emerged, in terms of state support, for those older people who need some – but not much – support, but who need this provided over the long-term rather than delivered in short courses or sessions. It is this group – those with mild problems – whose numbers appear to be rising (Wanless, 2001). This group, who prior to the community care reforms were likely to be among those receiving the more traditional home help service (see Chapter 3), may increasingly be trying to organise and pay for this care themselves.

It is important to place all these changes within the context of the demographic picture in the UK. Although overall the numbers of older people continue to rise, between 2000–2004 the number of people aged 85 and over will have fallen. This reflects the corresponding drop in birth rates during the First World War. This more detailed picture should be borne in mind, especially in terms of planning services for the future, whether short- or long-term.

Of course, there are a huge range of factors that affect whether individuals need, or receive, care. Indeed, there is an entire debate, not reflected here, about how 'need' is variously defined by central and local government and the NHS, and by individuals. At present, more older women than older men receive social care services and support. This is not so surprising given that there are currently greater numbers of older women than men in the population. Other factors include whether people are living alone, and socio-economic factors such as the level of income in retirement years. Indeed, studies such as the Black Report (1980) and the Acheson Inquiry (1998) have highlighted that the link between poverty and ill health increases in old age.

The UK's ageing population

It is the ageing of the UK's population over the next 20–50 years that has tended to attract most attention in terms of policy debate. People's life expectancy has been rising in the UK throughout the last century. For example, in 1901, life expectancy for men was just 45.7 years, but by 1998 this had risen to 74.9 years (Table 1.3).

TABLE 1.3 LIFE EXPECTANCY, 1841–1998

Year	Males' life expectancy (years)	Females' life expectancy (years)
1841	41	43
1901	45.7	49.6
1931	58.1	62.1
1961	67.8	73.7
1981	70.9	76.8
1991	73.2	78.8
1998	74.9	79.8

Source: *Social Trends*, ONS, 2001

Concerns have been raised about the impact of this increased longevity on the demand for care services, particularly in terms of suggestions that the UK is facing a 'demographic time-bomb' of the 'baby boomer' generations. This phrase describes two very large birth groups (or cohorts) of people born between 1946–51, and 1960–66. It is the likelihood that most of these two 'baby boomer' generations will live to old age that appears to cause most consternation.

There are a number of elements to this concern. The first is whether old age necessarily equates to illness or disability. It is still not entirely clear whether increased years means more years of illness, or whether the actual amount of time spent ill remains constant but happens at an increasingly later age. Most recent studies suggest that, while healthy life expectancy (the number of years spent 'disease-free', for want of a better term) has improved, it has not improved as much as overall life expectancy (ONS, 2001). However, it does seem that the proportion of older people experiencing severe illness and difficulties is reducing, while the number with mild problems has increased (Wanless, 2002). This is, of course, an overall picture of average older people, and so does not necessarily reflect any patterns for working-age adults with existing conditions and illnesses who are increasingly reaching retirement age and beyond. (There is also a wider debate about the negative portrayal of people with disabilities and illnesses – of whatever age – as a 'burden', which is not explored here.)

The second, and perhaps more important element, is as follows. While recent decades have meant significant increases in the numbers of older people surviving to much greater ages, this appears to have had less impact on NHS budgets (for example) than many people think (Wanless, 2001). This is because it is the beginning and end years of life that are most expensive in terms of health care – *regardless* of the age at which those last years occur. Indeed, there is evidence to suggest that the amount spent by the NHS on older people in their last year is less than that spent on those people who die before retirement age, during their last year of life (Wanless, 2001). This might be, in part at least, because of the far greater likelihood (compared with working-age adults) of an older person moving to live in a means-tested residential or nursing home, to which cost the older person contributes from their own resources.

A third element concerns the extent to which the expectations of these 'baby boomer' generations will be different from those of current older people. It appears to be taken almost as fact that those currently in their 50s (for example) will have significantly higher expectations than those in their 70s or 80s, although this tends to be based on assumptions rather than on hard evidence. These anticipated changes include expecting more prompt services, greater individual control and choice, and a wider range of care options. In the future, it is believed, older people will be more likely to raise concerns and make complaints because of their experiences as working-age adults in a consumer-led and consumer-driven society – although health and social care systems will by then be being implemented and run by another, younger, adult group that also has significant consumer experience.

Another change often cited concerns the pattern of the ethnic make-up of the older population. In some areas, this is likely to change significantly over the next decade – especially in parts of London (Lowdell *et al*, 2000), and other areas that have, in the past, attracted high numbers of particular immigrant populations. This tends to reflect the ageing of these more established populations. Ethnic origin can affect people's health needs – for example, coronary heart disease is high among people from South Asia, prostate cancer is high in black Caribbean and black African groups, and other cancers are more commonly found amongst white groups (Lowdell *et al*, 2000). The 2001 census returns may well provide more information about the health and care needs amongst different minority populations. Studies from the 1990s suggest that some pensioners from ethnic groups are less likely than their white counterparts to live in communal establishments such as care homes. This is particularly true for South Asian groups. This may reflect a traditional concentration on service provision and design for older people from white British and European backgrounds. A 1998 study by the Social Services Inspectorate, *They Look After their Own, Don't They?* found that widespread assumptions about the availability of family care for older people from black and ethnic minority populations was leading to their being offered fewer formal support and care services.

Finally, there are potential changes that are sometimes overlooked. These relate to emerging concerns about the health of the overall population, and how this may impact on current and future older people. Concerns include the rise in obesity, and the increasingly sedentary lifestyle being led especially by men, and more particularly by men from some ethnic minority groups (DETR, 1998).

Attention is often focused on changes for the future without necessarily fully recognising the extent to which change may already have taken place. In many areas, there are already significant numbers of ethnic minority pensioners; the expected change here is only the increase of an existing trend. Similarly, it is important to bear in mind that levels and type of expectation amongst today's older users and their carers may already be substantially different from even a few years ago. Present-day older service users are now nine years on from the implementation of the community care reforms. Their experiences – and expectations – will be further affected by the wide-scale modernisation plans currently underway.

2 Where are we now? Themes and priorities

This chapter gives an overview of the ways in which NHS and local authority systems are being modernised. It explores some of the key themes and priorities that have developed in the last few years. It begins by outlining some of the structural changes that have taken place within health, housing and social services organisations, the legislative framework for which was set out in Chapter 1.

Box 2.1 Use of terms – NHS and social services departments

Reference is made throughout the book to 'the NHS', and to 'social services departments'.

Social services departments are:

- Part of local authorities (sometimes also called local councils)
- Run by County Councils, Metropolitan and London Boroughs and, in some areas, Unitary Authorities
- Sometimes also called 'social services authorities' or, simply 'social services'

The NHS:

- Refers to the range of bodies and organisations that make up the National Health Service
- Includes Primary Care Groups and Trusts, as well as health authorities

---

Changes within the NHS include the replacement of GP fundholders with Primary Care Groups (PCGs); the ongoing development of Primary Care Trusts (PCTs); changes to the powers, numbers and sizes of health authorities and the development of Special Health Authorities; and the formation of the NHS Modernisation Agency, and related Teams and Change Agents, to oversee the implementation of *The NHS Plan* between 2000 and 2010. Table 2.1 gives a brief overview of some of these structural changes.

These changes come under the Government's broad aims to modernise the NHS and local government.

Changes to local government

Many of the structural changes made to local government relate to arrangements for elected members (or councillors) to make decisions on service provision, budgets and other matters. The Local Government Act 2000 set out a variety of new arrangements, which act to separate the executive (or decision-making) councillors from non-executive councillors. These replace the former committee structure, which consisted of elected councillors opting (or being co-opted) to serve on a committee with one councillor acting as Chair (e.g. social services committee). The new options include:

- an elected mayor, who then appoints a cabinet from the elected councillors;
- a leader elected internally, who then appoints a cabinet from the elected councillors;
- an elected mayor and a local authority-appointed council manager executive.

Overview and Scrutiny Committees (OSC) have also been established. These consist of non-executive councillors, who act to hold the executive to account, and assist in matters of policy and strategy. OSCs also scrutinise health bodies. The White Paper, *Strong Local Leadership, Quality Public Services* (DTLR, 2001), set out plans for a national framework of standards and accountability, including new Comprehensive Performance Assessments (CPA) for all councils. The 2001 White Paper also set out plans for the Local

TABLE 2.1 STRUCTURAL CHANGES WITHIN THE NHS

What change, when?	Relevant legislation	What does this mean?	Special notes
Primary Care Groups (PCGs), replaced GP fundholders from April 1999	Section 1 of the Health Act 1999 repealed Sections 14–17 of the NHS and Community Care Act 1990, concerning GP fundholding practices	PCGs are responsible for the health care needs of those living in each PCG area (this can range between 46,000 to 257,000 patients, although originally patient numbers above 100,000 were expected to be unusual). PCGs operate at one of two levels: **Level 1** Advising the health authority about the NHS care it commissions for patients **Level 2** Managing the NHS budget for their patients' care, acting as part of the health authority	Patients are represented through a lay member of each PCG governing body (Boards). Social services are also represented on the Board, as are GPs and community nurses
Primary Care Trusts (PCTs), first established April 2000	Section 2 of the Health Act 1999	All PCGs are expected to be PCTs by April 2004. PCTs will operate at one of two levels: **Level 3** A free-standing body that commissions care for its patients **Level 4** A free-standing body that commissions care and provides NHS community services (e.g. district nursing) for its patients. Under both models, PCTs are accountable to health authorities	By 2004 (when all PCGs are expected to be PCTs), PCTs will be responsible for at least 75 per cent of the NHS budget. A PCT Development Team is part of the NHS Modernisation Agency (continued)

41

What change, when?	Relevant legislation	What does this mean?	Special notes
	National Health Service Reform and Health Care Professions Act 2002	NHS Reform and Health Care Professions Act contains the legislative change for NHS resources to be paid directly to PCTs, rather than through health authorities	
Strategic Health Authorities (StHAs), established in 2002	NHS Reform and Health Care Professions Act 2002	In England in 2002–2003, 28 Strategic Health Authorities (StHAs) replaced the previous 95 health authorities. PCTs have the lead responsibility for assessing the overall health needs of local populations, and plan and commission services. PCTs also provide most community services, including GPs and dentists, and NHS Walk-in Centres. StHAs will be responsible for the overall strategic development of health services in their area. They will also manage the performance of PCTs and NHS Trusts	
NHS Community Health Trusts absorbed by relevant PCTs from April 2002	NHS and Community Care Act 1990; Health Act 1999; NHS Reform and Health Professions Act 2002	PCTs take responsibility for providing NHS community services (e.g. district nursing) starting from 2002. NHS Trusts will continue to provide most NHS hospital secondary care and specialist services, commissioned by PCTs or Special Health Authorities	

(continued)

What change, when?	Relevant legislation	What does this mean?	Special notes
Special Health Authorities, most established in 1999	Statutory Instrument, 1998, No.1577	Special Health Authorities are NHS organisations that provide particular services to the whole country	NICE (National Institute for Clinical Excellence) is a Special Health Authority. Some high security hospitals are Special Health Authorities, as is the National Blood Authority
Care Trusts, first established April 2002	Section 45 of the Health and Social Care Act 2001; Section 31 of the Health Act 1999	PCTs or NHS Trusts can apply to become Care Trusts if they take on health-related services from the local authority social services departments, delegated under the 'funding flexibilities' of the Health Act 1999. This means Care Trusts can provide both health and social care services	Health services provided by Care Trusts would still be free to NHS users, but social care may be subject to a charge
NHS Foundation Trust hospitals, expected in shadow form July 2003, fully operational April 2004 (subject to legislation)	*Delivering the NHS Plan* White Paper, 2002	Foundation status proposed for highest performing NHS hospitals, Trusts and PCTs. Will have greater freedom from central government on issues such as some finance matters (e.g. staff pay) and involvement of patients and others in boards and governance structures	NHS foundation bodies would still form part of the NHS and be subject to inspection and other usual NHS requirements. Requires new legislation

43

Government Association (LGA) to draw up a single list of priorities for local government to meet central government's main areas of concern, including health.

In the summer of 2002, the Government published a further White Paper *Your Region, Your Choice* (DTLR, 2002). This sets out proposals to create elected Regional Assemblies throughout England. These Assemblies would take on some powers devolved by central government and develop regional strategies on issues such as housing and transport.

In general, changes for local authorities tend to involve increased statutory responsibilities, such as new powers and duties.

Themes and priorities

It is possible to identify a number of common themes and priorities relating to older people's health, housing and social care services. Some are explained briefly here, but are explored in more detail in later chapters.

KEY THEMES

Key themes include:

- standards of services, and standards and quality of staff;
- evidence-based practice;
- promoting independence;
- working in partnership;
- plans and initiatives;
- involving users and carers;
- tackling age discrimination.

There are also a number of priorities, relating both to services and specific client groups and conditions, set by the government for the NHS and social care.

KEY PRIORITIES

These include:

- improving emergency services;

- reducing waiting times and delays (including reducing unnecessary hospital admissions and readmissions for people aged 75 and over; and reducing 'delayed discharges' amongst this same age group);
- improving cancer services; coronary heart disease (CHD) services; mental health services; and services for older people;
- increasing the proportion of social services-supported older users who receive care services in order to remain at home (see Chapter 3).

(HSC 1999/242, LAC (99)39, *National Priorities Guidance 2000/01–2002/03*; HM Treasury, 2002)

Arguably, some of the items listed as 'themes' could appear as 'priorities'; certainly there is some inter-relationship. For example, some of the improvements to services for older people may be dependent on developing services that promote independent living; these services may, in turn, help improve appropriate access to emergency services and reduce some aspects of waiting times. The relevant changes developed in response to these themes are outlined below.

Standards of services and staff

A great deal of emphasis has been placed by the Government on standards, including:

- standards of care in residential and nursing homes, and other personal care services;
- standards of NHS care;
- standards of care from health and social care professionals.

CARE STANDARDS ACT 2000

The Care Standards Act 2000 replaced the Residential Homes Act 1984, and the Residential Homes (Amendment) Act 1991. It came into effect in April 2002. The Act set up a new system of national minimum standards for services such as private and voluntary sector residential and nursing homes and, for the first time, extended the registration requirement for care homes to local authority 'Part III' homes. The Care Standards Act 2000, which is implemented by the National Care Standards Commission (NCSC), also extended regulation to personal domiciliary services (for example, assisting someone to wash or dress), and included nurses' agencies. It established a General Social Care Council (GSCC) to regulate people working in social care. More detail about the Care Standards Act 2000, the NCSC, and the minimum national standards, is contained in Chapter 4. However, whilst the Care Standards Act 2000 also regulates independent sector hospitals and clinics, it does not cover NHS provision. This is dealt with instead by the Commission for Health Improvement (CHI).

In April 2002, shortly after the NCSC began its new role, the Government published the White Paper *Delivering the NHS Plan*. This set out a range of proposals that will change the work of a number of organisations, including the NCSC and CHI (see Box 2.3 on page 48).

COMMISSION FOR HEALTH IMPROVEMENT (CHI)

CHI was set up under the Health Act 1999, and began operating on 1 April 2000. It covers England and Wales (Scotland has a separate body, the Clinical Standards Board; CHI may become involved in Northern Ireland in the future).

When CHI was first set up, a significant part of its work focused on monitoring the quality of patient care delivered by the NHS. It did so by undertaking clinical governance reviews through a rolling programme, that planned visits to every NHS Trust and health authority (including PCGs, PCTs and GP practices) every four years. Each NHS organisation must have clear lines of accountability for clinical quality systems and effective processes for identifying and managing risk, as well as for addressing poor performance (Box 2.2).

Box 2.2 What is clinical governance?

Clinical governance is a term first set out in the 1997 White Paper, *The New NHS: modern, dependable*. In very broad terms, clinical governance relates to the responsibility to provide good quality health care – NHS bodies have a duty to do this. A commonly used definition of clinical governance is as follows:

'A framework through which NHS organisations are accountable for continually improving the quality of their services and safeguarding high standards of care by creating an environment in which excellence in clinical care will flourish.'

Scally, G. and Donaldson, L. J. (1998)

Changes brought about through the NHS Reform and Health Care Professions Act 2002 have strengthened CHI's role as an inspector of health care services. It is through its inspections that CHI considers matters of clinical governance or the quality of services provided by NHS organisations. CHI also has powers to investigate serious service failures in the NHS, when requested to do so by the Secretary of State for Health in England (and by the National Assembly for Wales). It can designate any health services it defines (following inspection) as failing, and as being in need of 'special measures'. (This approach has been used for some years in the context of state schools.)

The NHS Reform and Health Care Professions Act 2002 also increased CHI's powers to inspect health care services provided by the independent sector for NHS patients (for example, operations undertaken at a private clinic for NHS patients under an NHS contract). This creates some overlap with the NCSC's role to regulate independent sector hospitals and clinics, and may lead to further changes to both organisations. This was highlighted in the 2002 White Paper *Delivering the NHS Plan* (see Box 2.3). There are also other proposals for CHI to take over some of the Department of

Health's work on information for performance data and indicators. Timetables for these changes should be clear from early 2003. The Government has said that it intends that contracts with overseas providers will require that CHI (and other bodies, as appropriate) has reasonable access to these providers, and that patients will have the same rights of redress as other patients (*The Government's Response to the Health Committee Report on the Role of the Private Sector in the NHS*, DH, 2002).

CHI reports are available from The Stationery Office, or over the Internet (www.chi.gov.uk. See also the Useful Contacts list on page 249).

Box 2.3 Delivering the NHS Plan proposals

The White Paper *Delivering the NHS Plan* (2002) included proposals to create two new organisations to inspect health and social care. This would change the roles of a number of organisations already involved in this work. The proposed new organisations are:

- Commission for Healthcare Audit and Inspection (CHAI). This would bring together the work of CHI, the private healthcare role of the NCSC, and the health 'value for money' work of the Audit Commission. CHAI would have responsibility for inspecting both the public and private health care sectors;
- Commission for Social Care Inspection. This would bring together the Social Services Inspectorate (part of the Department of Health), and the NCSC, and take on the responsibility for inspecting social care services.

These changes will require further legislation. In July 2002 the Secretary of State for Health announced that the Commission for Social Care Inspection would begin in shadow form by the end of 2002 (DH, 2002). Newspaper advertisements for the post of Chair of CHAI were also placed in July 2002 (*The Guardian*, 2002).

REGULATION OF SOCIAL CARE WORKERS

The General Social Care Council (GSCC) was established under the Care Standards Act 2000. It is responsible for promoting high standards of conduct and practice amongst social care workers, and high standards in their education and training. It covers England, but works closely with the Care Council in Wales, the Northern Ireland Social Care Council, and the Scottish Social Services Council.

One of the main roles of the GSCC is to set up, and regulate, a register of social care workers. This register includes people with professional social work qualifications, as well as untrained staff working in social care services. It covers people who work in the public, private and voluntary sectors. The GSCC will be able to investigate complaints into registered workers, and will have the power to remove people from the register. Consultation on the details of the register took place in mid-2002. Professionally qualified social workers are expected to be the first group to be registered, from spring 2003. It is likely that priority will then be given to registering residential child care workers, and managers of care homes. This is the first time social care workers, qualified or otherwise, have been registered in this way. It brings social care closer to the regulatory models for health care professionals.

REGULATION OF HEALTH PROFESSIONALS

In 2001, a Public Inquiry into the high rates of death in children's heart surgery at Bristol Royal Infirmary between 1984 and 1995 published its recommendations (*Learning from Bristol*, 2001; this is also known as the Kennedy Report, after its Chair, Professor Sir Ian Kennedy). Although concerned with one specific aspect of children's NHS services, many of its recommendations applied across the NHS, to all patient groups. These included recommendations about the involvement of patients and the public in health care, and about the information patients need in order to make informed decisions. The Inquiry also recommended changes to the regulation and education of health care professionals.

The Government responded by announcing the formation of a new Council for the Regulation of Healthcare Professionals. This brings together bodies regulating healthcare professionals, such as the General Medical Council (GMC), the Nursing and Midwifery Council (NMC) and the Council for the Regulation of Healthcare Professionals (for Professions Supplementary to Medicine).

There are also proposals for GPs and other doctors to be subject to a re-registration process every five years, in order to ensure their knowledge and work is up-to-date and of good quality. The Shipman Inquiry, which began in 2001 and continued its investigation into the case of the GP Dr Harold Shipman throughout 2002, may also recommend further changes affecting GPs and other health and associated professionals – for example, how deaths are recorded, and arrangements for cremation. (Dr Shipman was convicted in court of the murder of 15 of his patients and, the Inquiry concluded in 2002, killed up to 260 of his patients.)

NATIONAL PATIENT SAFETY AGENCY

Proposals for this Special Health Authority were set out in the Department of Health's *Building a Safer NHS for Patients* (2000). The remit of the National Patient Safety Agency (NPSA) is to co-ordinate the efforts of all those involved in healthcare, and to learn from adverse incidents that occur in the NHS (for example, deaths caused by staff administering the wrong drugs). It does this by collecting and analysing information on adverse events from local NHS organisations, NHS staff, patients and carers. It then highlights the lessons to be learnt, and ensures any change is put into practice. The aim is to make sure that problems in one part of the NHS are not replicated elsewhere; and to reduce the number of multiple investigations into what is often, essentially, the same problem. A series of national targets have been set, including reducing by 40 per cent the number of serious errors in the use of prescribed drugs, by 2005.

AUDIT COMMISSION/SOCIAL SERVICES INSPECTORATE JOINT
REVIEWS

In 1998, the Audit Commission and Social Services Inspectorate
(SSI – part of the Department of Health) were given new powers
to carry out Joint Reviews of local social services departments.
These Joint Reviews identify strengths and weaknesses, compare
the inspected authority with similar authorities' performances, and
make recommendations for service improvement.

In doing so, they draw on two sets of data: Social Services Performance Assessment Framework (PAF); and, increasingly, the Best
Value Performance Indicators. These contain a number of targets
and issues on which social services departments are judged annually. For older people, these include:

- percentage of items of equipment and adaptations costing less
  than £1,000 provided within three weeks;
- average gross costs of residential care and of intensive home care
  services;
- households receiving intensive home care to remain at home,
  per 1,000 of the population aged 65 and over.

(The Department of Health defines intensive home care as more
than ten contact hours and six or more visits each week.)

The Department of Health (DH) publishes both these Joint
Reviews and the Social Services PAF annual reports. The Office of
the Deputy Prime Minister (ODPM – formerly part of the Department of Transport, Local Government and the Regions (DTLR))
publishes the Best Value performance framework, and issues guidance on Best Value reviews.

In July 2002, the Secretary of State for Health announced new targets for social services (*Expanded Services and Increased Choices
for Older People*, DH, 2002). By the end of 2004, social services
departments will be expected to:

- make first contact with individuals referred for assessment of their needs within 48 hours;
- complete these needs assessments within one month;
- make available equipment to support people in their own homes within one week following assessment.

See also Chapters 3, 5 and 6. It is also likely that the Joint Reviews role will be taken over by the proposed Commission for Social Care Inspection from 2004.

BEST VALUE REVIEWS

'Best Value' was introduced under the Local Government Act 1999 and implemented from 2000. It replaced the previous Compulsory Competitive Tendering (CCT) arrangements, which had applied to some (but not all) local authority functions. It also replaced proposals from the last Conservative government to introduce 'Value for Money' (VfM) tests to social services' provision (*Social Services – Achievement and Challenge*, DH, 1997).

Initially, all local authority services were to be subject to a Best Value review over a five-year period. Guidance issued in 2002 removed this absolute requirement, although each local authority still has a legal requirement to review all its services at some stage. However, authorities have been given greater discretion over which services they review, and when. This means they have greater control over which services they decide to prioritise, in order to meet local and national targets (Statutory Instrument 2002, No. 305).

Since 2002, each authority has had to produce an annual Best Value Performance Plan. This should set out what services the authority will deliver locally; how it will deliver them; what standards are currently in place; how these should change for the future; and the steps the authority will take to meet these new targets (see page 67, Figure 2.2).

Best Value is based around four main questions (the 'four Cs'). Local authorities must apply these questions to each service under review.

Box 2.4 Best Value – the 'four Cs'

Challenge – Why is the service provided? Who is it for? Could it be provided in a better way? Should it change if people's needs are changing?

Consult – What do users and local citizens, council employees, and other organisations think about the service?

Compare – Do similar councils or organisations give a better service? In what ways is it better?

Compete – Could another body – such as another local organisation – provide a better quality, or more suitable, or cheaper service? Can partnerships be formed with other public bodies, or other organisations, to achieve this?

Best Value is an opportunity to take a strategic (or overall) view of a particular type of service – for example, residential provision; day care; sheltered housing. The aim behind Best Value reviews for social services and housing departments is to consider whether services best meet the needs of current and future users. The cost-effectiveness and quality of these services are also compared with other providers' services, or with other service solutions. Each local authority decides whether (and how) to change a service following its Best Value review.

Many authorities have considered each service from the point of view of the different client groups – for example, older people; adults with physical disabilities; adults with learning difficulties. Best Value reviews have also looked at particular elements of social services' work such as assessment and care management arrangements, as well as some of the infrastructure of local authority organisations. The Audit Commission and the Social Services Inspectorate (SSI) inspect Best Value reviews; annual Best Value Performance Indicators are also set, against which local authorities' performance is measured.

The Office of the Deputy Prime Minister (ODPM) is responsible for issuing guidance on Best Value reviews. In its guidance on the framework for Best Value in Housing (BVH), it stressed the need for local authorities and other partners to bear in mind the number of ways in which housing, care and support are inextricably linked (*Best Value in Housing Framework*, 2000).

BETTER CARE, HIGHER STANDARDS

Introduced in 2000, *Better Care, Higher Standards* (DETR/DH, 1999, also called the Long Term Care Charter) replaced the Community Care Charters established during the 1990s. It sets out a framework under which social services and housing authorities, agreed with health, set and publish local standards on services, and their availability via eligibility criteria. Local *Better Care, Higher Standards* charters are expected to be one of the major sources of information for older people and their carers seeking community and continuing health services. Housing services should also be included. Charters should be published each June, and contain information relevant for that financial year (April to March). See Chapter 7.

Evidence-based practice

Basing policy decisions on what appears to work in practice (what is known as 'evidence-based practice') has been a continuous theme across health, housing and social care services for some years. To a certain extent, Best Value reviews consider the available evidence base for service design, now and in the future. However, two specific types of initiative have developed around this issue. The first relates to formalising (and centralising) the sharing of good practice information between the NHS and local authorities – for example, the Beacon services (see Box 2.5 on page 57).

The second relates to creating distinct national services to give formal consideration to, and advice about, the evidence for particular treatments or services. An organisation such as the National Institute for Clinical Excellence (NICE) is an example of this.

NATIONAL INSTITUTE FOR CLINICAL EXCELLENCE (NICE)

The Special Health Authority, NICE, was set up on 1 April 1999 to cover England and Wales. Its role is to provide patients, health professionals and the wider public with guidance on current best practice in terms of health technologies (including medicines, medical devices and techniques) as well as the clinical management of specific health conditions. It does so by considering the available evidence, and the views of interested parties. These latter can range from pharmaceutical companies to charities and patients' groups. There is an appeal process against NICE's decisions. The topics for NICE's work programme are chosen by the Department of Health and Welsh Assembly Government.

Since its inception, NICE has issued guidance on a number of procedures and medicines, including, in 2001, recommending that the NHS make available certain drugs for people with mild to moderate Alzheimer's disease in specific circumstances. NHS organisations must follow NICE's advice, and make drugs and treatments available within three months of NICE issuing its recommendations.

The NHS Plan (DH, 2000) recommended that NICE establish a Citizens' Council to offer advice reflecting the general public's perspective. The Citizens' Council will advise on social, moral and ethical issues relating to NICE's work. People working for patient or healthcare groups, the Department of Health, the National Assembly for Wales or healthcare industries will be excluded from the Council, which is expected to start in late 2002. (See Chapter 7 for information on involving users and carers.)

SOCIAL CARE INSTITUTE FOR EXCELLENCE (SCIE)

As one of the proposals initially set out in the Department of Health consultation paper *A Quality Strategy for Social Care* (2000), the Social Care Institute for Excellence (SCIE, pronounced 'sky') was formally set up at the end of 2001. Like NICE, SCIE covers England and Wales and is expected to work with those countries' respective regulatory bodies – the National Care Standards Commission and the Care Council – as well as other organisations, users, practitioners and carers. Some staff from the

National Institute for Social Work (NISW), part of whose role was absorbed into the General Social Care Council (GSCC), transferred to SCIE. Unlike NICE, which is part of the NHS, SCIE has been set up as a not-for-profit company limited by guarantee (a term with which much of the voluntary sector will be familiar, as many voluntary groups are constituted in this way). This means it is an independent organisation responsible to its own Board. SCIE will create a knowledge base of what works in social care through assessing existing practice and expertise, and producing good practice guidelines, tools and other materials, including information on the Internet. (See the Useful Contacts list on page 249.)

'MODERNISATION' ORGANISATIONS, AND BEACON SERVICES

Proposals to set up an NHS Modernisation Agency were outlined in *The NHS Plan* (2000). A Modernisation Board was subsequently established to draw up the detailed implementation programme. The Modernisation Board acts in an advisory capacity, and is headed by the Secretary of State for Health.

A separate body, the NHS Modernisation Agency, was also set up to spread best practice. It includes a number of other Department of Health-established specialist teams and programmes. These are:

- National Patients' Action Team;
- Primary Care Development Team;
- Clinical Governance Support Unit;
- Beacons Programme;
- NHS Annual Awards programmes;
- Collaborative programmes.

The Modernisation Agency is also leading Local Modernisation Reviews (LMRs). LMRs involve both local NHS and social services authorities, as the aim of an LMR is to set out how the targets of *The NHS Plan* will be achieved in each local area. Stage One of the LMR process was completed at the end of July 2001 and looked at all *The NHS Plan* targets. Stage Two, carried out in 2001–2002, focused on the key issues on which more detailed work is needed to make sure *The NHS Plan* targets are met locally. These issues are:

- older people;
- mental health;
- capital and capacity;
- workforce;
- information management and technology.

Those involved in LMR in local areas have been advised to learn from organisations that have already tackled some aspects of these issues and have been identified under the NHS Beacons Programme. This Programme aims to spread good practice through identifying and publishing details of NHS organisations and services that have developed good practice examples relevant to *The NHS Plan* (Box 2.5).

In 1999, the Department for Transport, Local Government and the Regions (DTLR) also established a Beacons Programme for local councils (including social services and housing authorities). This is now run by the Office of the Deputy Prime Minister (ODPM).

Box 2.5 Beacon services in the NHS and local government

The aim of Beacon services in both the NHS and local government is to identify areas (or services) of excellence, from which other NHS bodies and councils can learn.

The NHS Beacons programme focuses on issues such as:

- stroke services
- palliative care.

Themes for 2002–2003 local government Beacon services include:

- community cohesion
- quality of the built environment
- tackling homelessness.

A Local Government Modernisation Team, also run by the ODPM, was set up to promote the implementation of the 1999 *Modernising Government* White Paper. This formed the basis for the Local Government Act 1999, and includes the introduction of Best Value reviews.

Finally, and again in order to secure the implementation of *The NHS Plan*, the Department of Health set up ten taskforces, each concentrating on one of the following key target areas in the Plan:

- access;
- cancer;
- capital and capacity;
- coronary heart disease;
- children;
- mental health;
- quality;
- older people;
- public health and reducing inequality;
- workforce.

These ten taskforces, consisting of representatives of key, interested organisations and experts, are also supported by two further groups (one specialises in communications and the other in performance improvement). The older people's taskforce is concentrating on:

- assuring standards of care;
- extending access to services;
- ensuring fairer funding;
- promoting independence;
- helping older people to stay healthy;
- developing links between health and social services.

Working in partnership

A theme that has appeared repeatedly over many years – certainly since the Griffiths Report of 1988 – concerns the effect on older services users of the barriers between health, housing and social services. Many people with ongoing care needs require the expertise and services found within these organisations at some stage. However, differing priorities, varied criteria for services, professional differences and a contrast in emphasis, not to mention varied funding cycles, budgetary constraints and charging regimes, have caused significant problems for both users and carers. The Department of Health's White Paper *Modernising Social Services* (1998) set out the view that one key way to 'bring down the Berlin Wall' between health and social services was through the creation of new joint funding arrangements.

Joint funding

Section 28A of the NHS Act 1977 had made it possible for local NHS bodies to provide funds towards social services authorities for health-related activities: for example, in helping to fund hospital discharge teams. However, these funds could only come from the NHS to social services, not vice versa, and did not necessarily tackle some of the organisational and professional barriers between the two bodies.

Under sections 29–31 of the Health Act 1999, since April 2000 local authorities and NHS bodies have been able to work in partnership through a wider range of financial possibilities commonly known as the 'funding flexibilities' (HSC 2000/10, LAC (2000)09, *Implementation of Health Act Partnership Arrangements*; Statutory Instrument 2000, No. 617).

POOLED BUDGETS

Health and social services put a proportion of their funds into a joint budget to create more integrated care. Both can access the funds equally.

LEAD COMMISSIONING

One organisation (either the NHS or local authority) delegates responsibility and transfers funds to the other authority to purchase both health and social care.

INTEGRATED PROVISION

One organisation provides both health and social care. This would mean an NHS Trust or a PCT could provide social care as well as NHS services; or that a social services' own (or in-house) service provider could provide some community health services on behalf of the NHS.

Care Trusts

Section 45 of the Health and Social Care Act 2001 gave the Secretary of State for Health the power to form a Care Trust, following local consultation on such a proposal. Care Trusts are NHS bodies which combine either a PCT or an NHS Trust with local authority services, using the power to delegate functions set out in Section 31 of the Health Act 1999. Care Trusts were first established in April 2002. They are accountable to the Strategic Health Authorities that came into being in 2002. As they also deliver functions that have been delegated to them by a local authority, Care Trusts are accountable to that local authority for that delegated function. Care Trusts will also be scrutinised by the relevant local authority Overview and Scrutiny Committee (OSC).

Each Care Trust is supported by a Board. Four Care Trusts were established in April 2002, in Northumberland; Manchester; Camden and Islington; and Bradford. It is expected that older people's health and social care will increasingly be provided by Care Trusts.

Local Strategic Partnerships

New powers for local authorities also mean that the notion of 'partnership' has moved beyond that of the relationship between health and social services. Part I of the Local Government Act 2000 created a new discretionary power for local authorities in England and Wales to take any action they consider will promote or improve the economic, social or environmental well-being of their area. This power came into effect in October 2000, and is fulfilled by Local Strategic Partnerships (LSP). Each LSP is established within local authority boundaries, and should involve all and any relevant parties – for example, environmental groups, schools, shopkeepers, local neighbourhood watch schemes, GP services, public transport, and social services departments. Public and private organisations, as well as individuals and community groups, should be involved. LSPs consider a wide range of issues, including social exclusion, neighbourhood renewal, and the drawing up of local community strategies (see also Figure 2.2 on page 67). They should establish common priorities and targets, and ensure that member organisations are aligned with the aims and objectives of the LSP.

Overview and Scrutiny Committees (OSC) were also introduced under the Local Government Act 2000. The powers of OSCs were extended, under the Health and Social Care Act 2001, to include the scrutiny of health bodies as part of local authorities' wider role in health improvement and in reducing health inequalities.

Other arrangements

Other partnership arrangements are more closely linked to the private and voluntary sectors, and take a variety of forms.

COMPACT WITH THE VOLUNTARY SECTOR

In November 1998, the Home Office published the framework between Government and the voluntary and community sector. This framework, *Getting It Right Together*, is commonly called 'the Compact'. Arising from the Deakin Commission's report on the future of the voluntary sector (NCVO, 1996), the Compact describes voluntary and community groups as society's 'third sector'. It sets out a number of shared principles for the voluntary sector: the intention to develop good practice guidelines for funding by government departments (particularly in regard to long-term funding); to consult the sector; to recognise its independence and right to campaign; and for this approach to be adopted by other public bodies, including local government, in their areas. In 2002 the Spending Review White Paper *Opportunity and Security for All* (HM Treasury, 2002) announced plans for a new investment fund for the voluntary and community sector. This fund, worth £125m over three years, is expected to help build capacity in the sector, amongst other objectives.

THE CONCORDAT WITH THE NHS

In 2000, the Department of Health and the Independent Health-care Association jointly published details of the partnership relationships the NHS should develop with private and voluntary healthcare providers, known as the Concordat. This national framework, *For the Benefit of Patients*, set out the range of possible partnership arrangements. These include: PCGs/PCTs renting or commissioning accommodation from the private and voluntary health care sector; an NHS Trust 'sub-contracting' the provision of a service to the private or voluntary health care provider; or PCGs/PCTs directly commissioning from one of these providers. Intermediate care services were one of the areas especially identified for developing the role of the independent sector (see Chapter 3). The Concordat reminded providers that, where services are provided under contract to the NHS, the appropriate quality standards set by NICE and CHI for NHS Trusts will also apply. It signalled a commitment from the NHS towards planning the use of private and voluntary health care providers on a longer-term basis.

In 2002, the Health Select Committee published the results of its inquiry into the relationship between the NHS and the private sector. This included consideration of the use of the Private Finance Initiative (PFI) within the NHS, a subject that is not covered by this book. The Select Committee expressed concerns that the NHS's capacity directly to provide acute services should be developed; and that Concordat arrangements should not mean the NHS becomes so dependent on the independent sector that contract prices for treatments cannot be protected. It also recommended that Concordat arrangements be reviewed to ensure the NHS is always getting 'value for money' from independent providers. In its response, the Government set out its continued commitment to strengthening relationships between the NHS and the independent sector.

The White Paper, *Delivering the NHS Plan* (DH, 2002) set out expectations on the NHS to become more involved in forming individual partnerships with the private and voluntary sector. A further document, *Growing Capacity* (DH, 2002), identified a specific role for independent sector healthcare providers in developing new surgical and diagnostic clinics, using medical staff from abroad, to assist the NHS in reducing waiting times in key surgical areas. This builds on developments from late 2001, when the Secretary of State for Health signalled his approval for the NHS to contract for treatment with European healthcare providers. In January 2002, the first patients (most over the age of 60) received treatment, including hip and knee operations, in French hospitals and clinics. It is expected that further initiatives involving hospitals, clinics and clinicians from European and other countries will develop. It is likely that commissioning of overseas services will be handled by key, named, individuals within the NHS, who will act on behalf of the whole NHS (*Treating More Patients and Extending Choice: draft guidance*, DH, 2002).

PARTNERSHIPS IN PRACTICE AND PLANNING

Other requirements on health and social services and other agencies, to work together in partnership, include identifying and agreeing eligibility criteria for NHS continuing health care, and implementing the Single Assessment Process for older people (sometimes called 'SAP'). These are dealt with in more detail in later chapters. In addition, these bodies are involved locally in developing and implementing a wide range of plans and initiatives. The government itself signalled a commitment to working across agencies, by creating an Inter Ministerial Group for Older People. This was intended to ensure that initiatives from different government departments that affect older people – for example, the Departments of Health, Work and Pensions, Transport, and the Office of the Deputy Prime Minister – are co-ordinated and designed in a complementary way.

PARTNERSHIPS WITH OLDER PEOPLE

One interesting area, in terms of partnership working, concerns proposals for local councils to be obliged to offer direct payments to older people (DH, 2002). The issue of direct payments is explored in more detail in Chapter 3, but is essentially a system whereby individuals can receive money instead of (or as well as) services to meet the needs social services have assessed them as having. Individuals use these funds to organise their own care to meet these needs, subject to the various restrictions set out in Chapter 3. The proposals, set out in July 2002, would mean that older people are always offered the option of receiving direct payments from social services departments (DH, 2002). This would include those identified as ready to leave NHS hospital care, but who need some form of post-acute care. It suggests new partnership arrangements with individual older people in two respects. Firstly, the onus to access care as quickly as possible would fall on the older person rather than social services. Secondly, as direct payments cannot be spent on services provided by the statutory sector, it suggests a range of new individual arrangements between older people and the independent sector – perhaps particularly with the private sector, which has far greater experience compared with the voluntary sector of providing care services to people under private, individual arrangements.

PARTNERSHIPS WITH HOUSING

A key issue that emerged strongly during the 1990s is the importance of meeting the housing needs of older people, especially in the context of their other needs for treatment, care and support. The Housing Green Paper, *Quality and Choice: a decent home for all* (DETR, 2000), drew particular attention to the needs of older people, as well as the rest of the population, to have both good quality housing and a choice of housing options. Chapter 6 details the ways in which the funding of supported housing (such as sheltered housing for older people) and associated support services (such as community alarm schemes) change from April 2003, under the *Supporting People* proposals (DETR, 2001). An older people's Listening Event, set up through the *Better Government for Older People* (BGOP) programme and under the auspices of the Inter Ministerial Group, was held following the publication of the Housing Green Paper. This reported a number of concerns and led, for the first time, to the Departments of Health and Transport, Local Government and the Regions jointly publishing a housing framework for older people. This stressed the need for increased insulation, help with heating and other energy saving measures; practical help around the garden and home and better transport facilities; better quality in sheltered housing, and less time spent waiting for adaptations and equipment, and when moving home (DTLR/DH, 2001). Other concerns were voiced about the extent to which new housing design takes the needs of older people into account, although many of these issues should be being addressed under Part M of the Building Regulations. These came into effect in October 1999, and cover a range of standards aimed at producing 'lifetime homes' – accessible housing for all age groups and for able-bodied and disabled people.

From these concerns, the Government identified five key areas for improvement:

- diversity and choice;
- information and advice;
- flexible service provision;
- quality;
- joint working.

In addition, local Housing Investment Programmes (HIPs) for 2001–2002 drew attention to how the needs of older people would be considered and met through local authority housing strategies.

Plans and initiatives

There are a wide range of plans (e.g. HIMP, JIP, SaFF) and initiatives (e.g. HAZ, HLC, BGOP), which have shaped the development of the way local authorities and the NHS have been working in each area. These are explained in detail in the sections below.

Plans

Figures 2.1 and 2.2 set out some of the key inter-relationships between the various plans, for the NHS and for local government. Many of these plans have developed over time. The Joint Investment Plan (JIP) developed from the 1997 initiative, *Better Services for Vulnerable People* (BSVP), and initially concentrated on older

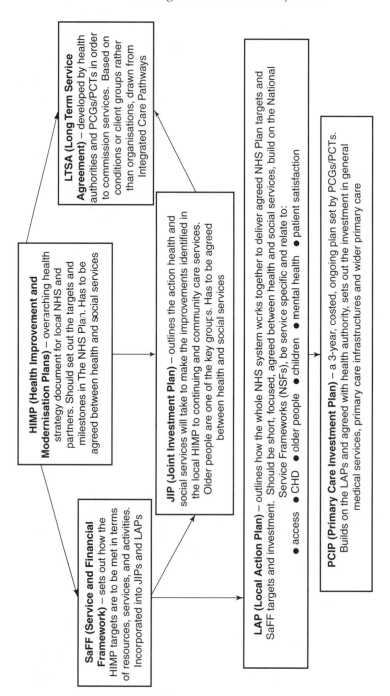

HIMP (Health Improvement and Modernisation Plans) – overarching health strategy document for local NHS and partners. Should set out the targets and milestones in The NHS Plan. Has to be agreed between health and social services

LTSA (Long Term Service Agreement) – developed by health authorities and PCGs/PCTs in order to commission services. Based on conditions or client groups rather than organisations, drawn from Integrated Care Pathways

SaFF (Service and Financial Framework) – sets out how the HIMP targets are to be met in terms of resources, services, and activities. Incorporated into JIPs and LAPs

JIP (Joint Investment Plan) – outlines the action health and social services will take to make the improvements identified in the local HIMP to continuing and community care services. Older people are one of the key groups. Has to be agreed between health and social services

LAP (Local Action Plan) – outlines how the whole NHS system works together to deliver agreed NHS Plan targets and SaFF targets and investment. Should be short, focused, agreed between health and social services, build on the National Service Frameworks (NSFs), be service specific and relate to:
● access ● CHD ● older people ● children ● mental health ● patient satisfaction

PCIP (Primary Care Investment Plan) – a 3-year, costed, ongoing plan set by PCGs/PCTs. Builds on the LAPs and agreed with health authority, sets out the investment in general medical services, primary care infrastructures and wider primary care

Figure 2.1 Plans: the NHS perspective

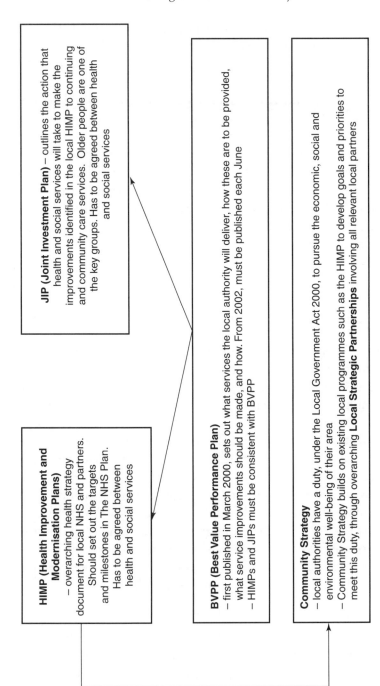

HIMP (Health Improvement and Modernisation Plans)
– overarching health strategy document for local NHS and partners. Should set out the targets and milestones in The NHS Plan. Has to be agreed between health and social services

JIP (Joint Investment Plan) – outlines the action that health and social services will take to make the improvements identified in the local HIMP to continuing and community care services. Older people are one of the key groups. Has to be agreed between health and social services

BVPP (Best Value Performance Plan)
– first published in March 2000, sets out what services the local authority will deliver, how these are to be provided, what service improvements should be made, and how. From 2002, must be published each June
– HIMPs and JIPs must be consistent with BVPP

Community Strategy
– local authorities have a duty, under the Local Government Act 2000, to pursue the economic, social and environmental well-being of their area
– Community Strategy builds on existing local programmes such as the HIMP to develop goals and priorities to meet this duty, through overarching **Local Strategic Partnerships** involving all relevant local partners

Figure 2.2 Plans: the local government perspective

people. Health Improvement and Modernisation Plans (HIMPs) began life in 1998 as HImPs (Health Improvement Programmes), intended to draw up a local plan of action to improve health and modernise services. The emphasis now, as set out in many documents, is for NHS and social services bodies to respond to the targets in *The NHS Plan* at a local level. As HIMPs and JIPs – amongst other initiatives and plans – have superseded Community Care Plans, the Department of Health decided to repeal section 46 of the NHS and Community Care Act 1990 as of April 2002. This had set out the duty on local authorities to prepare and publish Community Care Plans (*Community Care Plans (England) Directions*, 2002). It is possible that, in the future, JIPs will be subsumed under the more detailed requirements of the National Service Framework for Older People.

Initiatives

WINTER PRESSURES FUNDING

In 1996, the Conservative government announced the first 'winter pressures' money. This was a specific block grant for health and social services to develop services to tackle problems generated by increasing numbers of patients, especially older patients, in NHS hospitals during winter months. Many of the initiatives and responses developed at that time – Rapid Response Teams, Early Discharge Schemes, intensive home support and social care rehabilitation – have formed the basis for intermediate care services (see Chapter 3). Winter Pressures Funding and service responses have also developed into year-round funding. The *Building Capacity and Partnership in Care* initiative in 2001–2002 was designed further to develop services to accommodate older patients waiting to be discharged to alternative care arrangements. (This is one of the Government's responses to the issue of 'bed blocking' – see Chapter 3.)

BETTER SERVICES FOR VULNERABLE PEOPLE (BSVP)

BSVP was launched in October 1997, in conjunction with winter pressures money for that year. It set out early requirements to improve the multi-disciplinary assessment of older people, and develop opportunities for recuperation and rehabilitation. It also created the Joint Investment Programme (JIP) for health and social services authorities. Subsequent monitoring of the BSVP initiative identified the need to develop a range of intermediate care services (see Chapter 3), offering a bridge between home and hospital care for older people.

HEALTH ACTION ZONES (HAZS)

HAZs were set up in 1998, covering geographical areas identified as experiencing deprivation and poor health. They range in size, but all aim to tackle health inequalities, and link health, regeneration, employment, education, housing and anti-poverty initiatives. They are co-ordinated locally by a partnership board, which also helps agree the health and service needs of each HAZ. Some HAZs have focused on one particular client group (including older people, in some areas) and set short, medium and long term goals for local agencies to improve the overall health of that group in the HAZ area.

HEALTHY LIVING CENTRES (HLCS)

HLCs are funded though the New Opportunities Fund, the lottery distribution body set up under the National Lottery Act 1998, which gives grants for educational, environmental and health-related initiatives. The HLC initiative began in January 1999 and, like HAZs, forms part of the Government's public health initiatives, set out in the Department of Health White Paper, *Saving Lives: Our Healthier Nation* (1999).

BETTER GOVERNMENT FOR OLDER PEOPLE (BGOP)

This programme initially ran between 1998 and 2000, and was formed through a partnership between the Cabinet Office, Age Concern England, Anchor Trust, and the Carnegie Third Age programme, Help the Aged and Warwick University. There was an Older People's Advisory Group to the programme, and input from the Local Government Association. The programme aimed to improve public services for older people by encouraging and recognising their contribution, listening to their views, and meeting their needs more effectively.

Pilot projects involving older people, local government and the private and voluntary sectors were launched by 28 local authorities. These projects covered issues such as health care, transport, housing and leisure facilities, as well as opportunities to volunteer and contribute to the community. Some pilots considered the information needs of older people, including avoiding the use of jargon in order to make clearer how people can gain access to systems of help. In some areas, local authorities have expanded and continued with these pilot projects. In its report, *All our Futures* (Better Government for Older People Steering Committee, 2000), the BGOP programme concluded that there was a need to combat age discrimination, engage older people more effectively, improve decision-making, meet older people's needs more effectively, and promote a strategic, joined-up approach to an ageing population. One important message was that improving services for older people brought benefits for the whole local population. Since 2001, the work has continued via a network of BGOP members and the Older People's Advisory Group.

Involving users and carers

Chapter 7 explains at length how service users and carers, as well as the general public, are increasingly involved in consultation and discussion about services and organisations. These include new arrangements and responsibilities, especially within the NHS, to obtain the views of people who use services as one way of improving provision.

Tackling age discrimination

Concerns about age discrimination within health care services have focused on both the quality and quantity of support received. In 1998, the Health Advisory Service 2000 noted the poor quality of care received by some older NHS hospital patients, and raised concerns about age discrimination in its report *Not Because They Are Old*. Other organisations have identified concerns about upper age limits on breast cancer screening for women; about NHS hospital policies and practice on resuscitating older patients; and about upper age limits on access to some specialist services such as heart units (Age Concern England, 1998).

In social care, most attention has been focused on differences in the *quantity* of support available to older people compared with younger adults (Age Concern England, 1998a; Help the Aged 2002). Most social services departments divide users into separate client groups. Typically for adults, these are:

• adults aged 18–64 with physical disabilities;
• adults aged 18–64 with mental health problems;
• adults aged 18–64 with learning disabilities;
• adults aged 18–64 with substance abuse problems;
• older people (65 and over).

Some concerns have centred on whether older people are able to access as much support as working-age adults. This issue is complicated, partly because some services (especially places in residential care) tend to be much more expensive for younger adults than for older people; and partly because some state financial support to help people with disabilities is not generally available to older disabled people. In addition, some working-age adults with disabilities receive support in employment, which tends not to be relevant (or available) to retired people with disabilities.

The Government has responded to these concerns in a variety of ways. For example, *The NHS Plan* extended the age at which women are automatically invited for breast cancer screening from 65 to 70 (and made clear that women can still request such a screening after that age but will not be automatically invited). In 2000, guidance on 'Do Not Resuscitate' (DNR) decisions was issued to the NHS (HSC 2000/028, *Resuscitation Policy*), reminding staff not to make such decisions without involving patients and their families. Standard One of the National Service Framework (NSF) for Older People set out a requirement on health and social services to 'root out age discrimination' (see Chapter 3). In addition, social services departments have been told they must use the same eligibility criteria for all adult groups by 2003, when deciding to whom to offer social care services (see Chapter 5).

Some organisations have been campaigning to change the law to outlaw age discrimination in everyday life. However, the Government's response has been limited to a voluntary code of conduct aimed at tackling age discrimination in employment. From 2006, following a Directive from the European Union (EU), it will be unlawful to discriminate against workers on the basis of their age.

Some of the Government's themes and priorities apply to adults of all ages, some are more relevant to older people. One priority that considers issues for children as well as adults of all ages is the commitment to tackle health inequalities (*Saving Lives: Our Healthier Nation*, DH, 1999). Inequalities in health can mean some sections of the population, or people who live in certain parts of the country, become ill earlier in their lives, and die sooner. For example, in 2002, the Office for National Statistics (ONS) published details showing that people in the southwest of England tend to live longer than those in the northeast of England (ONS, 2002). The Government's targets to tackle such health inequalities include reducing the rate of serious injury from accidents (such as falls amongst older people) by one-tenth by 2010 (*Saving Lives: Our Healthier Nation*, DH, 1999). There are also targets to reduce the death rates from coronary heart disease (CHD) and stroke amongst adults under the age of 75, also by 2010. This is a particular issue for some ethnic minority groups. CHD rates are high amongst South Asian populations, and hypertension and strokes are also very high among people of African-Caribbean origin (Lowdell *et al*, 2000). Men from lower socio-economic classes (such as unskilled manual workers) are also more likely to die from CHD. Meeting these targets may well have implications in terms of which sections of the population begin to reach much older ages.

As explained above, some of the themes identified in this chapter will be explored in more detail in later chapters. These include the emphasis on involving users and carers. The National Service Frameworks (NSFs), especially those relating to services for older people, are outlined in detail in Chapter 3.

3 Treatment, care and support for older people

This chapter considers some of the main service issues for older people seeking treatment, care and support for their ongoing needs. It looks at how some of the most commonly-used services have been changing; the local and national policy decisions that have affected services; and the development of responses to specific conditions and experiences – for example, stroke, cancer, coronary heart disease, mental health (including dementia), and falls amongst older people. Further sources of information are given in the chapter.

Chapter 1 outlined how, since April 1993, services have increasingly been targeted on those 'most in need'. This chapter considers how such targeting, and the emphasis on supporting people to live in their own homes, has affected home care services (see pages 83–4), services to promote independence (see page 85), and the use of residential care (see page 98). Services for older people have been further affected by two additional factors:

- the increasing role played by the statutory sector as a purchaser;
- the policy imperative to tackle the discharge of older patients from NHS hospital beds.

These issues are also discussed, below.

The statutory sector – provider or purchaser?

Chapter 1 outlined how the provision of services has changed over the past twenty years. The majority of residential and nursing homes for older people are now provided by the independent sector (especially by the private sector), rather than through local authority Part III homes, or NHS long-stay wards. Similar changes have taken place, since the full implementation of the community care reforms in April 1993, in non-residential services such as home help or home care. In 1993, 95 per cent of home care services were provided directly by local authorities, and only 5 per cent by the independent sector under a contract with social services departments. By 2000, 56 per cent of these home care services were provided by the independent sector (Laing and Buisson, 2001).

Local authorities as purchasers

There are a number of reasons why local authorities have moved away from their more traditional role as direct providers of many social care services for older people (and other groups), towards a role as purchasers (or commissioners) of services from the private and voluntary sectors.

One of the key reasons concerns requirements placed on social services departments by central government in the first few years following the community care reforms. After April 1993, local councils were given additional funding by central government in recognition of their new responsibilities to fund care services (especially the responsibility to assist in the funding of means-tested places in nursing homes – see Chapter 6). This additional funding was called the Special Transitional Grant (STG). Prior to April 1993 (as outlined in Chapter 1), most of the state's funding for independent sector residential and nursing homes came from the Department of Social Security (DSS – now the Department for Work and Pensions). This was accompanied by significant increases in the number and use of independent sector homes. In order to maintain (and build upon) this pattern, the then Conservative government required local authorities to spend 85 per cent of their STG allocation in the independent sector. This figure did not have to be spent exclusively on residential services – local authorities also used the money to purchase day services (such as home care, meals-on-wheels and places in day centres). The independent sector therefore began to provide more and more of the state's social care support to older people because there was a clear central policy – and financial imperative – to do so.

Importantly, a 1996 court case helped to confirm that local authorities were not obliged directly to provide services. The case, *R v Wandsworth London Borough Council ex parte Beckwith*, dealt with the provision of residential care for older people. The court ruled that, under the National Assistance Act 1948, local authorities could meet their legal duties entirely through contracting for places in homes run by the independent sector, rather than through running their own, 'Part III' (see page 2), residential accommodation.

Other factors have also played a part. In some instances, services directly provided by the independent sector cost the local authority less than its own ('in-house') services. Between 1993–2002, independent sector residents could claim more state benefits as income than could 'Part III' residents (these benefit rules changed after April 2002 – see Chapter 6). This additional income was included in the means-test applied to such care. The net effect was that this reduced the cost to local authorities of independent sector home places – but did not apply to those living in its own Part III homes.

In some areas, local authorities decided to change the amount and range of services they provided directly to older people and other users. One example concerns the re-development, in some areas, of local authority residential homes into extra care sheltered housing (see page 108), with ownership and management for the new schemes often transferred to housing associations. Elsewhere, some local authorities transferred the ownership and management of existing directly-provided services, such as home care services and residential homes, to specially established 'not-for-profit' companies. Such changes are reflected statistically only as a general decrease in local authority services, and a general increase in voluntary sector services.

The current pattern of social care services is further affected by the independent sector's own history of providing services. The voluntary sector, in particular, has long played a significant role (for example, providing such services as meals-on-wheels to older people over many decades). As a result, local authorities could purchase increasing amounts of services, such as meals-on-wheels, from the voluntary sector because this provision already existed. Because local authorities have not been able, in law, to own and run means-tested nursing homes, this type of care has necessarily developed within the independent sector. In this case, the development of private sector nursing homes has, in part at least, also resulted from the reduction in NHS long-stay provision for older people. (See Chapters 1 and 6 for more detail.)

Some concerns have been raised as to whether local authorities have gone too far in reducing their role as direct providers of services. This is a particular concern in relation to social services' abilities to meet their statutory responsibilities towards individual older people – see pages 98–9.

The NHS as a purchaser

Arguably, it has taken longer for the NHS to embrace the idea of being a purchaser in any large-scale way, although GP fundholders were purchasing health care for their patients from private providers from the early 1990s. However, in other areas of NHS care it appeared there was a view that the NHS could not be responsible for any service or treatment it did not directly provide. This was one of the major barriers facing older people trying to access fully-funded NHS continuing health care services at a time when long-stay care provided directly by the NHS was diminishing. As Chapter 6 explains, in these circumstances, older people were faced with a *fait accompli* – no long-stay NHS care could be provided if the local NHS service had been closed.

Even now, when the health service does purchase increasing numbers of places for patients meeting local criteria for fully-funded NHS continuing health care from independent sector homes, this represents a small proportion of the overall number of places in such homes.

Chapter 2 set out some of the Government's plans to increase the partnership arrangements between the independent sector and the NHS. These include the commissioning of treatment in overseas clinics, and the Concordat with the independent sector for intermediate care services (see page 94). Chapter 6 also explores new arrangements for the NHS to take on the funding of some care in nursing homes. In the future, it is expected that substantial changes in NHS provision will be subject to the scrutiny of Independent Reconfiguration Panels. These will take account of the impact of the proposed change on the whole health and social care system.

Statutory responsibilities

One concern, arising from this increased purchasing role, relates to the statutory sector's responsibilities towards individuals. Local authorities and (albeit to a lesser extent) the NHS hold certain statutory responsibilities towards individual older people and others. This means they have duties in law. For example, local authorities have a duty to assess the care needs of certain people, and provide services in particular instances (see Chapter 5). The local authority still holds these responsibilities even if another organisation provides the services on behalf of the local authority, under a contract. This is because it is the local authority that must *either* provide the service itself, *or* make the arrangement for another organisation to do so. This was also confirmed in the court case, *R v Wandsworth London Borough Council ex parte Beckwith*, outlined above.

Another legal case heard by the Court of Appeal in 2002 (*R v Leonard Cheshire Foundation (a charity) and HM Attorney General ex parte Heather; Ward; Callion*) raised other matters concerning statutory responsibilities. This case concerned the closure of a home run by the independent sector (in this case, a charity), and the impact on the residents – some, but not all, of whom were financially supported by local authorities. It centred on whether, by taking on the functions of a public body (i.e. a local authority), the charity was subject to the Human Rights Act 1998. In particular, it considered whether the charity was subject to Article 8 of the

Act, which sets out the right to respect for private and family life, home and confidentiality. By closing the home, it was argued, the charity was in breach of Article 8. The Court of Appeal concluded that the charity was not performing 'public functions', because legislation did not provide the charity with statutory powers. However, a local authority did retain its legal obligations, including meeting the requirements of Article 8, even if services were provided by a third party under contract (as was the situation in this case). At the time of writing, an appeal to the House of Lords was pending. However, this case helps to illustrate that the statutory sector retains its statutory responsibilities. (The issue of home closures is discussed in more detail later in this chapter.)

Other difficulties that have arisen for older people, where one organisation purchases services from another on their behalf, relate to the regulation of care and the pursuit of complaints. These are discussed in Chapters 4, 5 and 7.

This reduction in direct state provision may, arguably, be linked with concerns about pressures within the system of care. Chief amongst these pressures is the need to tackle delays in discharging older patients from hospital. There has been little analysis to date as to whether or not the increased growth in the numbers of different post-acute care providers is adding to, or reducing, these pressures.

Tackling hospital discharge

Pressures on the statutory sector, in terms of available budgets and service targets, have also affected the pattern and nature of services. For example, the reduction of NHS waiting times for operations has been a priority for both Conservative and Labour governments for over a decade. Despite the growing proportion of older people in the UK's population prior to and during this time, the overall number of hospital beds fell, including those designated for older patients (Audit Commission, 1997; National Beds Inquiry, 2000). However, the National Beds Inquiry found that the amount of time older patients spent in hospital had fallen significantly in recent years. In 1990, the average length of stay for a patient aged

85 or older was 30 days; by 1999, it was 17 days; similarly, for patients aged 65–74, the average length of stay had fallen from 21 days (1990) to 12 days (1999) (*Shaping the Future NHS*, DH, 2000). In addition, the proportion of emergency admissions had risen sharply. Across all age groups, by 1999 emergency admissions to hospital accounted for 60 per cent of all admissions.

Pressures on NHS hospital beds tend to become worse during winter months, especially in January and February when illnesses and falls, for example, in older people often increase. This was a particular problem over the winters of 1998 and 1999, when there were significantly increased numbers of influenza cases, especially among older people. This resulted in a rise in hospital admissions. Since then, the Government has expanded its flu vaccination programme, to include everyone over the age of 65. Additional funding to deal with these winter pressures was first introduced in 1996 (see Chapter 2). The then Conservative government issued extra funds to the NHS and social services to help them deal with the short-term difficulties. Many of these grants were used to set up, and commission, services such as Hospital Discharge schemes, and Rapid Response services. This 'Winter Pressures' money developed, from 2001–2002, into the annual 'Building Care Capacity' grant programme.

One service response to these pressures has been the development of intermediate care (see page 94). Intermediate care is a term now frequently used to describe a range of services intended to ensure people (especially older people) do not enter hospitals or residential homes unnecessarily, and – in particular – to speed up their discharge from hospital back to their own homes. This is frequently referred to as 'bed-blocking', now more commonly called 'delayed discharge'. In April 2001, the Department of Health began to use the phrase 'delayed transfer of care'. This was defined as follows:

'A delayed transfer occurs when a patient is ready for transfer from a general or acute hospital bed but is still occupying such a bed. A patient is ready for transfer when:

- a clinical decision has been made that the patient is ready for transfer
- a multi-disciplinary team decision has been made that the patient is ready for transfer
- the patient is safe to discharge/transfer.'

(*Delayed Discharges*, Health Select Committee, 2002)

Delayed discharge, or delayed transfer of care

Despite the Department of Health's recent definition, there are widely ranging views as to what constitutes a 'delayed discharge' – and, indeed, whether patients so identified are always inappropriately taking up a hospital bed. An unpublished study of a Midlands hospital in 1995 revealed that many older patients identified as 'blocking beds' were, in fact, waiting for other hospital interventions (including pharmacy supplies, or specialist opinions) before they could be discharged. Some patients had not been identified as ready to be discharged by hospital doctors. Elsewhere, some older patients' appropriate discharge from hospital was held up by problems or delays in accessing the help and support needed after hospital care. In some instances, this was caused by local councils' lack of resources; in others, by a lack of suitable local services – or, at least, suitable services with immediate vacancies. In certain parts of the country, for example, this was especially true of nursing home places for the care of older people with dementia.

Other problems arose from what some older users and their families experienced as pressure from hospital staff to leave the hospital. Even the term 'bed-blocking' is emotive and somewhat demeaning, which may explain why the terms 'delayed discharge' or 'delayed transfer of care' have been adopted more recently. There were concerns that some older people were being 'rushed' into making the major (often irreversible) step of leaving hospital to move to live permanently in a residential or nursing home. This was compounded by individuals' concerns about paying for care in homes (especially in circumstances when the value of their former home would be included in the amount they had to contribute – see Chapter 6). Despite the implementation of explicit criteria for NHS continuing health care services in April 1996, some older people experienced considerable difficulty in securing any kind of needs assessment for fully- or partially-funded NHS continuing health care *except* while in hospital. Rightly or wrongly, during the mid–late 1990s some older NHS patients saw their continued stay in hospital as one of the few 'levers' remaining to them with which they might influence what happened next in terms of receiving services. Equally, many NHS Trust hospitals found themselves – as providers – with patients needing care, which they neither provided at that hospital nor had the responsibility (or ability) to purchase from other Trust hospitals or providers, and whose attempts to meet targets on waiting lists, for example, were being frustrated. These problems were arguably exacerbated by the lack, since April 1996, of detailed formal guidance to the NHS on how it should handle hospital discharges. Although the Department of Health had published the *Hospital Discharge Workbook* in 1994, this lacked the status of formal guidance. In reality, it was often regarded as good practice that could – but did not have to – be followed.

Concerns about 'delayed discharges' continue to abound. *The NHS Plan* (DH, 2000) included a target to end widespread 'bed-blocking' by 2004 (see Chapter 1). The £300 million 'Building Care Capacity' grant, announced in autumn 2001, was specifically aimed at tackling delayed discharges from hospital. This was to be achieved by stabilising the care home sector, and so secure necessary post-hospital residential services. It was also used to purchase intermediate care beds and intensive care packages to support people at home. In June 2002, the Government announced that, by 31 March 2001, this grant had succeeded in reducing by 1,000 the numbers of beds blocked at any one time. An additional £475 million has been allocated for the same purposes for 2002–2003.

In July 2002, the House of Commons Health Select Committee published its report of an inquiry into the problem of delayed discharge. This raised a number of issues. Most of the evidence – and the policy imperative – related to the delayed discharge of patients over the age of 75. However, the Committee had received evidence of problems of delayed discharge for younger patients, especially those with mental health needs and brain injury. The Committee noted that, despite the policy and media attention afforded to the issue of 'blocked beds', it is estimated that these accounted for only 6 per cent of all acute beds, although local figures varied significantly around the country (*Delayed Discharges*, Health Select Committee, 2002).

The Health Select Committee made a number of recommendations. These included the issuing, as a matter of urgency, new statutory guidance on health and social care responsibilities for hospital discharge; and the development of service responses that promote the avoidance of inappropriate admissions to hospital. The Select Committee concluded that, although nearly one-third of delayed discharges can be attributed to waits for care home placement, this did not mean that the best response was the rapid development of further residential and nursing homes. Rather, the closure of care homes should act as a further spur to the development of care in other contexts. Greater attention should be paid to developing the necessary alternative service models to ensure that 'the right care, in the right place, at the right time, is available' (*Delayed Discharges*, Health Select Committee, 2002: para. 145). The Select Committee's report also emphasised the importance of community equipment, the provision of adequate housing and adaptations, and the need for further debate on the integration of health and social care and their links with related services, especially housing.

Also in July 2002, the Government published details of proposals to charge social services departments, in circumstances where they hold responsibility for care after hospital treatment, for the costs of delayed discharge of NHS patients. These proposals, first reported in the 2002 White Paper *Delivering the NHS Plan*, build on earlier suggestions set out in the Wanless Report (see Chapter 1). The Department of Health consulted on the detail of this change over the summer and autumn of 2002.

The proposals set out a protocol for the hospital to notify social services and the PCT, and to draw up a care plan. A strict time limit (proposed at three days) would apply to drawing up the care plan. Any 'delay' would be counted from the end of the three days in which the discharge plan is prepared, or from the day after the decision is made that the patient is ready and safe to transfer, whichever is the later. Delays after that time would result in a charge to social services, it is proposed, of £100 per day in most of the country, and £120 per day in London and the southeast. The consultation document sets out the intention that new legislation – required to effect this change – would be framed in such a way that regulations could extend this reimbursement system to patients in intermediate care and community hospitals, as well as in acute care (*Consultation on Proposals to Introduce a System of Reimbursement around Discharge from Hospital*, DH, 2002). The Government has said it hopes the necessary new legislation will be in place from April 2003.

It is worth noting that *Delivering the NHS Plan* also set out plans to impose financial penalties on the NHS if other targets – to reduce the numbers of emergency readmissions amongst patients aged 75 and over within 28 days – are not met. This reflects pressures in some areas whereby older patients are discharged too soon, and have to be quickly returned to hospital as a result; rather than older patients whose fluctuating condition may necessitate such admissions. These changes will also require new legislation.

These varied approaches to tackling the discharge of older NHS patients from hospital are part of an overall policy imperative to maintain older people at home, and away from institutional care, for as long as possible. This continues the direction for health and social care for older people begun through the community care reforms.

Home help and home care

One of the major changes since 1993 has been the increasing shift, within home help services, from the traditional 'housekeeping' services of shopping, light housework, and collecting pensions or benefits, towards personal care such as help with washing and dressing. This has been reflected in the increasing use of the term 'home care' rather than 'home help'. While the overall numbers of older people who receive home care services has reduced in recent years, there has been an increase in the intensity of services provided.

These changes make for dramatic reading. The Department of Health's *Community Care Statistics* for home care in England in 2001 show that the proportion of households receiving more than five hours (or six separate visits) of home care each week rose from 11 per cent in 1992 (the year before the community care reforms) to 39 per cent by 2001. In contrast, the proportion of households receiving only one weekly visit of fewer than two hours home care each week fell from 42 per cent in 1992 to 17 per cent in 2001. In short, fewer people each receive more services. This development has been in line with the expectations on local authorities set by the then government in 1993 to prioritise those 'most in need'. In 2002, the Government set a new target for social services to increase the proportion of older people who receive intensive home care. By March 2006, such older people must make up 30 per cent of the *total* number of older people supported by social services, whether in residential care or at home (HM Treasury, 2002). (The Department of Health defines intensive home care as more than ten contact hours and six or more visits each week.)

In some areas, this prioritisation led to changes in criteria for help, and the withdrawal of, or reductions in, the 'housekeeping' elements of the home help service. Increasingly, these 'housekeeping' services are provided only for those older people who need personal care as well. This development has led to concerns about whether sufficient attention is being paid to what are sometimes called 'low level' services. These are often precisely those services that can help older people stay at home for longer by promoting their independence.

Box 3.1 Further information on home care services

❋ **Age Concern England**
Factsheet 6, *Finding help at home*
❋ **Help the Aged**
Provides a range of information leaflets on staying at home

Services to promote independence

In 1998, the Government announced a three-year programme of grants for local councils under the 'Promoting Independence' theme. This included grants aimed at the provision of preventative services, to help older people and others maintain existing levels of independence. A number of voluntary sector organisations have particularly been developing preventative services.

Research involving older people found the following:

- help with housework, gardening, laundry, home maintenance and repair enhanced older people's quality of life and helped them maintain their independence;
- older women value housework as skilled work;
- the appearance of their home is particularly important to older women;
- older people defined personal and domestic assistance as 'help' not 'care';
- being 'looked after' meant losing independence;
- what older people saw as important to maintain their independence changed as their capacities, abilities and circumstances changed;
- older people valued having an alternative to always having to ask their families, which could undermine their sense of independence;
- older people needing home maintenance and repairs wanted access to help from reputable organisations.
(Clark, Dyer and Horwood, 1998)

Lewis and colleagues (1999) suggest that, in order to promote older people's independence, agencies need to do the following:

• tackle 'ageist' attitudes towards people's abilities to contribute, and do things for themselves;
• develop a wide range of preventative services (this was easiest in areas with a strong local voluntary sector);
• move staff and services away from a 'look after' attitude where care is 'done to' a person, towards a 'promoting independence' attitude where care is 'done with' the person.

As a result of the Government's plans to reduce the rates of serious injury and deaths following falls (*Saving Lives: Our Healthier Nation*, DH, 1999), in 1999 the Department of Trade and Industry began a three-year campaign, *Avoiding Slips, Trips and Broken Hips*. The campaign identified ways older people can play a part in promoting their own good health, and reducing the chances that they will fall. There is evidence that strengthening lower leg muscles, improving balance, and making sure that an older person can easily see the edge of each step in a flight of stairs, for example, can help minimise the risk of falls.

Box 3.2 Further information on promoting independence

❉ **Department of Trade and Industry,** *Avoiding Slips, Trips and Broken Hips* **campaign**
Produced a range of reports and leaflets aimed at preventing falls, and minimising injuries from falls
❉ **Anchor Trust**
Has published a range of reports about promoting independence
❉ **Health Development Agency** (a Special Health Authority)
Identifies practical ways to improve people's health

Day care and day opportunities

Day care services have tended to follow a traditional model in which older people attend a centre in the day time (generally 10 am–4 pm) during the week. Here, they take part in activities such as crafts and activities, and may perhaps be bathed. Centres tend to be run by social services or the voluntary sector – very few are run by the private sector. Within the NHS, there are a number of day hospitals offering diagnostic, clinical and therapeutic services to older patients. Although there are currently no nationally agreed standards for day care provision, some professional associations have developed guidelines about the range of activities or interventions that might usefully be provided in day hospitals (British Geriatric Society, 1998; Health Advisory Service, 1999).

In some areas, local authorities have begun to review social care day centres and day care as part of their rolling programme of Best Value reviews. Some concerns have been voiced as to the need to provide a broader range of what is sometimes called 'day opportunities', as well as daytime care services, activities and health promotion opportunities. Arguably, day care for older people has, in the recent past, tended to suffer from a lack of attention in terms of service development. In some areas, local councils are looking to provide or commission a range of resource centres geared towards older people's needs, which are also accessible to the wider local population. In other areas, buildings-based day care is being seen as an opportunity to provide, in one centre, a range of health and social care provision for older people. This might include physiotherapy, chiropody and GP clinics, together with welfare advice, activities and hobbies, exercise opportunities and personal care.

Elsewhere, services such as outreach day care facilities (not based in particular buildings) are being developed. Outreach day care can involve sharing an activity with someone in their own home, or supporting older people (sometimes in small groups) to access mainstream services, such as leisure centres, cafes or cinemas. Outreach day care is sometimes targeted at older people whose fluctuating condition means they are not always able to leave home to attend a centre. This can include older people with dementia, clinical depression, or conditions such as agoraphobia.

Many of the changes in day care services are also developing as local councils and NHS bodies begin to consider the immediate and future needs of two sub-sections of their local older populations: active retired people (some of whom may have illnesses and disabilities) and those in 'greatest need'. This reflects a growing concern that these two 'types' of older people appear broadly to reflect the experiences of the current older population; and because of concerns that the health of those with 'low level' needs should be maintained and improved, alongside service provision for those with higher levels of care needs. Further changes in day opportunities may also arise through the use of direct payments (see below).

In some areas both the NHS and social services remain concerned that services cater for those who are being supported in their own homes with increased levels of need. This may mean, in the future, that more of the services and opportunities for older people with fewer health or care needs will be provided by the independent sector, with statutory bodies tending to concentrate their funding and provision of services on those with the highest level of needs.

Box 3.3 Further information on day opportunities

❋ **Age Concern England**
Factsheet 6, *Finding help at home*
Factsheet 30, *Leisure and education*

Direct payments

The Community Care (Direct Payments) Act 1996 came into force in 1997; its provisions were extended to older people in 2000. Strictly speaking, the provision of direct payments is not a service: it is money – paid by local councils to those who qualify – provided instead of services (or as well as some services).

There are 'rules' about who can receive direct payments. They can only be offered to support those living at home or in sheltered housing. As Chapter 5 describes, people must first have been assessed as being in need of community care services, and must use the direct payments money to meet those assessed needs. They must also:

- be aged 18 or over (there is no upper age limit);
- meet the definition of disability set out in Section 29 of the National Assistance Act 1948. (This includes people who are deaf or hard of hearing, people with partial or full sight loss, those with a learning disability; and people with illnesses or conditions such as multiple sclerosis, arthritis, or Parkinson's disease);
- not be subject to certain criminal justice or mental health legislation that carry elements of compulsion (for example, being compelled to accept treatment in a psychiatric hospital under the Mental Health Act 1983 – sometimes called 'being sectioned');
- be willing to accept a direct payment;
- be able to manage a direct payment, with or without some assistance.

Users can receive a combination of some community care services and some money, or they can receive money only. They can use the money to arrange their personal care, for example, or to attend their own choice of daytime activities instead of going to a day centre. It is intended as a way for people with disabilities to gain more control over their daily lives. Some people have chosen to use direct payments to employ someone to meet their personal care needs – usually called a personal assistant (or 'PA').

The money for direct payments comes from public funds. Policy and practice guidance from the Department of Health states that, while local authorities must check the money is being spent appropriately, they should make sure they do not stifle any innovative ways individual people find to meet their own needs. However, there are some restrictions. For example, people cannot use direct payments to buy social services' own in-house services. Neither can they use it to pay for care received from a spouse or close relative, from the NHS or housing services, nor for permanent residential care. It can be used to buy periods of respite care, although there are some rules about how often respite is bought, and for what length of time.

The system of direct payments took several decades to develop and be implemented in law, and was led by younger, working age adults with disabilities. In practice, few older people have accessed direct payments to date. Its use in general around the country is still highly variable, ranging from a handful of people in some local authority areas to several hundred recipients in others. This may be because local authorities have not, in the past, been *obliged* to offer direct payments – it is simply that they have had the *power* to do so. People who have been assessed by their social services departments as needing community care services can request a direct payment, and can pursue this through the local authority complaints system if they are refused (see Chapters 5 and 7). Local authorities have been told that they must consider each case on its own merits, and should not have a blanket policy to refuse everyone.

In the summer of 2002 the Government announced it intended to *oblige* local authorities to offer direct payments to older people, rather than leaving it up to local authorities to decide whether or not to offer this option (*Community Care (Draft Payments) Act 1996 Consultation Paper*, DH, 2002). This would include offering direct payments to older people about to be discharged from hospital, so they could arrange their own care. It seems likely that local authorities will have to implement this change sometime after April 2003. At the time of writing, it is not clear whether this new obligation will be accompanied by changes in the rules governing which services can be bought through direct payments. This may be particularly important in terms of any rehabilitation services needed after hospital treatment. In some areas only the NHS and social services departments may provide such services, but direct payments cannot be used to purchase services from either of these two organisations.

Since 1 April 2001, carers who have been assessed as needing services in their own right have also been able to receive direct payments, under the Carers and Disabled Children Act 2000. To qualify, carers (who provide unpaid care, and are usually the family or friends of the cared-for person) should be providing regular and substantial care for someone who might need a community care services arranged or provided by the social services department. The carer and cared-for person do not need to be living in the same household for the carer to qualify. Nor does the cared-for person have to be receiving community care services before the carer can receive a direct payment.

The provisions in law for direct payments tend to exclude older people with dementia. Anyone holding an Enduring Power of Attorney for someone with dementia can access direct payments only if this is specifically mentioned in their EPA arrangement. (An Enduring Power of Attorney is an arrangement whereby one person may lawfully make financial decisions on behalf of another.)

Box 3.4 Further information on direct payments

* **The National Centre for Independent Living**
  Offers advice and information leaflets about direct payments
* **Carers UK (formerly the Carers' National Association)**
  Provides information for carers wishing to seek a direct payment
* **Alzheimer's Society**
  Provides information for people with dementia, and their carers
* **Age Concern England**
  Factsheet 24, *Direct payments from social services*
  Factsheet 22, *Legal arrangements for managing financial affairs*

Support for carers

Aside from provisions for carers to receive services in their own right, and direct payments in lieu of services, the Carers and Disabled Children Act 2000 also created voucher schemes for short breaks (the term increasingly being given to respite care). Voucher schemes build on the 1998–2001 programme of Carer's Grants issued for short-term breaks to local councils, as part of 'Promoting independence' initiatives. This grant programme has been extended to 2004.

In 1999, the Department of Health published the Government's National Carers Strategy, *Caring for Carers*, which included many of the proposals outlined above. At the same time, the Government began to outline its interest in supporting policies to create what is sometimes called a 'work–life balance'.

This issue is important for carers who are also in employment. Of the 5.7 million carers estimated in the UK (Rowlands, 1998), 47 per cent also undertake some kind of paid work (DH, 1999), whether full- or part-time, or in self-employment.

In 1999, the Department of Trade and Industry (DTI) launched its entitlement for employees, *Time Off for Dependants* (or emergency relief provision), which applies to any employee with a dependant. This definition can include both children and older people. A dependant is classed as anyone who reasonably relies on the employee for assistance, and becomes ill, suffers an injury or whose care arrangements break down (DTI, 1999). Importantly, the dependant and the employee do not need to be related: this benefits working adults who help support older neighbours or friends. While emergency relief provision is an entitlement employees can take, there is no fixed amount of time that can be claimed – unlike parental leave. DTI guidance states that one or two days should be sufficient. Again unlike parental leave, it is up to employers whether or not to pay for this emergency leave.

However, one of the problems with this, and other work-based schemes, is that they tend to be developed for the parents of able-bodied children who may – as given as one example in the DTI guidance – catch chicken pox. A different approach may well be needed for older dependants with ongoing health and care needs.

A few employers have developed day provision for their employees' older dependants, but this is still very unusual. Research published by the Joseph Rowntree Foundation found that, although at least in one in ten employees was caring for an older adult in an informal capacity, they were reluctant to ask for help from their employers (Phillips *et al*, 2002). Working-age employed carers may also need quite different support to the spouses and cohabiting partners of older people – for example, support services during working hours. However, it is important to note that it is this latter group, spouses and partners, that provides the most intensive carer support to older people in terms of the average hours of care given each week (Rowlands, 1998).

In 1998, a report from the Social Services Inspectorate (SSI – part of the Department of Health) found many social services departments assumed a significant amount of family care to be provided within ethnic minority families. The report, *They Look After Their Own, Don't They?* highlighted the need to challenge such assumptions, and to provide a range of appropriate support services. Provision to older people from ethnic minority populations is likely to become a much bigger issue in the next decade, especially in parts of London, the Midlands and Yorkshire (see also Chapter 1). In 2002, the SSI published an audit tool to help social services authorities develop their services for minority ethnic older people, and for planning further developments (*From Lip Service to Real Services: audit tool*, SSI, 2002).

In response to concerns that, in some areas, statutory bodies offer less help to people with a carer, the Royal Commission's report (DH, 1999) into long-term care funding for older people stressed the need for what it called 'carer-blind' services. It called for local authorities and the NHS to provide services for the older person as if the carer were not there, in terms of the amount and type of support being made available.

Box 3.5 Further information on support for carers

❋ **Carers UK**
   Offers advice and information leaflets for carers
❋ **Princess Royal Trust for Carers**
   Provides information and practical support to carers

Intermediate care and rehabilitation services

In its 1997 report, *The Coming of Age*, the Audit Commission reported that the NHS and social services departments had become locked into a 'vicious circle' of care. The pressure on hospital beds and the high use of residential and nursing homes was making it hard to 'free up' alternative resources for services that might ease the situation, and improve the outcome for older people. Such alternatives included rehabilitation, and intermediate care services.

Since 1997, growing emphasis has been placed on the development of intermediate care services. These are sometimes called 'step-down' services, and are intended to provide a bridge between home and hospital. Such services can also help older people avoid unnecessary hospital admission and lengthy stays, or premature moves to permanent residential home care. In some areas, the NHS and social services departments have increasingly looked to intermediate care services to help deal with localised delays in hospital discharge.

The Department of Health has defined intermediate care services as those that meet all the following criteria:

• they are targeted at people who would otherwise face unnecessarily prolonged hospital stays or inappropriate admission to acute inpatient care, long-term residential care or continuing NHS inpatient care;
• they are provided on the basis of a comprehensive assessment, resulting in a structured individual care plan that involves active therapy, treatment or opportunity for recovery;

- they include a planned outcome of maximising independence and typically enabling patients/users to resume living at home;
- they are time-limited, normally no longer than six weeks and frequently as little as 1–2 weeks or less;
- they involve cross-professional working, with a single assessment framework, single professional records and shared protocols.

(HSC 2001/001, LAC (2001) 01, *Intermediate Care*)

Although intermediate care services may offer elements of rehabilitation, the King's Fund has drawn a distinction between the two:

'Rehabilitation is always an active process of building up a person's capacity to live independently. It tends to last for a relatively short period of time – weeks or months. Intermediate care, on the other hand, describes a range of services designed to divert people from unnecessary admission to hospital, or speed up discharge from hospital, easing the transition back to normal life.' (King's Fund, 2000:1)

Many intermediate care services have developed from initiatives first funded under Winter Pressures Funding (see page 68). These include Rapid Response Teams, which aim to maintain an older person at home rather than their having to be admitted to hospital, by providing (sometimes intensive) support from health and social care professionals for short periods of time during health crises. This is provided in people's own homes. Hospital discharge schemes work – in broad terms – the other way around, providing similarly time-limited intensive support when someone first leaves hospital to return home.

Some elements of rehabilitation may take place within these schemes. The development of rehabilitation services was one of the main requirements under the *Better Services for Vulnerable People* (BSVP) initiative outlined in Chapter 2. In 2000, the Audit Commission reviewed rehabilitation and remedial services for older people who had experienced a stroke. It found that access to comprehensive assessments, co-ordinated services and the continuity of care received were essential factors in providing effective rehabilitation services (Audit Commission, 2000). In some areas, local authorities have developed short-term residential schemes offering a strong emphasis on enabling older people to return to their own homes by concentrating on enhancing their abilities to undertake daily tasks, and improving their confidence in doing so. Sometimes these schemes are called 'social rehabilitation', and may consist of the local authority providing the accommodation and some staff, with therapeutic staff (such as physiotherapists, speech and language therapists) provided by the NHS. *A Guide to Contracting for Intermediate Care Services* (DH, 2001) highlighted the potential for intermediate care services to be commissioned by the NHS and social services from the voluntary and private sectors. These services should be contracted for within Long Term Service Agreements (LTSA). These agreements aim to provide a longer-term framework within which the NHS and local councils commission services (see also Figure 2.1, page 66). It is expected that many of the additional intermediate care beds will be provided in private nursing homes.

Overall, the development of intermediate care services forms a significant part of *The NHS Plan* (DH, 2000) and the National Service Framework (NSF) for Older People (see below, including stroke rehabilitation services). In 2000, the Government announced it was allocating £900 million by 2003–2004 to social services and the NHS to develop (or commission) new intermediate care and related services to promote independence. *The NHS Plan* sets out the Government's intention for this additional funding to provide an extra 5,000 intermediate care beds by 2003–2004, and 1,700 non-residential care service places. Doing so will be critical to meeting the Public Service Agreement (PSA) targets also set out in *The NHS Plan*, and reiterated in the 2002 *Spending Review* (HM Treasury, 2002). These build on targets first developed in 1997, and on similar priorities from previous Conservative administrations to achieve:

- reductions in the readmission of people aged 75 and over to hospital within 28 days of leaving hospital;
- reductions in the delaying of discharge from hospital of patients aged 75 and over.

Moving Forward, the Department of Health's (2002) review of intermediate care services, found growing evidence of reduced acute hospital admissions and fewer care home placements in areas with established intermediate care services. However, it also found a need to ensure timely access to medical assessments. It also pointed to the need to develop intermediate care that meets mental health needs, as most intermediate care services currently concentrate on physical problems.

In April 2002, *Delivering the NHS Plan* set out the Government's expectations of a 30 per cent expansion in intermediate care by 2005–2006. In July 2002, the Secretary of State for Health stated that, by 2005, an additional 70,000 older people a year should be helped to receive rehabilitation services provided by local councils. This announcement also contained proposals for new legislation to make all rehabilitation and intermediate care services free of charge, regardless of whether they are provided by the NHS or social services (*Delivering the NHS Plan*, DH, 2002; see also Chapter 6).

There has been some criticism that some intermediate care services are merely existing services that have been re-labelled. The Health Select Committee raised concerns that what it called the 're-badging' of NHS services as intermediate care, if widespread, represented a failure to use the skills, knowledge and wider experience of statutory and independent sector partners for maximum benefit (*Delayed Discharges*, Health Select Committee, 2002).

Box 3.6 Further information on intermediate care and rehabilitation

❊ **King's Fund**
Has published a range of reports and papers on intermediate care and rehabilitation services

❊ **Stroke Association**
Offers advice and information to people who need rehabilitation and care following a stroke.

Residential and nursing homes

Aside from issues about the quality and regulation of care homes, discussed in Chapter 4, there are arguably three main issues affecting the provision of places in residential and nursing homes, Broadly, these relate to:

- the closure of homes, and the loss of places;
- the actual costs of care in homes;
- the future direction of the service.

These issues are discussed below.

Home closures and loss of places

Much attention has been placed, in the last few years, on the closures of homes and the consequent loss of places. Certainly, by 2002 the numbers of places in long-stay care had fallen by 64,000 from its peak of 575,600 in 1996 (Laing and Buisson, 2002). Commentary on these changes often concentrates on the losses in the independent sector (particularly private sector provision), but this decline has occurred across all sectors – including local authority 'Part III' homes and NHS long-stay facilities.

In 2002, compared with 2001, there were 13,146 fewer places in all types of long-stay care. Of this total, 9,600 places were lost from the independent sector; 2,300 from Part III homes; and 1,200 from NHS continuing care places in hospitals. However, 8,000 fewer residents received state financial support over the same period of time; as some new care home places have also been registered during this time, it seems that the *demand* for this type of care has also fallen by a similar rate (Laing and Buisson, 2002). It is worth noting that, in 2002, occupancy rates in private sector homes were very slightly higher than pre-1993 levels. In short, although there has been a loss of beds, the remaining homes have more residents living there more of the time, and thus have fewer vacancies (Laing and Buisson, 2002).

WHAT IMPACT DOES THIS HAVE?

When homes close, it is inevitable that most of the impact falls on existing residents. In general, it is the handling of closures by the statutory sector that has tended to attract most criticism, rather than closures amongst the independent sector. Importantly, governmental guidance that has developed as a result of these concerns is directly aimed at the statutory sector. This guidance cannot, as a general rule, be enforced on the independent sector (see also page 77). This difference may become a greater concern, given that it is the independent sector that is currently closing most places in care homes.

Some local authority home closures, and the closure of long-stay NHS wards have been especially criticised for their poor handling. The deaths of some NHS long-stay patients shortly after transfer from closing geriatric or psychogeriatric long-stay wards have, for example, attracted much media attention. This issue of whether residents will die following the closure of a home and the subsequent relocation of residents in different homes, tends to be one of the main objections raised to such proposals. It is important to note that fears about residents' premature deaths as a result of such closures tend to be based on a small number of cases, often concerning the closure of long-stay NHS settings. The majority of older residents who do move between long-term care settings (who may move for a variety of reasons) do so successfully.

Two of the more significant cases concerning deaths following the closure of long-stay NHS services, took place in the 1990s. In the first, the Select Committee on Public Administration published a report, in 1997, on an inquiry it held into the death of an older patient in 1994, transferred from a closing long-stay psychogeriatric ward in Basingstoke. This transfer had taken place against the specific medical advice of the consultant, and in her absence. The report followed an investigation, reported in 1996, into the incident by the Health Service Commissioner (the Ombudsman). The Select Committee severely criticised the relevant health authorities for ignoring the consultant's expert advice, that the patient was too ill to be moved. It recommended that the then Secretary of State for Health review the suitability of those responsible to continue to hold posts in the NHS (Select Committee on Public Administration, *Second Special Report*, 1997).

The second case concerned the deaths of several long-stay patients transferring from another closing long-stay hospital ward, to a purpose-built nursing home in Barnet, north London in 1997. As a result of this case, guidance was issued to the NHS on how it should transfer frail older NHS patients to other long-stay settings, in the event of the planned closure of NHS facilities (HSC 1998/048, *The Transfer of Frail Older Patients to Other Long Stay Settings*). This applies to NHS patients whose care would continue to be funded by the NHS but in another setting – under NHS contract in a private nursing home, for example. (This requirement should not be confused with the usual discharge of patients from NHS hospitals – it is specific to those for whom the NHS has an ongoing responsibility but where NHS facilities are to be closed.) The guidance sets out a range of factors that those involved in such closures should address, including the numbers of people moved at any one time; issues about the handover of medical, nursing and personal care, and continuity of care workers; and about the practicalities of the move.

In some areas, local authorities that have closed their own residential homes have also used this NHS guidance, although they are not obliged to do so. The guidance is specific to NHS-funded patients who, it is expected, will be significantly more frail and dependent than local authority-funded residents. However, local authorities are obliged to carry out consultation with the residents and other interested parties in the homes that are being proposed for closure (*R v Wandsworth London Borough Council ex parte Beckwith* 1995). Subsequent court cases have ruled that individual residents' needs should be assessed before, and considered at the time when, the decision is taken to close a local authority home. More recently, cases have also explored issues under the Human Rights Act 1998 (especially Article 8, the right to respect for private and family life, home and confidentiality), as in the case outlined on page 77.

Despite the guidance and case law, it is important to note that many of these statutory responsibilities are not shared by the independent sector, which provides most of this type of care. Although there are some provisions under the Care Standards Act 2000, these tend to relate to what happens to homes in the event of the death of the person registered to run the home, or the bankruptcy or liquidation of the home. Residents in independent sector homes may find there is little they can do to prevent closures. This may be the case even though their contract with the home (also required under the Care Standards Act 2000, from April 2002) sets out a minimum period of notice the home must give prior to their leaving. Although many of those who own and run closing independent sector homes will try to follow good practice in the transfer of residents to other establishments, in practice there are few sanctions that can be applied to those who choose not to do so. One such sanction, however, is a requirement on care home owners to give three months' notice to cancel the registration of their homes (which they must do in the event of its closing). Failure to do so would be an offence for which the owners could be prosecuted (National Care Commission Registration Guidelines, 2002).

Other issues that arise for older people as a result of the closure of homes relate more to the impact on future residents. Fewer homes, it can be argued, leads to less choice for older people (see Chapter 5). Concerns have also arisen that gaps are beginning to arise in the type and range of care provided. There is a particular concern about whether there are currently sufficient long-stay nursing care places for older people with dementia, especially in the south of England.

The loss of more specialist care, and the reduced choice for older people, because of homes closing are leading to concerns that government targets to reduce the delayed discharge from hospital of older patients may not be met. However, this is not a view shared by the Health Select Committee, whose 2002 report suggested that the current closures of homes present an ideal opportunity for the state to encourage, and develop, alternative forms of care (see page 82). In 2001, the Government responded to concerns about whether home closures were exacerbating 'bed-blocking' problems, by introducing a Building Care Capacity grant programme. Some of this grant was spent by local authorities on securing places in care homes for older NHS patients, in order to help reduce delayed discharges from hospital. It has also been used, in some areas, significantly to increase the amount paid to independent sector homes for the care they provide (see page 104).

WHY HAVE PLACES IN HOMES DECLINED?

The reductions in the numbers of long-stay places, and the concerns about closures of homes, can be viewed in a number of ways. For example, the social care market of the 1990s may simply be levelling out. If more older people are being supported at home for longer, it follows that fewer will need residential care. Given that a main aim over the past decade (straddling both Labour and Conservative governments) has been the reduction in inappropriate and unnecessarily early admissions to homes, it would be more surprising if there had been no reduction in the number of places. Equally, as has been set out in earlier chapters, between 2001–2004 the numbers of people aged 85 and over will have fallen. As Chapter 1 described, it is those in the oldest age groups who are most likely to receive care in homes. If their numbers have dropped demand will also, quite naturally, have declined. One overriding reason for the loss of places, therefore, may simply be that the care home market is adjusting to reduced demand.

A second set of explanations relates to the specific reasons why individuals, and organisations, might decide to close (or re-provide) care homes. For private individuals who own and run care homes, reasons could include their own ill health; their own retirement; or divorce settlements. Organisations (across the statutory and independent sectors) may decide to concentrate on different client groups, or to completely redesign the care services they offer. One example of the latter is the development of extra care sheltered housing schemes from some previous Part III accommodation (see page 108).

Two issues arise from these reasons to close homes. The first relates to concerns that, in some parts of the country, private care home proprietors have found it difficult to 'sell-on' the care home as an ongoing business. It has been much easier to sell it instead for redevelopment as private housing, particularly in parts of the south of England. That some care home owners have decided to take advantage of the significant increase in property prices in recent years in this way seems to be confirmed, at least in part, by a reduction in numbers of new care homes currently being established. There also appears to be a growing imbalance in long-stay care provision across the country, with most problems in terms of shortages arising south and east of a line from the Severn to the Wash (Laing and Buisson, 2002). The second issue is that the closure of homes does not necessarily always mean fewer care services, although it may mean that care needs are met in different ways (see page 108).

One reason for home closures that is frequently cited concerns the costs of providing care in homes. Such concerns include the view that the state does not pay sufficient amounts for such care; that the anticipated post-2002 regulatory requirements would place excessive burdens on care home owners, without recompense; that for the private sector, the profit margin may be too low at current fee levels; and that, for the voluntary sector, charitable funds may not continually be available to provide for increased care needs. Issues about the actual costs of care, and the state's response to this, are discussed below.

The actual costs of care

This section considers three of the key aspects to the issue of the costs of care provided in care homes.

'Underpayments' from social services

A view expressed by some private sector home providers over many years is that they offered better value for money than the equivalent local authority homes. This drew attention to the fact that, in some areas, local authorities were paying less for places in independent sector homes than the cost of care in one of their own 'Part III' residential homes. An important response to this was the last Conservative government's White Paper, *Achievement and Challenge* (1997), that emphasised the role of private sector homes in securing value for money (VfM) for taxpayers.

Other sections of the independent sector have raised concerns about the amounts paid by local authorities for the costs of places in homes. Rather than their homes offering 'better value' because they cost less, these providers have argued that social services departments have not been paying enough for independent sector care. Their argument is that, if older people are being maintained at home for longer, then it is highly likely the level of care needs among those who do enter homes has risen. This means that the cost per place is also likely to have risen, if more care is required. The concern is that these care needs, and associated costs, have increased more, and faster, than the amounts local authorities have been willing to pay in some parts of the country. This gave rise to particular problems in parts of the country where local authorities followed closely the 'preserved rights' amounts set by central government under the pre-1993 system. Such 'preserved rights' residents were believed to have lower levels of care needs than their post-1993 local authority-funded counterparts. This led to concerns that the state was trying to pay the same rates for increasingly dependent residents.

In 2002, many local authorities were reported to have significantly increased the amount of fees they agree to pay for places in care homes – some by as much as 10 per cent (Laing and Buisson, 2002). Most were using the Building Care Capacity grant to do so. In the summer of 2002, the Secretary of State for Health said that additional funds, to be made available from April 2003, would also allow local authorities to pay increased care home fees, if that was what was needed in order to stabilise the local care home market (*Expanded Services*, DH, 2002).

'Overpayments' by residents

The other side of 'underpayments' by the state relates to the extent to which some homes may have come to rely on 'top-ups' from residents' own resources. Two studies from the 1990s considered this issue. One highlighted the extent to which older self-funding residents were effectively subsidising state-supported residents, by paying higher fees (Laing, 1998). The other revealed the extent to which older residents, funded under the 1993–2002 'preserved rights' system, were having to find an additional contribution from their reduced income and capital to meet 'top-up' amounts over and above the maximum Income Support levels available to pay for their homes' fees (Age Concern England/Association of Charity Officers, 1996).

The Age Concern/ACO (1996) report found that a high proportion of elderly people were facing a shortfall between the maximum paid by the DSS (now the Department for Work and Pensions) in benefits and the cost of the home, equal to the amount of their weekly personal expenses allowance (PEA). PEA is the sum ignored from income in the means-test for care in homes. It is used by residents to pay for their personal items not covered in the home's fees, such as toiletries, stationery, and clothes. In April 2002, it was £16.80 per week.

However, the reforms to the system of paying for care in homes after April 1993 specifically prevented residents from using their PEA to pay these 'top-up' demands, if they were receiving financial support from their local authority. Instead, if residents chose to live in a home that cost more than the authority could show it could pay for care in a home that met the resident's assessed needs, then a 'third party' (often a relative) had to agree to meet the extra cost. After 1993, it became more difficult for homes to increase their fees to state-funded residents without some degree of state sanction via the local authority contract, and without formal arrangements with someone other than the resident. In some parts of the country, however, some residents have been using their PEA to pay for other services not included in the home's fees, or not available locally from the NHS – for example, chiropody (Easterbrook, 2001). In 2002, the Government issued guidance to reiterate that the PEA should be used for personal items, and not to pay for care services (LAC(2002)11, *Charges for Residential Accommodation, CRAG amendment no. 17*).

Concerns have also been expressed over the way some nursing homes have responded to the introduction, in October 2001, of NHS funds to pay for the nursing care element of self-funding residents. Designed to reduce the amount such residents' pay for care from their own resources, some care homes increased their fees to reflect this additional funding. This effectively 'wiped out' the financial benefit to residents. The Government reacted to concerns about this practice by amending the care home regulations that oblige homes to provide a breakdown of their fees, and make clear which aspects of fees relate to nursing care, and which to residential care (*Letter*, DH, 2002). Since April 2002, NHS bodies (primarily Primary Care Trusts) have been using a new central core contract. This sets out how homes account for any NHS nursing contribution they receive, and also sets out how the NHS will reimburse nursing homes for the costs of continence products used by residents (see Chapter 6).

The actual cost of providing care

It is clear that many of the concerns, and the reasons given for homes closing, relate to the actual costs of providing care. This includes the cost of premises, staffing, and facilities. For example, after the 1997 general election, concerns were raised by the managers and owners of care homes about the cost to them of introducing the minimum wage, and stakeholder pensions, amongst other increased employee rights.

More recently, concerns have been expressed by the independent sector home market about the cost to them of implementing some of the quality standards set from April 2002 by the National Care Standards Commission. However, the more costly elements (the installation of lifts, and the minimum size for bedrooms) were not originally intended to come into effect until April 2007 for homes already in existence prior to April 2002. During the summer of 2002, the Government said it would not require existing homes to meet some of these environmental standards (see page 135).

On the private sector side, concerns are often raised about the levels of profit that can be achieved through providing homes. On the voluntary sector side, concerns are often raised about the proper role of charitable funds in supporting otherwise state-funded residents.

A study published in 2002 considered the range of costs associated with providing such care: staffing, including levels of pay; non-staffing costs, including utilities and grounds maintenance; and capital costs, including the investors' and operators' return (Laing, 2002). This suggested that a 16 per cent rate of return on capital would be reasonable. It also suggested a mechanism whereby local authorities could link the fee rates they pay with the extent to which care homes comply with the national minimum quality standards.

There is clearly a need to better understand, and agree on, the legitimate costs of care in homes, especially to agree the proper amount that should be paid by the state and by self-funding residents for such care.

The future for care homes

The situation for care home provision for the future appears mixed. On the one hand, the independent sector is now expected to play a role in the overall planning of care for people in local areas. From 2001–2002, part of local strategic commissioning has had to include the NHS and social services working with the independent sector to determine the future needs for places in homes (CI (2001)5, *Health and Social Care Planning*, 2001–2002). The National Care Standards Commission, and the proposed Commission for Social Care Inspection (see Chapter 4) may also play a part in future planning for this type of care.

On the other hand, the Government continues to signal the priority given to care to support people living in their own homes (including sheltered housing). In the summer of 2002, the Secretary of State for Health announced proposals for increased places in sheltered housing; for more packages on intensive home care to support people at home; and for further rehabilitation services However, especially in some parts of the country, local authorities may need to increase the amounts they pay for care in homes, or tackle gaps in provision, especially for the more specialist care (*Extending Services*, DH, 2002). In short, there is no indication that care homes will not continue to play a significant role in the provision of health, housing and social care options for older people, but that at present it is expected that a greater number of alternatives will be developed alongside current provision.

Supported housing

Supported housing for older people (sometimes called 'assisted living') usually means housing schemes that offer self-contained housing with care services. These are sometimes called 'extra care sheltered housing', 'close care', or 'very sheltered housing'. Many of these schemes offer communal facilities such as lounges, restaurants or laundry facilities, as well as individual flats, maisonettes or bungalows. Recently, this type of housing provision has been affected by two issues.

Changes in the regulation of care

The first is the change in the regulation of care services, especially the definition in law of what constitutes a care home (see Box 3.7).

Box 3.7 Definition of a care home

The law defines a care home as an institution that meets the following criteria:

- it provides accommodation, together with nursing or personal care, for any of the following persons:

(a) persons who are or who have been ill
(b) persons who have or have had a mental disorder
(c) persons who are disabled or infirm
(d) persons who are or have been dependent on alcohol or drugs
- But an establishment is not a care home if it is:
(a) a hospital
(b) an independent clinic
(c) a children's home

or if it is of a description excepted by regulations.

(Section 3, Care Standards Act 2000)

In theory, this definition could have applied to those living in supported housing schemes, although this was not the intention of the Care Standards Act 2000. Nor was it intended that these provisions would apply to accommodation that is owner-occupied (whether freehold or leasehold). These are therefore exempted, in order to make sure that individual older owner-occupiers who receive care in their own home (whether ordinary housing, or some kind of sheltered or retirement flat) are not inadvertently affected by the framework for regulating care homes. The Government has also made it clear that extra care housing will not be affected by the Care Standards Act. Sheltered housing schemes that offer personal care services also avoid regulation as a care home if they either arrange for the care services to be provided by another organisation, or register their own care service as a domiciliary care agency. In this latter case, their agency will come under the domiciliary care regulations of the Care Standards Act 2000.

Funding of sheltered housing

This avoidance of regulation as a care home is crucial in terms of the overall funding arrangements for sheltered housing and the financial impact on older residents. Tenants in non-regulated sheltered housing schemes (and individual owner-occupiers), by avoiding regulation, also avoid the means-test imposed on those living in (regulated) residential and nursing homes. This gives them significantly greater control over their financial affairs by leaving most of their income and savings intact (depending on personal circumstances), to be spent by them on daily living expenses such as rent, fuel bills, food and council tax. In some cases, they may be asked to pay towards any care services they receive. This would occur if care services have been arranged or provided by their local authority following a community care assessment, and if their local authority has a policy to set a charge for services that support people staying at home. However, these charges are often nominal when compared with the national mandatory means-test for places in homes (see Chapter 6).

It is the desire for greater financial control, and control over other aspects of their lives through living in their own flat (rather than a room in a home) that many older people find attractive in sheltered housing. As set out earlier, some local authorities have decided to withdraw from residential home provision in favour of sheltered accommodation. Many sheltered flats also offer warden services, personal and practical care, and communal facilities – in order to provide more older people with this option, especially schemes to rent. Private sector developments have tended to concentrate on purpose-built leasehold flats available for sale, which may offer some caretaker or janitor services but not usually care services.

More recently, some voluntary sector organisations have also been developing 'retirement villages'. These tend to provide a range of flats or bungalows within grounds that also offer a variety of activities and facilities, such as small sports centres, hairdressing salons, a grocery, along with a variety of care services frequently including a nursing home. Although such 'villages' are still relatively few in number, the original idea dates back at least a century. One of the main ideas behind such developments is that, by providing a range of services, older people can be enabled to carry on living in that community despite changes to their care needs.

Box 3.8 Information about sheltered housing

* **Elderly Accomodation Counsel**
  A charity providing advice and leaflets. Has a national database that can be searched for details of local retirement and sheltered housing schemes to buy or rent.

Changes to the way supported housing schemes are funded by the state will be implemented in full from April 2003. These changes, under the *Supporting People* initiative (DSS, 1998) outline the ways in which housing-related support services will be funded (see Chapter 6). These new arrangements do not apply to regulated care homes. The *Supporting People* changes also require local authorities to consider how they will decide who is most suited to rented sheltered housing. Councils are expected to provide opportunities to recognise and meet the culturally specific needs of black and ethnic minority elders; and to further develop alternatives to institutional care. In addition, the Government has announced plans to increase the amount of sheltered, or supported, housing available to older people (*Expanded Services*, DH, 2002).

Aids, equipment and adaptations

The Audit Commission (2000) report *Fully Equipped* criticised health and social services' arrangements for providing community equipment. Its findings included poor co-ordination between the two organisations, both of which provide aids and equipment. In addition, many users were waiting a long time to receive equipment – which, when finally supplied, was sometimes found to be unsuitable or inadequate in quality.

An updated version of this report, *Fully Equipped 2002 – Assisting Independence*, found some improvements in the system. However, users were still reporting long delays; service commissioning was not integrated with wider health and social care services; and equipment services were often commissioned to match a limited budget rather than to meet need (Audit Commission, 2002).

Equipment from the NHS is generally intended to meet home nursing needs, such as pressure relief mattresses and commodes. In general, it is local authorities that provide aids for daily living such as grab rails and raised toilet seats. However, there is no central 'list' that determines, in absolute terms, which items are provided by which organisation. This can lead to difficulties for people trying to get equipment and aids. It can also cause confusion in terms of whether or not individuals have to pay towards equipment. However, in the summer of 2002, the Secretary of State for Health announced plans to exempt equipment from charges (*Expanded Services*, DH, 2002; see also Chapter 6).

The NHS Plan (DH, 2000) set out the Government's intention to create Integrated Community Equipment Services (ICES) by 2004. A National Implementation Team, providing support and advice to NHS Trusts and local councils, was established in 2001. These measures form part of the intermediate care programme (HSC 2001/008, LAC(2001)13). It is expected local NHS bodies and local councils will manage and fund these integrated services under one of the Health Act 1999 partnership arrangements.

The system of state support to pay for adaptations in people's own homes (whether rented or owner-occupied) is explained in Chapter 6.

Box 3.9 Further information about equipment

* **Help the Aged**
  Information sheet 15, *Equipment for daily living*
* **Age Concern England**
  Factsheet 42, *Disability equipment and how to get it*
* **Disabled Living Foundation**
  A charity that specialises in providing information on disability equipment and improving the independence of people with disabilities

---

Mental health services

There are three aspects of mental health provision that are particularly pertinent to older people with mental health issues:

- the National Service Framework (NSF) for Older People;
- integration of the Care Programme Approach (CPA) with care management;
- the draft Mental Health Bill (2002).

The Government has identified improvements to mental health as one of its key health targets, alongside coronary heart disease and cancer (*Saving lives: Our Healthier Nation*, DH, 1999; *The NHS Plan*, DH, 2000). It has published an NSF for Mental Health, but this only applies to adults up to the age of 65. It is the NSF for Older People – which specifically includes depression and dementia – that has been designed for people with mental health problems over 65 years old. Despite this, the CPA and the provisions of the mental health White Paper apply to everyone over the age of 16. There is no upper age limit. This may, therefore, cause some confusion in circumstances when older people have mental health problems other than depression or dementia. Government guidance sets out, however, that – with a few exceptions – for older people with mental health problems, the single assessment process should be followed rather than the CPA (HSC 2002/001; LAC(2002)1). These exceptions apply to older people with severe mental illness such as schizophrenia. In such cases, agencies should apply CPA using mental health practitioners, but base the assessment on the four levels of assessment set out in SAP (see Chapter 5) (*Single Assessment Process: SAP and CPA*, DH, 2002).

Older people with dementia

In common with the NSF for Older People, the Audit Commission's 2000 and 2002 reports on mental health services for older people (*Forget-me-not* and *Forget-me-not 2002*) concentrated on depression and dementia, as the most frequently found mental health conditions among older people. Of the two, depression is the more common, especially among older women, although men over 85 with depression are more likely to commit suicide (Kelly and Bunting, 1998). Some older people from black or Asian ethnic minority backgrounds experience particularly high rates of depression compared with white older people (Lowdell *et al*, 2000). Studies during the 1980s found that as many as 40 per cent of older people living in residential and nursing homes may have been clinically depressed, although only a small minority received drug treatment or counselling. There are also problems with diagnosis. Depression can be ignored or symptoms, such as lack of concentration or some memory loss, mistaken for dementia.

The prevalence of dementia rises with age, with approximately one-quarter of people aged over 85 believed to have the disease (Audit Commission, 2000). Around one-third of people with dementia are estimated to be living in residential or nursing homes, or hospitals. It is expected that the number of older people with dementia living in hospitals and homes will have risen by 14 per cent by 2010, if current eligibility criteria for this care is unchanged (Audit Commission, 2000). The updated Audit Commission report – *Forget-me-not 2002* – found that GPs needed more support, especially around diagnosing dementia and depression; and that specialist teams for older people with mental health problems were only fully available in less than half of all areas.

In 2001, the National Institute for Clinical Excellence (NICE) gave its approval for the NHS to provide certain drug treatments for older people in the early stages of dementia, which can slow down the progression of the disease. Trade names include Aricept, Exelon and Reminyl. It is not clear how widely available these are, despite instructions from the Department of Health to the NHS to follow NICE's guidance.

The use of other drugs, particularly neuroleptic medication, amongst older people with dementia has been viewed with some concern, however. In broad terms, neuroleptic drugs act as tranquillizers, having a sedative effect. Such drugs have been used as a way of controlling behaviour such as 'wandering' among those living in residential settings (Levenson, 1998). Alternative approaches have concentrated instead on the advantages of therapeutic approaches (such as music therapy and gentle swimming exercises) with people with advanced dementia.

Work carried out over several years with older people with dementia living in a variety of care homes has also uncovered a wide range of communication possibilities, including a variety of non-verbal contact (Killick and Allan, 2001). This is particularly important for the consultation with, and the provision of information to, older people whose advanced dementia can otherwise mean they are offered few opportunities to take part in consultation exercises (see Chapter 7). These developments are likely to prove particularly helpful if there is an increase in the number of older people with dementia in the future.

Box 3.10 Further information about mental health

* **Alzheimer's Society**
  Produces information about, and provides services for, people with all forms of dementia
* **MIND**
  Provides information and support for people with mental health problems

---

Care Programme Approach (CPA)

This approach describes the ways patients (of whatever age) of consultant psychiatrists should be assessed and reassessed if they either live in the community or are being discharged from psychiatric hospital. CPA was first introduced in 1990, partly to aid the resettlement of people with severe mental health difficulties from long-stay hospitals into supported or ordinary housing.

Changes were made to the CPA system in 1999. It was extended to everyone over the age of 16 under the care of the secondary mental health service (provided by health and social care), regardless of where that care was being provided. CPA was also incorporated with care management, through the integration of mental health services for those people with mental illness who live in areas where geographical boundaries are shared between a health and a social service (*Effective Co-ordination in Mental Health Services*, DH, 1999). It is important to ensure that the needs of patients over the age of 65 with mental health problems are dealt with as thoroughly under the single assessment process as under CPA; and that problems do not arise when people who have previously come under CPA turn 65. (See also Chapter 5.)

(It is worth noting that the Government has also begun to use the abbreviation CPA to indicate the Comprehensive Performance Assessment programme, which measures the performance of health and social services bodies.)

Mental health legislation

People with mental health needs (including some older people) may, after assessment, receive services under Section 117 of the Mental Health Act 1983. This requires health authorities and social services departments, in co-operation with relevant voluntary agencies, to provide after-care services for eligible patients. Unlike other services to help support people living at home, local councils cannot charge for these after-care services (see Chapter 6).

Since the implementation of the community care reforms, much attention has centred on a small number of highly publicised murders and attacks committed by a handful of people with severe, often complex, mental health difficulties. In 1998, the Government published a White Paper, *Reforming the Mental Health Act* (Home Office, 1998), suggesting a raft of changes to provide more opportunities to compel people to receive treatment. These proposals have been highly criticised by some organisations. Consultation on the subsequent draft *Mental Health Bill* was to be completed by the autumn of 2002. This draft Bill sets out two main aims:

- to provide a legal structure for requiring mentally disordered people to submit to compulsory treatment (whether or not this takes place in a hospital)

- to bring the law more closely into line with modern human rights legislation.

Proposed changes include requiring that all decisions compelling people to have treatment be taken by an independent judicial body. Services provided compulsorily would be free to individuals under these proposals. This would include any aftercare received following a period under compulsory powers. The proposed Commission for Healthcare Audit and Inspection (CHAI – see Chapter 4) would, it is planned, scrutinise the proper application of the resulting new Mental Health Act. The draft Bill has attracted some early public criticism, particularly concerning the suggested new broad definition of 'mental disorder'.

Proposals for arrangements to protect vulnerable adults, who may lack the capacity to make decisions, are outlined in Chapter 4.

Health care services

Aside from NHS continuing health care services, which are discussed in detail in Chapter 6, and intermediate and mental health care services outlined above, there are a number of ways in which health care for older people has been affected by changes in policy and practice.

A key concern for the NHS in recent years has been the inappropriate accessing of its services by the general public – especially GP services, hospital accident and emergency (A&E) departments, and services such as NHS ambulances. So, in March 1998, the government opened the first of two 'screening' services, aimed at helping people better to care for themselves in the first instance, and directing them to other services where needed. These are NHS Direct and NHS Walk-in Centres. They are described below, together with other health care services.

NHS Direct

This is primarily a telephone service for use by members of the public. Staffed by nurses, it aims to provide advice and reassurance to callers, as well as direct people to the right service – calling an ambulance, if needed. NHS Direct also has a website, with information about the most common illnesses (see Useful Contacts on page 249).

However, a report by the House of Commons Public Accounts Committee (HPAC) has suggested that some sections of the population are either less aware of NHS Direct, or use it less despite having an equal need for the service. This includes older people, and those from ethnic minority groups. From the end of 2002, NHS Direct is expected to run a specially tailored campaign to improve awareness of the service amongst older people (HPAC, 2002).

NHS Walk-in Centres

The first Walk-in Centres were opened in January 2000. By mid-2002, they were available in 42 sites across England. They are open seven days a week, although opening hours may vary. Walk-in Centres offer the following.

- assessment by an NHS nurse;
- treatment for minor injuries and illnesses;
- information on out-of-hours GP, dental, and pharmacy services;
- advice on other services, and on staying healthy.

The nurse also advises visitors whether they need to seek further treatment from a GP or A&E department, for example.

Research carried out in 2001 suggests that these NHS Walk-in Centres are relieving pressure on other NHS services. For example, 74 per cent of consultations were managed entirely in the Centres, with 45 per cent of patients saying they would have contacted their GP if the centre had not been available (Salisbury *et al*, 2002).

Services such as NHS Direct and the Walk-in centres potentially (if somewhat distantly), raise the issue of whether GP and A&E services should be considered as specialist services, to which access may always require some prior screening.

Care Direct, which aims to provide information about health, housing and social care services, was piloted in several local authority areas during 2001–2002 (see Chapter 5).

Exemptions from charges for NHS treatments and services

In 1997, shortly after the general election, the Government reinstated free eyesight checks for everyone over the age of 60. The qualifying age for other support, such as exemption from prescription charges, is also set at 60 for both men and women. Older people on low incomes (including those in receipt of Income Support or the Minimum Income Guarantee – MIG) may also be eligible to help with the costs of dentistry, spectacles, and wigs.

It is possible that the equalisation of the pension age at 65 in 2020 may result in a review of the relevant qualifying age. On the other hand, reform in this area may take place more quickly. The Wanless review, published in 2002, particularly suggested that the current policy of offering exemption on prescription charges to some groups of people was illogical, and recommended that this be re-examined.

GP services

Under the NHS reforms of the early 1990s, GPs became responsible for offering an annual health check to all their patients aged 75 and over. There were initially mixed views about this initiative. Whereas older people were generally pleased and reassured to receive such a check, some GPs raised concerns about whether this was an effective use of their time. Negotiations between GPs and the Government on their overall contracts, including the provision of this annual check, have been proceeding during 2002, and further guidance is expected in 2003. In the meantime, the over-75s health check has been identified within the Single Assessment Process (SAP – see Chapter 5) as one way in which different aspects of older people's needs can be recorded and shared, and – where appropriate – people put in touch with other relevant agencies.

During the late 1990s, and the turn of the millenium, it became apparent that a number of residential and nursing homes were being asked by GPs to pay retainer fees for the services they were providing to residents. In some areas, there were problems finding GPs willing to accept older residents in homes onto their NHS patient lists, especially in areas with a high proportion of homes. Older people living in these care homes have the same entitlements to GP services from the NHS as people living in their own home, and these services should be provided without charge. However, homes were – inevitably – passing on the costs of these extra, retainer fees to their residents.

In response, in 2001 the Department of Health's Health and Social Care Joint Unit issued a guide to care home managers on GP services for their residents. This reminds managers of the role of the health authority in finding GPs who will register residents as NHS patients, and that those residents should not be charged for services (such as immunisation against influenza) provided to everyone else as part of a personal medical service. However, the guide also states that GPs can enter into private, professional arrangements with any body or institution, including residential or nursing homes. These arrangements would be for services to the *care home* – such as the safe management and control of medicines, occupational health of staff at the home, and the management of patients with problems of mobility or on infection control – not services to *individual patients*. Homes may need to make clear if there are any services it receives from GPs for which a fee is paid, and which may be recouped through the fees charged to residents, as a GP's registered NHS patient should not be charged for individual, direct patient services.

Recent research has found that, in some areas, GPs are continuing to charge homes for at least some of the services provided to older residents. There are also suggestions that, as these payments have to be met through the fees charged by homes and there are generally limits to the amounts local authorities will pay, it is self-funding residents who are paying these extra costs for all residents in any one home (Glendinning *et al*, 2002).

Day surgery

Another change for patients, that particularly affects some older patients, is the increased use of day surgery, for which patients do not need an overnight stay. This is especially useful for treating such conditions as hernias, varicose veins, and cataracts. A study by the Audit Commission (*Day Surgery Report*, 2001) found that patients having day surgery rather than inpatient surgery often have shorter waiting times because more people can be treated, spend less time in hospital, and receive care that is better suited to their needs. In addition, hospital costs are lower.

The NHS Plan set out the Government's expectations that 75 per cent of all planned (or elective) operations would be carried out as day cases, but figures for 2000–2001 suggest this target is not yet being met. In response, and as part of an overall drive to bring down waiting times for operations, *Day Surgery – Operational Guide* (DH, 2002) aims to improve efficiency in day surgery units.

National Service Frameworks (NSFs)

Set out in the White Paper *The New NHS* (1997) and the 1998 consultation document *A First Class Service*, a rolling programme of National Service Frameworks was launched in 1998. These are intended to set national standards and define service models for a defined service area (e.g. cancer) or care group (e.g. older people). They set out a timescale for improvements, and a strategic framework to support any necessary changes. The first four NSFs to be published were:

- Mental Health (1999);
- Coronary Heart Disease (2000);
- Cancer Plan (2000);
- Older People (2001).

A draft NSF for Diabetes was published in late 2001. Other planned NSFs include Long Term Conditions (focusing on neurological conditions), Renal Services, and Children's Services. It is expected that additional NSFs will be developed at the rate of one per year.

With the exception of those covering Mental Health and Children's Services, NSFs apply equally to older people and to other adults. Similarly, while the NSF for Older People focuses on the conditions that are particularly significant for older people (and that are not addressed elsewhere), its standards on stroke and dementia, for example, also apply to younger adults experiencing these conditions. It will be important to ensure that everyone involved in the delivery of the different NSFs understands this relationship.

National Service Framework for Older People

This is the key NSF, in terms of older people's experiences and services, and is based on eight standards, developed from four themes (Box 3.11).

Box 3.11 The standards and themes of the NSF for Older People

Theme 1: Respecting the individual

Standard 1: Rooting out age discrimination

NHS services will be provided, regardless of age, on the basis of clinical need alone. Social care services will not use age in their eligibility criteria or policies to restrict access to available services.

Standard 2: Person-centred care

NHS and social care services treat older people as individuals and enable them to make choices about their own care. This will be achieved through the single assessment process, integrated commissioning arrangements and integrated provision of services, including community equipment and continence services.

Theme 2: Intermediate care

Standard 3: Intermediate care

Older people will have access to a new range of intermediate care services at home or in designated care settings, to promote their independence by providing enhanced services from the NHS and councils to prevent unnecessary hospital admission and effective rehabilitation services to enable early discharge from hospital and to prevent premature or unnecessary admission to long-term residential care.

Theme 3: Providing evidence-based specialist care

Standard 4: General hospital care

Older people's care in hospital is delivered through appropriate specialist care and by hospital staff with the right set of skills to meet their needs.

Standard 5: Stroke

The NHS will take action to prevent strokes, working in partnership with other agencies, where appropriate.

People who are thought to have had a stroke have access to diagnostic services, are treated appropriately by a specialist stroke service, and subsequently, with their carers, participate in a multidisciplinary programme of secondary prevention and rehabilitation.

Standard 6: Falls

The NHS, working in partnership with other councils, takes action to prevent falls and reduce resultant fractures or other injuries in their populations of older people.

Older people who have fallen receive effective treatment and rehabilitation and, with their carers, receive advice on prevention, through a specialised falls service.

Standard 7: Mental health in older people

Older people who have mental health problems have access to integrated mental health services, provided by the NHS and councils to ensure effective diagnosis, treatment and support, for them and for their carers.

Theme 4: Promoting an active, healthy life

Standard 8: The promotion of health and active life in older age

The health and well-being of older people is promoted through a co-ordinated programme of action led by the NHS with support from councils.

Source: *National Service Framework for Older People* (DH, 2001)

Every NHS organisation and local council has been told to ensure that older people's views are properly represented on local Modernisation Boards (see Chapter 2); to designate older people's champions to lead health and social services organisations; and to ensure professional development within organisations. In addition, NHS Trusts have been told to designate a champion for older people through the Patients' Forum to look after patient interests (see Chapter 7). An inter-agency group, involving older people and their carers, will oversee the implementation of the NSF locally.

It is expected that implementation of the NSF will take place over several years – some examples are set out in Table 3.1.

TABLE 3.1 TIMETABLE TO IMPLEMENT NSF FOR OLDER PEOPLE STANDARDS

Year	Action	Standard
2001	• Audit of all age-related policies	1
	• Intermediate care co-ordinator appointed by health and social care in each health authority area	3
2002	• Councils review social care criteria to ensure no age discrimination	1
	• Best practice benchmarks on outcome for older people's health needs, and outcomes analysed	1
	• Single Assessment Process introduced	2
	• Additional intermediate care services available	3
2003	• Development of integrated continence service included in HIMPs (Health Improvement and Modernisation Plans) and other local plans	2
	• All general hospitals with older patients completed a skills profile of staff in relation to care of their older patients, and training/ education needs identified	4
	• Programme to promote healthy ageing and prevent disease included in HIMPs, SaFFs (Service and Financial Frameworks) and other local plans	8

Year	Action	Standard
2004	• Single integrated community equipment service in place	2
	• Further additional intermediate care services in place	3
	• Every hospital caring for older people with stroke has a specialised stroke service	5
	• Health and social care agreed protocols in place for care and management of older people with mental health problems	7
2005	• All local health and social care systems' integrated falls service in place	6

Standards have also been set for the review of older people's medication. From April 2002, everyone over the age of 75 should have their medication reviewed at least annually. Those taking four or more medicines should have a six-monthly review.

The NSF for Older People is a detailed initiative that is likely to form the focus of much service, organisational and staff development over the next three years. It represents a major shift in the recognition of the needs of older people for health and social care services, and in setting standards for their care that go beyond clinical priorities.

4 Regulating services, protecting users

This chapter focuses on the key changes to the system of regulating older people's care services, implemented in April 2002, and, for the most part, set out in the Care Standards Act 2000. It also discusses some measures designed to protect vulnerable users.

A brief history of regulation

The Residential Homes Act 1984 and Residential Homes (Amendment) Act 1991 set out a system of registration and inspection of private and voluntary sector residential and nursing homes for adults, including homes for older people. This system was used until April 2002. Homes offering fewer than four places were included in this regulatory system, although under a simpler version of it. Local authority residential 'Part III' homes, and NHS long-stay nursing homes (there are relatively few of these) were not covered by this legislation. Other homes were specifically excluded under the legislation – for example, homes established under Royal Charters.

Under the NHS and Community Care Act 1990, a new system for inspecting homes was established. Implemented from April 1991, this set out the following arrangements:

- private and voluntary sector residential homes (now known as 'care homes', under the Care Standards Act 2000) were registered and inspected by units run by local authorities in each area;

- nursing homes run by the private and voluntary sector (now known as 'care homes with nursing', under the Care Standards Act 2000) were registered and inspected by units run by each health authority.

Local authority registration and inspection units inspected their own 'Part III' care homes, but these were not subject to the same registration requirements that applied to private and voluntary sector residential homes. Under the NHS and Community Care Act 1990, local authority registration and inspection units were intended to be at 'arms length' from social services departments, although they were the responsibility of the Director of Social Services in each area. Because social services had, from April 1993, roles as both purchasers and providers of services, it was felt that the inspection role should be separate from these other, potentially conflicting, responsibilities.

Concerns during the 1990s

Following the full implementation of the community care reforms in April 1993, criticisms and concerns about these regulatory arrangements began to grow. For example, there were concerns that, despite attempts to keep these separate, local authorities' roles as the regulators, the inspectors *and* the purchasers of care created an unhealthy conflict of interest. There was growing resentment, particularly from some private sector providers, that local authorities were expecting independent sector homes to meet standards of provision that did not apply to their own, unregulated (although inspected) Part III homes. Indeed, some argued that Part III homes would not be able to meet these standards, if they were imposed. This issue became intertwined with the concerns of some in the private sector that places in Part III homes cost the local authority more to provide than it would pay for places in private sector care homes. In short, many private sector home providers believed they were offering better quality care for less money. The counter-argument over costs was that Part III homes' staff received better pay (including pension arrangements) and more training, and that the ratio of staff to residents was higher than in the private sector. These concerns about costs were discussed in more detail in Chapter 3.

Other concerns were that each of the local and health authority inspection and registration units set their own standards within the broad framework set out in legislation. This meant that some of the detail in the standards varied both between units, and across the country. In particular, the larger independent sector providers who had several homes in various parts of the country, found it increasingly difficult to respond to widespread local variations. There were concerns – especially at health authority inspection and registration units but also on the part of local authorities – that the annual minimum number of two inspection visits to each home (one announced, one unannounced) was not always taking place, because of a lack of resources. Units were supposed to be able to cover their costs from the annual registration fees paid by care home owners, but these fees – set by Parliament – had not been increased for several years. In addition, there were concerns that some dual registered homes – offering both residential and nursing home care places – were receiving inspections from both units, creating unnecessary duplication, overlapping assessments and, sometimes, conflicting advice. Finally, the growth in providing personal care to people in their own homes, created disquiet about the potential abuse of older people from those working in this unregulated, uninspected service. As a result, there were also calls for care at home to begin to be regulated in some way.

Local standards

In drawing up local standards for registration, many local and health authority units used various publications about standards for people living in homes. The Social Services Inspectorate's publication, *Homes are for Living In* (SSI, 1989), set out some basic values for residents:

- privacy;
- dignity;
- independence;
- choice;
- rights;
- fulfilment.

Other reports used by inspection units included two from the Centre for Policy on Ageing – *Home Life: A code of good practice* (1984) and *A Better Home Life: A code of good practice for residential and nursing home care* (1996) – and one from the National Association of Health Authorities and Trusts (NAHAT – now called the NHS Confederation) – *Registration and Inspection of Nursing Homes: A handbook for health authorities*, and its supplemented version, published in 1985 and 1999.

The Burgner Report

In October 1996, the then Conservative government published Tom Burgner's report on the future regulatory system. Drawing on an earlier consultation document, the Burgner report – *Moving Forward* – made a number of recommendations for change:

- local authority responsibilities for inspecting residential homes should be moved, after the necessary preparation, from social services to either the Chief Executive's department or the Trading Standards department;
- local authority homes should be subject to the same rules as homes run by the voluntary and private sectors;
- new national benchmarks should form a basis for standards for all homes;
- the extension of regulation to domiciliary care services should be considered.

In March 1997, two months before the general election that year, the Conservative government published its White Paper, *Social Services – Achievement and Challenge*. This built upon the Burgner Report. Indeed, many of Burgner's recommendations were incorporated in full. The White Paper proposed:

- extending regulation to domiciliary care services;
- extending regulation to include local authority services;
- removing regulatory functions from social services departments;
- moving towards a single regulatory authority for each area;
- moving towards a single category care home, rather than separate categories for residential and nursing homes.

Modernising social services

In 1998, the New Labour Government published its own White Paper, *Modernising Social Services*, which included proposals for changing the regulatory system. This also accepted and built on many of the recommendations in the Burgner Report. It included proposals to create eight regional Commissions for Care Standards, independent statutory bodies that would regulate services. Domiciliary services would be included in regulation requirements, as would local authority Part III homes and homes created under a Royal Charter. The Government commissioned the Centre for Policy on Ageing to advise on proposed national standards for the largest group of regulated services – residential and nursing homes for older people. After a long process working with key interested parties, the Centre for Policy on Ageing issued its consultation document on standards for residential and nursing homes, *Fit for the Future*, in 1999, with the final version published in March 2001. The issue of national minimum standards in care homes is explored in more detail later in this chapter.

Other reports

Two other reports drew attention to particular aspects of care home provision, and the need for new regulatory requirements. In 1998, the Office for Fair Trading (OFT) published *Choosing a Care Home*. This considered the issue of residents as consumers and citizens. It recommended that all residents should have a contract with the home in which they lived, specifying what care and facilities were to be provided, and setting out their rights to continue to live in the home.

Part of the report of the Royal Commission on long-term care, *With Respect to Old Age* (DH, 1999) also included recommendations on regulation. It called for a National Care Commission with wide-ranging responsibilities for services for older people. Key amongst these were:

- to take a strategic overview of care services;
- to act as an ombudsman to deal with complaints and reflect user's views to government;
- to publish and monitor national benchmarks of quality of services, eligibility criteria and national systems of assessment.

However, the Royal Commission did not see its proposed National Care Commission as responsible for day-to-day regulation of care homes or care workers. This, it expected, would be carried out by the new regulatory bodies set out in *Modernising Social Services* (DSS, 1998), and which subsequently developed separately into the National Care Standards Commission (NCSC). The background to, and key recommendations of, the Royal Commission are discussed in more detail in Chapter 6.

Regulation from April 2002

Following extensive consultation, the Government announced its detailed plans for the new regulatory system and set out the legislative framework in the Care Standards Act 2000. This established the National Care Standards Commission (NCSC), whose powers began in April 2002 to inspect and regulate:

- care homes (including 'care homes with nursing');
- children's homes;
- domiciliary care agencies;
- independent fostering agencies;
- day centres (for children);
- nurses' agencies;
- private and voluntary hospitals;
- residential family centres;
- voluntary adoption agencies.

Box 4.1 Key elements of the Care Standards Act 2000

Part I of the Care Standards Act 2000

- Sections 2 and 3 give the definitions of 'independent hospital' and 'care homes'
- Section 4 gives the definition of 'domiciliary care agency' and 'nurses agency'
- Sections 5–10 set out the establishment of the National Care Standards Commission (NCSC) for England (for Wales, the registration authority is the National Assembly for Wales); the relationship between these bodies and the Commission for Health Improvement (CHI) and the National Institute for Clinical Excellence (NICE); and the NCSC's general duties

Part II sets out the requirements of establishments and agencies to register; the registration procedure; and offences under the Act

Part III extends regulation to local authority establishments and agencies

Part IV establishes the General Social Care Council (GSCC) for the regulation of social care workers

Parts V and VI deal with children's services

Part VII covers the protection of vulnerable adults and children

Part VIII deals with miscellaneous items, including nurses' agencies

---

In short, the Care Standards Act 2000 set out to deal with many of the issues raised during the 1990s and responded to by both Conservative and Labour governments. These included calls for national quality standards in care homes; for local authority homes to be subject to the same system of regulation as independent sector providers; and for personal domiciliary care services to be regulated.

In its response to the Royal Commission, the Government stated its belief that improving the standards of care, and fair access to services, would benefit older people's health more than would implementing the Royal Commission's main recommendation, of making personal care free to people in all settings (*The NHS Plan – the Government's Response to the Royal Commission on Long Term Care*, 2000).

How is regulation carried out?

There are three tiers to the National Care Standards Commission (NCSC):

- the head office, in Newcastle upon Tyne;
- eight regional offices;
- a further 71 area offices.

NCSC's head office has overall responsibility for the organisation. The eight regional offices are responsible for ensuring the quality of the registration and inspection work undertaken by the 71 area offices. This structure replaced the previous health and local authority inspection and registration units in April 2002. In practice, many of the staff from these former units joined the NCSC at national, regional or local levels. The files and records of the former units were transferred to the NCSC, together with any ongoing cases.

From April 2002, establishments that were already registered under the Registered Homes Act 1984 and Registered Homes (Amendment) Act 1991 were automatically registered under the 2000 Act. So, too, were services that were required, as a result of the Care Standards Act 2000, to register for the first time (for example, local authority residential homes). In April 2002, the NCSC began inspecting existing services (those regulated under the previous system, as well as those now regulated under the new system) against the new National Minimum Standards (see below).

Services that would have been subject to regulation before April 2002 (for example, a private sector residential home with ten places), but which were not set up as new establishments until after April 2002, have to meet these new national minimum standards from the outset.

Under the previous regulatory system, lay assessors (members of the public) were involved in inspection visits. The Government has said it expects the NCSC to continue to involve lay assessors in this role.

One of the other changes brought about through the new regulatory system, is the development of new training courses and qualifications for inspection staff. The qualification, the Regulation of Care Services Award, is based on new National Occupational Standards produced by the national Training Organisation for Personal Social Services (TOPSS). This has been developed in conjunction with the General Social Care Council (GSCC).

Proposals for change

Shortly after the NCSC began to fulfil its role in April 2002, the Government published another White Paper, *Delivering the NHS Plan*. Chapter 2 described some of the ways this is expected to change the respective roles of the NCSC and CHI, among other organisations. This included plans for a new organisation, the Commission for Social Care Inspection, which would take over much of the work of the NCSC. These changes will require new legislation. In July 2002, the Secretary of State for Health announced plans to create the Commission for Social Care Inspection in shadow form by the end of 2002 (DH, 2002). At the time of writing, the timetable for further reform of this new regulatory system was unclear. However, until these changes are effected in law, it is expected that the NCSC will continue to operate as set out in this chapter.

National minimum standards

The minimum number of inspections for services has been set out in regulations (The National Care Standards Commission (Fees and Frequency of Inspections) Regulations 2001), as have the annual fees to be paid by agencies and establishments to be registered. As with the previous system, care homes will be inspected at least twice every financial year (between 1 April and 31 March). Independent hospitals, clinics, nurses' agencies, and domiciliary care agencies will each receive a minimum of one visit each financial year. Again, in common with the previous regulatory system, a great deal of emphasis is placed on the person who is registered to run the home or agency (often called the 'fit person'), to ensure standards are met.

It is important to note that there is no direct requirement in the Care Standards Act 2000 to comply with the national minimum standards. However, there is a requirement on homes (and other regulated services) to comply with the Regulations issued under the Care Standards Act 2000, which expect the national minimum standards to be taken into account when inspecting and registering homes.

NATIONAL MINIMUM STANDARDS IN CARE HOMES FOR OLDER PEOPLE

These standards were the first of the series relating to the different services to be published, in March 2001 (*Care Homes for Older People, National Minimum Standards*, DH, 2001). There are 38 standards, which form the basis for judgements made by the NCSC regarding registration decisions. They are intended to provide a tool for judging the quality of life of residents in homes. Not all the standards were expected to apply from April 2002. Indeed, in January 2002, the Minister for Health wrote to the Chair of the National Care Standards Commission, suggesting that some standards not be applied until 2007; and further suggesting that the Commission respond flexibly to the individual circumstances of homes (*Letter*, DH, 2002). As a result, it was expected that standards relating to shared rooms and to minimum room sizes would not apply until 2007.

In July 2002, the Secretary of State for Health announced plans for further consultation on the environmental standards applying to care homes. These include the provision of single (rather than shared) rooms, minimum room sizes and the numbers of lifts and baths provided in the home (*Expanded Services*, DH, 2002). The Secretary of State for Health set out his view that existing care homes should not be required to meet these environmental standards. If agreed, this would mean care homes aspiring to these standards as good practice. They would be required to make clear to residents whether or not they met these standards. The announcement was made as part of the Government's response to concerns, raised especially in the media during 2002, that care homes have been closing as a direct result of the new minimum standards (this issue has been discussed in detail in Chapter 3). At the time of writing, it is unclear whether the proposed changes to these particular quality standards will encourage potential providers to *open* new homes, which analysts have suggested may be the more serious problem (Laing and Buisson, 2002; see also Chapter 3). The Secretary of State has also announced that £70 million would be made available, by 2006, specifically to train unqualified social care staff, in order to enhance the quality of care provided to people in care homes and elsewhere (*Expanded Services*, DH, 2002).

During the autumn of 2002, consultation took place to develop new environmental standards (see pages 106–7). However other national minimum standards, covering issues such as contracts and complaints systems, apply to all care homes from April 2002.

Standards 1–6 cover information to be provided to service users, the contract with the home; needs assessment and meeting needs; trial visits; and the provision of planned intermediate care prior to someone returning to their own home.

Standards 7–11 outline the health and personal care services that a resident receives in the home. This includes setting out a plan of care and meeting all health care needs; policies on medication; arrangements to ensure residents' privacy; the care of residents when they are dying, and the handling of residents' deaths.

Standards 12–15 cover social activities and daily life, including maximising users' ability to exercise choice and control; ensuring meals are nutritious and varied, and mealtimes pleasant.

Standards 16–18 cover complaints and protection. The registered person must ensure there is a simple, clear and accessible complaints system; that residents' legal rights are protected; and that they are safeguarded from any form of abuse.

Standards 19–26 relate to the physical environment of the home – for example the layout of the home, size of rooms, bathroom facilities and adaptations and equipment. These standards were subject to further consultation during the autumn of 2002. At the time of writing, it seems likely that care homes will be asked to aim at meeting any new environmental standards as a matter of good practice rather than this being a requirement. However, they may be required to make information available so that residents and prospective residents know whether these standards have been met by individual homes.

Standards 27–30 cover staff skill mix, qualification levels and staff numbers; recruitment; and opportunities for training.

Finally, **Standards 31–38** set out the requirements for management and administration. This includes minimum qualifications to be achieved by managers by 2005. It also included a requirement for an annual development plan for the home, involving a survey of users, which should be published by, and available from, the home.

Box 4.2 Further information on standards in care homes

✳ **National Care Standards Commission (NCSC)**
   Has copies of the regulations and other relevant material on its website, and offers a telephone information service, particularly for service providers

---

NATIONAL MINIMUM STANDARDS FOR DOMICILIARY CARE AGENCIES

The debate about how to regulate domiciliary care agencies, and what constituted such an agency, went on for some time. The term 'domiciliary care' is generally used to mean care someone receives to help them stay at home. However, there were concerns early on not to develop a 'catch-all' definition that might inadvertently include people such as window cleaners, or someone who cuts grass for a living, some of whose customers might happen to be over retirement age or have disabilities.

There were also concerns about how to inspect the services, which are by their very nature delivered in people's own homes. Spot checks on care homes can be carried out reasonably easily, but spot checks on an 'individual household' basis would be significantly more problematic.

The Care Standards Act 2000 defines a domiciliary care agency as:

'an undertaking which consists of or includes arranging the provision of personal care in their own homes for persons who by reason of illness, infirmity or disability are unable to provide it for themselves without assistance'. (Section 4 (3), Care Standards Act 2000)

As with care homes, it is the person registered to carry on the domiciliary care agency who bears much of the responsibility. The registered person must be 'fit' to carry on the agency. This is expected to mean:

'Section 8 (3)(a) he is of integrity and good character

(3)(b) he is physically and mentally fit to carry on the agency; and

(3)(c) full and satisfactory information in respect of each of the matters listed in Schedule 2 is available in relation to him'. (LASSL (2001)10, *Regulation of Domiciliary Care*)

The Schedule 2 requirements include proof of identity, two written references, a full employment history, documentary evidence of qualifications and training, and matters relating to criminal records.

Standards cover the manager of the agency, records kept by the agency including the plan of care for the user; and the conduct of the agency, including the need for due regard to the sex, religious persuasion, racial origin, cultural and linguistic background, and any disability, of service users and the ways in which they conduct their lives. Also included are the skills and qualifications of agency workers; the provision of information to service users; and the requirement to establish a complaints procedure for service users to access. Other sections regulate the agency's premises, financial matters, and notification to the NCSC of serious injuries or incidents involving service users, agency premises or domiciliary care workers.

These standards are expected to apply from January 2003, to personal domiciliary care services provided by the local authority, private and voluntary sectors. There are three key aspects to this element of regulation:

- **first**, that it relates to 'personal care' (i.e. care that involves touching the person, such as help with bathing) as opposed to housework or housekeeping-type services;
- **secondly**, that social care staff themselves will become subject to registration over a period of time, under the General Social Care Council;
- **thirdly**, that these agencies differ from nurses' agencies.

NATIONAL MINIMUM STANDARDS FOR NURSES' AGENCIES

These are also expected to come into effect in January 2003, following the repeal of the Nurses' Agencies Act 1957 and associated regulations.

The regulations and minimum standards cover agencies that act as employment agencies (supplying nurses to organisations), as well as those directly providing nurse services to individuals. Section 4(5) of the Care Standards Act 2000 specifies that the staff being used be registered nurses, registered midwives or registered health visitors. It is proposed to exempt NHS nurse banks, at least for the foreseeable future. This would be in line with the exemption of directly provided NHS services from the NCSC regulatory system. The NHS Reform and Health Care Professions Act 2002 enhanced the powers of CHI to inspect NHS services (see Chapter 2).

The focus of the standards is on issues about the protection of people who receive care from agency nurses, such as ensuring the fitness of those carrying on agencies, and the fitness of nurses supplied by them. Aspects of running an employment agency will be separately regulated under the Employment Agencies Act 1973. The nurses' agency standards also cover the provision of information to users; the fitness of the registered person; the recruitment and qualification of nurses; complaints and protection; and management and administration.

Nurses' agencies that also supply non-nursing staff (for example, domiciliary care workers) will have to be separately registered for that side of the agency with the National Care Standards Commission.

NATIONAL MINIMUM STANDARDS FOR PRIVATE AND VOLUNTARY HEALTH CARE

The final area of the new regulatory system pertinent to older people, is private and voluntary sector health care facilities. These include:

- acute hospitals (including day surgery hospitals);
- hospices;
- private doctors.

In April 2002, standards for private and voluntary health care providers came into effect (Private and Voluntary Health Care (England) Regulations 2001). These standards cover the following areas:

- quality of treatment and care;
- management and personnel;
- complaints management;
- premises, facilities and equipment;
- risk management procedures;
- records and information management;
- research.

These standards are divided into core (or common) standards, and those that are specific to the different types of hospitals, clinics and other establishments.

Box 4.3 Further information on different aspects of regulation

✻ **National Care Standards Commission (NCSC)**
Has copies of the regulations and other relevant material on its website, and offers a telephone information service, particularly for service providers

---

Regulation and NHS services

Although the new regulatory system under the National Care Standards Commission brings together local authority directly provided (or in-house) services with those offered by the private and voluntary sectors, services run by the NHS continue to be exempt from regulation. This includes NHS nursing homes as well as NHS hospitals and primary care services.

Chapter 2 set out the role and work of the Commission for Health Improvement (CHI) in inspecting NHS services. The Care Standards Act 2000 creates powers for CHI and the National Care Standards Commission to take on each other's functions, subject to the necessary regulation. This is partly to allow for those NHS services that are funded by the NHS, but actually provided by the private or voluntary health care sector under contract with the relevant NHS body, being subject to the same checks enjoyed by other NHS patients. This would include instances when the NHS purchases operations or other treatments from private hospitals. In these circumstances, the NHS retains responsibility for the care of the patient for whom it has purchased treatment. The NHS Reform and Healthcare Professionals Act 2002 strengthened the arrangements for CHI to inspect independent sector organisations providing care to NHS patients under such an NHS contract. In theory, this could include independent sector nursing homes providing NHS continuing health care to individuals that the NHS funds in full (see Chapter 6). This is a good example of situations where the NCSC and CHI need to co-operate, as the regulation of the home comes under the auspices of the NCSC, but the quality of the care provided to any such NHS patient would fall to CHI. This helps illustrate some of the complexities in regulating health and social care services that are provided by such a wide range of organisations, and are funded in a variety of different ways.

Relationship between CHI and NCSC

The relationship between CHI and NCSC may be thrown into further relief with the development of intermediate care services. In December 2001, CHI and the Audit Commission published the report of their joint investigation into the care of cancer patients, following the implementation of the National Cancer Plan. Further joint studies are planned on the implementation of all the National Service Frameworks (see Chapter 3). Amongst the elements of the NSF for Older People, the development of intermediate care services is a major priority. The Government has already signalled its support to develop intermediate care services among private and voluntary sector providers (especially through the use of places in private sector nursing homes). This could therefore involve CHI and the Audit Commission considering whether NCSC-regulated independent sector provision is meeting statutory targets.

Further issues also arise. In January 2002, the first of 200 patients received planned operations in hospitals in France – mostly hip replacements and cataract treatment. It is not yet clear what the relationship will be between the NHS (the 'purchaser' and still statutorily responsible for this care) and the French clinic (the 'provider' of the treatment) in terms of the roles of CHI and NCSC. The development of Care Trusts may also further blur the distinction, and relationship, between unregulated but CHI-inspected NHS services, and regulated local authority social care provision. Such developments could be dealt with through new regulations under the Care Standards Act 2000, under the NHS Reform and Healthcare Professionals Act 2002, or through new legislation. However, despite some of these uncertainties, most health and social care services will be subject to some form of inspection.

Delivering the NHS Plan (DH, 2002) set out a range of changes to regulation and to the organisations involved in delivering this system (see Chapter 2). It seems likely that the proposal relating to CHI, to create a new Commission for Healthcare Audit and Inspection (CHAI), will come into effect sometime during 2003 (subject to the necessary legislation). It is important to note these proposals continue to describe two systems separately covering health and social care. Other government reforms have prioritised the need to bring down the barriers between health and social care. Within regulation, this distinction seems likely to continue. *Delivering the NHS Plan* states that the organisational upheaval required would not be justified by the creation of a single Commission to regulate health and social care, but that this situation will be kept under review.

Box 4.4 Further information on the regulatory systems for health and social care

* **Commission for Health Improvement (CHI)**
Produces copies of inspection reports and other materials
* **National Care Standards Commission (NCSC)**
Has copies of the regulations and other relevant material on its website, and offers a telephone information service, particularly for service providers

---

Other regulatory change – protecting users and patients

One other significant change within the regulation of social care is the development of a requirement for individual social care workers to hold a professional registration with the General Social Care Council (GSCC). This is a new development in social care, although nursing, medical and other health professionals have registered with their relevant bodies for many years. Adherence to a code of practice for social care workers, applying to both employees and employers, will be monitored in England by the National Care Standards Commission. In Scotland and Wales, this will be carried out by the Scottish Social Services Council, and the Care Council for Wales.

Chapter 2 has already described changes to the system of regulating and monitoring the quality of health care professionals. Many of these have been developed in response to serious concerns about the performance and behaviour of hospital doctors working in specialist services. The public inquiry established in 2001 into the case of Dr Harold Shipman has identified further recommendations for change.

Guidance has also been issued on the development of multi-agency policies to protect vulnerable adults from abuse. This applies to older people, who may – in some cases – experience a range of abuses including financial, physical, sexual and emotional abuse. The guidance, *No Secrets* (2000), requires local authorities to co-ordinate with the police and health services locally, and to develop a code of practice to militate against abuse. This includes being able to recognise when someone is being abused; dealing with abusive care regimes and individual abusers (including abusive relatives and neighbours); and criminal acts of abuse (Box 4.5).

Other measures that offer protection to users and patients include complaints systems. These systems include, from April 2002, the NCSC's role in investigating complaints about the quality of care in homes and other agencies, and are explained in Chapter 7.

Box 4.5 Further information on protection for vulnerable adults

✳ **Action on Elder Abuse**
Produces a range of booklets on different aspects of abuse, runs training courses and a telephone helpline

✳ **General Social Care Council**
Will be operating the new system of registering social care workers

---

5   Access to services

Having information about what sort of treatment, care and support might be available locally for older people is often the critical first stage in accessing services. In each area, the local authority's charter, *Better Care, Higher Standards* (see page 169), should contain details about the support it provides, who is eligible for services, and how to apply. Copies should be available from the local council's offices, as well as from venues such as libraries and GP surgeries.

In 2001, the Government piloted a new initiative, Care Direct, in parts of southwest England. The assessment of these pilots will include aspects such as the delivery of timely information and advice on housing aspects of care for older people. The Care Direct pilot schemes provide information on local care services, through a local rate telephone number and a website. These were developed following the national implementation of NHS Direct. In some areas, local councils have developed what are often called 'one-stop shops' – one point of contact for people to obtain relevant information about support from social services, as well as benefits advice, and information on NHS and housing services locally. Many of these 'one-stop shops' were originally developed under the *Better Government for Older People* (BGOP) initiative.

There are fewer requirements on the NHS to provide information about services in the local area, although the new Patient's Charter, *Your Guide to the NHS*, contains some details, and some health services will feature in local *Better Care, Higher Standards* documents. For some years now, NHS hospitals have been told by governments that they must have information to give to patients about hospital discharge procedures. Since 1996, health authorities have had to publish details of their criteria for NHS continuing health care services.

Having information is one thing, but translating this into receiving services can be quite another. The process of accessing community and continuing care services, forms what is known as an *assessment* (sometimes also called a care assessment, or an assessment of need).

Community care assessments

One of the main changes under the NHS and Community Care Act 1990 was that it gave individuals new rights, from 1 April 1993, to be assessed by their local authority for care services. Local authority care assessments are critical for older users and carers, since this is the first stage in getting services provided or funded by social services (including help towards the cost of places in care homes). These new arrangements signalled a major change from policies and practice before 1993, where many older residents gained state financial support towards the costs of places in independent sector care homes without first having their care needs assessed to ensure that this was the most suitable option for them (see Chapters 1 and 6).

There are currently three circumstances when individuals (including older people) have a right to an assessment:

- **first,** if the person 'appears to be in need' of community care services (NHS and Community Care Act 1990);
- **secondly,** if the person has a disability (Disabled Persons Act 1986);
- **thirdly,** if the person is a carer (Carers (Recognition and Services) Act 1995; Carers and Disabled Children Act 2000).

These are discussed further in the following sections, together with case law that has determined some of the details about social services' assessments since 1993.

If the person 'appears to be in need' of community care services

Section 47 of the NHS and Community Care Act 1990 sets out people's rights to an assessment for community care services, which social services departments may arrange or provide. The Act defines community care services as those provided under the following legislation:

- Part III of the National Assistance Act 1948;
- Section 45 of the Health and Public Health Act 1968;
- Section 21 of and schedule 8 to the NHS Act 1977;
- Section 117 of the Mental Health Act 1983.

Local authorities also provide certain services for people with disabilities, under Section 2 of the Chronically Sick and Disabled Persons Act 1970 (see Chapter 1). In addition, under the Community Care (Direct Payments) Act 1996, local authorities can provide people with money to buy their own community care services, after they have been assessed as needing support (see Chapter 3).

The precise wording of Section 47 of the NHS and Community Care Act 1990 is important, as it places the emphasis on whether someone 'might' need care, and services the council 'may' provide or arrange. In some areas, by the mid-1990s, local authorities had begun to limit assessments to people they already believed *would* 'qualify' for the services they were arranging or providing, even before the assessment had taken place. People who it was felt would not qualify, or might qualify but only for services the council had decided not to offer because of restricted eligibility criteria (see page 165), were being turned away. This led to concerns about the extent of 'telephone screening', and what might be called the 'cup of tea test'. Allegedly, some older people were told, on first contacting social services, that they would not qualify for any help if they were able to make themselves a cup of tea.

A court case in 1998 helped clarify the situation. The legal judgement, *R v Bristol City Council ex parte Penfold*, means that local authorities have to carry out care assessments of people seeking care services that they have the power to provide or arrange. This applies even if a local authority is not currently providing a particular service because it has tightened its criteria that determine who is eligible for support (see page 165). This case law also helped further embed the principle that there are three separate stages to accessing local authority support:

- **first**, the care assessment;
- **secondly**, the decision to provide particular services; and
- **thirdly**, the decision about whether (or how much) someone pays towards care services – the financial assessment (see Chapter 6).

Local authorities must not ask someone about their finances first, and then refuse to provide or arrange a service if someone could pay for themselves. This is particularly important in respect of means-tested care in homes.

If the person has a disability

The Disabled Persons Act 1986 sets out the rights of people with disabilities to be assessed for services provided under Section 2 of the Chronically Sick and Disabled Persons (CSDP) Act 1970. Section 47 of the NHS and Community Care Act 1990 strengthens this by setting out that, when local authorities are assessing someone's needs for community care services and it becomes clear that the person is disabled (because they meet the definition in law of 'disability'), the local authority *must* also consider their need for these services under CSDP Act 1970. Perhaps more importantly, the understanding has long been that this assessment should be comprehensive in nature. This may have implications for the application of the Single Assessment Process in these circumstances (see page 153).

Box 5.1 Definition in law of 'disability', for services under CSDP Act 1970

The exact definition dates back to the **National Assistance Act 1948**, and uses terms that some people might find offensive:

'persons who are blind, deaf or dumb, and other persons who are substantially and permanently handicapped by illness, injury or congenital deformity or who are suffering from a mental disorder within the meaning of the Mental Health Act 1983'.

This was added to by government guidance LAC(93)10:

'and people who are partially sighted or hard of hearing'.

The **Mental Health Act 1983** defines mental disorder as 'mental illness, arrested or incomplete development of mind, psychopathic disorder and any other disorder or disability of mind'.

In addition to the definition given under the National Assistance Act 1948, people with the following conditions are eligible to apply for Disabled Facilities Grants, to provide facilities and adaptations in their homes (see Chapter 6), under the **Housing Grants, Construction and Regeneration Act 1996:**

- their sight, hearing, or speech is substantially impaired
- they have a mental disorder or impairment of any kind
- they are physically substantially disabled by illness, injury, impairment present since birth, or otherwise.

More recently, a further definition of disability has been applied for the purposes of the **Disability Discrimination Act (DDA) 1995:**

- a person is disabled if 'he has a physical or mental impairment which has a substantial and long-term adverse affect on his ability to carry out normal day-to-day activities'.

If the person is a carer

The powers and duties to provide care assessments, under the Carers (Recognition and Services) Act 1995 and the Carers and Disabled Children Act 2000, relate to people who are acting as an unpaid carer to someone else – usually a spouse (or an unmarried partner) or other relative, sometimes a friend or neighbour. Carers are sometimes also called family carers, or informal carers, to distinguish them from people who provide care services for a living.

Section 8 of the Disabled Persons Act 1986 states that local authorities must take account of the carer's ability to provide care on a regular basis, when they are assessing the needs for services under CSDP Act 1970 of the person with a disability that they care for. The extent of this duty increased in subsequent legislation.

The Carers (Recognition and Services) Act 1995 gave carers a new right (from April 1996) to ask for their care needs to be assessed at the same time as the local authority is assessing the needs of the person they care for. The Carers and Disabled Children Act 2000 gave carers a further right to an assessment, even if the person being cared for refuses to be assessed. This Act also extended local authorities' powers to provide or arrange services that support carers in their caring role (see Chapter 3).

Box 5.2 Further information about community care assessments

* **Age Concern England**
  Factsheet 32, *Disability and ageing: your rights to social services*
  Factsheet 41, *Local authority assessments for community care services*
* **Carers UK (formerly the Carers' National Association)**
  Provides information for carers seeking assessments

It is important to be clear that the rights held by users and carers to care assessments, as set out above, are not affected by more recent service and organisation developments. Examples include the implementation of the 'funding flexibilities' (under Section 31 of the Health Act 1999), or the establishment of Care Trusts (under the Health and Social Care Act 2001). Although these developments change the ways health and social services can fund and provide services, they *do not* affect individuals' existing legislative rights to social services assessments. Social services' statutory duties to provide or fund care services remain unaltered by these changes. However, these rights and duties might be delegated to another body. For example, delegation might be to a local NHS organisation (perhaps a Primary Care Trust, or a Care Trust). This organisation would then take on the responsibilities to fulfil these rights and duties, including the rights to assessments of individuals' care needs, and the receipt of services. In this case, the organisation would be accountable to the relevant social services department whose statutory duties it was carrying out.

Assessing people's needs

In 1991, the *Practice Guidance on Care Management and Assessment* was issued by the Department of Health to social services departments. This was intended to inform them of the new assessment arrangements, prior to implementation from April 1993 under the NHS and Community Care Act 1990. Key elements of this 1991 guidance included:

- the need to take account of the wishes of individuals and their carers;
- the need to decide the level of assessment most appropriate to an individual's circumstances and needs.

It is not clear how many current social care practitioners are still fully familiar with the 1991 guidance. However, a major criticism of the community care reforms post-1993 centred on poor assessment and care management by social services departments.

Problems with care assessments

In setting assessments of individuals' needs as one of the corner-stones of the community care reforms, the NHS and Community Care Act 1990 also gave local authorities the responsibility to invite local health and housing authorities to be involved in the assessment, if the person appeared to have needs for those services. In addition, local authorities needed the consent of health author-ities before arranging the nursing home place for someone the local authority had assessed as needing that type of care.

In practice, arrangements on both fronts varied widely. In many areas, health authorities gave what amounted to an 'en masse' agree-ment to all nursing home placements, rather than being involved in the assessment of all potential residents' needs. The involvement of health and housing bodies in community care assessments also varied across the country. Often, these amounted to separate assessments. Later in this chapter, the ways in which eligibility criteria and deci-sions about services varied around the country, are discussed.

Another new requirement post-1993 was for local authorities to set out each individual's care plan, detailing the services they would receive. In reality, these tended to reflect the services being provided or funded by social services. Health and housing services the person might also need or receive were not always recorded, nor were these always known to social services.

A number of issues therefore arose. Firstly, users and carers found themselves having to repeat the same information to health, social services and housing – not just about their care needs and their health, but basic details such as their date of birth and with which GP they were registered (where appropriate). Secondly, the lack of a central record of the various assessments meant that sudden changes in an older person's circumstances – such as being admit-ted to hospital following a fall – tended to necessitate assessments starting again from scratch.

There were also problems about the timing of involving other pro-fessionals in the assessment process (especially for older people in hospital, where the pressure to release beds may not always be compatible with the need for thorough, timely assessments). Some professionals were unhappy accepting the assessment opinions of others, and sought to re-do elements of the assessment – this was a particular problem for some health and social care staff. There was a lack of a consistent approach to assessments around the country (Royal Commission on Long Term Care, 1999), and some confusion as to what should happen following an assessment, in terms of which organisation should then provide support. It was firmly believed that the need to improve working practices between health and social services included improving assessments and the assessment process (Health Select Committee, 1998).

The Single Assessment Process (SAP)

The Government responded to these criticisms by setting out, in Standard 2 of the National Service Framework (NSF) for Older People (DH, 2001), a requirement to develop a new Single Assessment Process. Initially, this has been developed for older people, but will subsequently apply to other client groups. Standard 2 of the NSF for Older People states:

> 'NHS and social care services treat older people as individuals and enable them to make choices about their own care. This is achieved through the Single Assessment Process, integrated commissioning arrangements and integrated provision of services, including community equipment and continence services'.

It is important to note that the Single Assessment Process sets out the detail of how assessments should be carried out – as set out above, it does not alter users' and carers' rights to assessments, or to care.

The Single Assessment Process (SAP) builds on the 1991 Practice Guidance referred to above. However, one major difference between the 1991 guidance and SAP lies in the Government's expectation that health care professionals, including doctors and therapists, will follow the latter whereas the 1991 guidance clearly laid the onus on social services staff. Some of the requirements and approaches in SAP may therefore prove unfamiliar to some health staff.

SAP concentrates on:

- ensuring that the scale and depth of assessments is in proportion to older people's needs;
- ensuring agencies do not duplicate each other's assessments;
- ensuring professionals contribute to assessments in the most effective way.

Local agencies began using SAP from June 2002, but the Department of Health has given them until April 2004 to refine the process and fully comply with all aspects of the guidance (HSC 2002/01; LAC(2001) 01, *Guidance on the Single Assessment Process for older people*).

The guidance establishes seven stages in the assessment process:

- publishing information about services;
- case finding (optional – to identify older people who have not been referred to social services, but who may need help);
- completing the four types of assessment;
- evaluating the assessment information;
- deciding what help should be offered, including eligibility decisions;
- care planning (leading to service delivery);
- monitoring and review.

The guidance does not set out a standard tool or method, although the relevant section of the Department of Health's website (www.doh.gov.uk/toolsandscales/) gives some illustrative examples. However, it does establish four 'levels' of assessment:

- contact;
- overview;
- specialist;
- comprehensive.

In 2002, the Department of Health published advice to local authorities on the relationship between SAP and the care programme Approach (CPA) for people with mental health issues (see Chapter 3).

During the summer of 2002, the Department of Health consulted over changes to how 'delayed discharge' from hospital is handled (see Chapter 3). This suggests that some assessments, begun in hospital, may need to be completed elsewhere (for example, in an intermediate care bed, or at home) in order to meet proposed new targets for discharging patients following hospital treatment. This suggests that the issue of the speed at which it is possible to complete a timely, thorough assessment has yet to be fully resolved.

CONTACT ASSESSMENT

This simplest of the four levels describes the first contact between an older person and health and social services where significant needs are first described or suspected. Basic personal information is collected, together with details of what is known as 'the presenting problem' or the 'presenting need'. This is the initial reason the older person gives for seeking help or advice – sometimes there is more than one problem or difficulty, but an older person may choose only to talk about one. Professionals need to find out:

1 The nature of the presenting need;
2 The significance of the need for the older person;
3 The length of time the problem has been experienced;
4 Potential solutions identified by the older person;
5 Other needs experienced by the older person;
6 Recent life events or changes relevant to the problem(s);
7 The perceptions of family members and carer.
    (HSC 2002/01; LAC(2001) 01, *Guidance on the Single Assessment Process for older people, Annex E*)

Some presenting problems will be straightforward – for example, information about services or request for a bath mat. These should be dealt with straight away. Other problems may not be so straightforward, because they are not clear-cut. They may lead to other problems being identified, or it may become apparent the person is asking for more help than these simple requests. In these circumstances, a more in-depth assessment will be needed. The guidance emphasises the importance of exploring the seven key questions listed above, especially about unsettling recent events in the person's life. How the person appears when they make contact – whether they are tearful, or appear confused, for example – should also be given due consideration. If an older person asks a GP or nurse about a specific health problem, this would provide an opportunity to carry out the annual over 75s health check, which lends itself to exploring wider health and social care problems. Further guidance on the over-75s health check is expected in 2003 (see also Chapter 3 on services).

Basic personal information can be collected or checked by staff that have been trained to do this, but who may not have other professional qualifications. A single professional should explore the problems. This professional could be any one of the following:

- social worker;
- nurse;
- GP;
- therapist;
- geriatrician;
- old age psychiatrist;
- other doctor;
- other professionals working with older people in community-based, hospital, and other settings.

The importance of SAP – and the contact assessment – is that the approach is the same no matter who asks the questions, what their professional training, or whether they work in hospitals, care homes, GP surgeries, or with older people living in their own homes.

If more investigation is needed, an overview assessment should be carried out.

OVERVIEW ASSESSMENT

Professionals carry out this second 'level' if they believe a more rounded assessment is appropriate. However, at this stage, it is up to each professional to decide whether to investigate several key issues, or just a few. These issues are called 'domains'. The domains (or categories) and sub-domains that apply to the overall SAP are set out in Box 5.3.

Box 5.3 Domains and sub-domains of the Single Assessment Process (SAP)

User's perspective

- Needs and issues in the user's own words
- User's expectations, strengths, abilities and motivation

Clinical background

- History of medical conditions and diagnoses
- History of falls
- Medication use and ability to self-medicate

Disease prevention

- History of blood pressure monitoring
- Nutrition, diet and fluids
- Vaccination history
- Drinking and smoking history
- Exercise pattern
- History of cervical and breast screening

Personal care and physical well-being

- Personal hygiene, including washing, bathing, using the toilet, and grooming
- Dressing
- Pain
- Oral health
- Foot-care
- Tissue viability
- Mobility
- Continence and other aspects of elimination
- Sleeping patterns

Senses

- Sight
- Hearing
- Communication

Mental health

- Cognition and dementia, including orientation and memory
- Mental health including depression, reactions to loss and emotional difficulties

Relationships

- Social contacts, relationships, and involvement in leisure, hobbies, work and learning
- Carer support and strength of caring arrangements, including the carer's perspective

Safety

- Abuse and neglect
- Other aspects of personal safety
- Public safety

Immediate environment and resources

- Care of the home and managing daily tasks eg food preparation, cleaning and shopping
- Housing – location, access, amenities and heating
- Level and management of finances
- Access to local facilities and services.

(HSC 2002/01; LAC(2001) 01, *Guidance on the Single Assessment Process for Older People, Annex F*)

Professionals do not have to follow these levels of assessment in some kind of numerical order. If a professional judges that *all* the domains should be investigated, this would constitute a comprehensive old age assessment (see page 160). Investigating one aspect in detail would be a specialist assessment (see page 159). An overview assessment might follow an in-depth assessment, or begin as soon as the basic personal information has been collected in the contact assessment. The guidance leaves this to the professional's judgement. It is also left to the professional carrying out the overview assessment of an individual's needs, to decide which domains to include. For example, if an older person is experiencing urine incontinence, then medication, mobility and access to the toilet should be explored. Once a particular domain has been identified for further assessment, however, then all its sub-domains should be considered.

The guidance states that it is possible for overview assessments to be completed by a single professional from either the NHS or social services, although who is competent to do this should be agreed locally. Any health or social care professional carrying out an overview assessment should check, in the first instance, on existing or past assessment – particularly for the domains of 'clinical background' or 'disease prevention'. Overview, and other assessments, may use tools and scales as part of identifying the presence or severity of a particular problem. The Department of Health (2002) has published examples of tools and scales currently being used in the UK (*The Single Assessment Process: assessment tools and scales*).

SPECIALIST ASSESSMENTS

Specialist assessments provide an opportunity to explore specific problems in detail. This is likely to mean a professional being able to confirm the presence, extent, cause and likely development of a health condition or problem, and establish links to other conditions and problems. A specialist assessment will not necessarily be carried out by the same person who conducted either the overview assessment or contact assessment, but it should draw on that information. Registered nurses, qualified social workers, occupational therapists, physiotherapists, geriatricians and old age psychiatrists, and other appropriately qualified and experienced professionals may carry out specialist assessments. The professional may use scales or other tests as part of the assessment, but the needs of each individual older person should determine how the specialist assessment is structured and organised at all times – including deciding which professional is most appropriate for each case. The Department of Health has particularly pointed out that therapists can offer a specialist contribution to aspects such as mobility, speech, drinking and eating, and the impact of the home and the wider environment on individuals' needs (HSC 2002/01; LAC (2001) 01, Annex E).

COMPREHENSIVE ASSESSMENT

In a comprehensive assessment, all the domains set out in Box 5.3 should be investigated. It may be clear that this is appropriate at the contact assessment, or at a later stage. However, if there is a strong likelihood that the person needs a level of support and treatment that will either be intensive or prolonged (for example, a year or longer), including a permanent place in a care home, intermediate care services or intensive services at home (see Chapter 3), then a comprehensive assessment must be carried out. For places in homes, additional sub-domains should be considered (see Box 5.4 below).

Box 5.4 Additional sub-domains for older people likely to receive intensive or prolonged support

User's perspective

- Personal fulfilment
- Spiritual fulfilment

Personal care and physical well-being

- Eating, drinking and swallowing
- Breathing difficulties

Relationships

- Personal relationships
- Lifestyle choices

It is expected that comprehensive assessments are carried out in respect of decisions about NHS continuing health care services. A comprehensive assessment should be completed before the NHS carries out its assessment to pay the Registered Nursing Care Contribution (RNCC) for people in nursing homes (see below, and Chapter 6).

The Single Assessment Process guidance says that, in individual cases, professionals may wish to err on the side of caution and carry out a comprehensive assessment, bearing in mind that many treatable health conditions and other problems often go undetected or are misdiagnosed for older people.

Comprehensive assessments will involve a range of different professionals or specialist teams, because of the wide-ranging nature of the domains. However, this should not mean professionals duplicate each other's work. It is expected that geriatricians and old age psychiatrists should play the leading or a prominent role in comprehensive assessments. The guidance also draws attention to the need for arrangements for care co-ordination to be agreed locally.

The Government has told local authorities that it expects them to review older people's care needs three months after the initial assessment, and every 12 months thereafter, or when there is a significant change in the needs or circumstances. This review timetable also applies to older people who are self-funding their care in nursing homes, for the purposes of assessment by the NHS for the Registered Nursing Care Contribution (RNCC).

Registered Nursing Care Contribution (RNCC)

Since 1 October 2001, the NHS has been responsible for funding the RNCC element of nursing home care for older self-funding residents, as part of the Government's response to the Royal Commission's inquiry into funding long-term care. This arrangement will apply to local authority-supported nursing home residents from April 2003. The Government has said that everyone moving into a nursing home on a permanent basis after 1 October 2001 should have their RNCC needs reviewed after three months, preferably at the same time as social services are reviewing the person's care needs, then every 12 months thereafter or until there is a significant change in the person's health status (HSC 2001/17; LAC (2001) 26, *Guidance on Free Nursing in Care Homes*). The assessment for the RNCC involves deciding which of three bands of financial support best describe the person's nursing needs. Chapter 6 explains this in more detail.

Box 5.5 Further information about the RNCC

✳ **Age Concern England**
Factsheet 20, *NHS continuing care, free nursing care and inter-mediate care*

✳ **Counsel and Care**
Provides information for older people about care in homes, including paying for care

---

Involving older people and carers in SAP

The SAP guidance stresses the importance of older people being given time to reflect on their situation and the issues they may want to raise. Overview, specialist and comprehensive assessments should be particularly concerned with learning about older people's personal history and life story, including problems they have faced in the past, important events in their lives, relationships, and their motivations and beliefs. Agencies are also reminded of the need to respond, at the earliest opportunity, to older people's needs for translators, advocates or interpreters. (Chapter 7 contains more details on communicating with older people.)

Where there is a family carer, two assessments may be needed, one for the older person and one for the carer in line with the legislation set out on page 150. Guidance on carers' assessments says that this should focus on what the carer identifies as the 'best outcome', that would most help them in their caring role and maintain their health and well-being.

Person-centred care

Standard 2 of the National Service Framework for Older People is also known as the Standard for Person-Centred Care. Person-centred approaches have been developed with younger adults with learning disabilities in particular (*Valuing People*, DH, 2001)

For people with learning disabilities, a key element of a person-centred approach is that the person sets out their own goals and aspirations, and takes control of their own lives:

'Understanding someone's aspirations cannot be achieved by functional assessments or using checklists. It can only come about through sustained intense personal contact, friendship and understanding – and a willingness to make informed guesses, accepting that we still get it wrong at times.' (Wertheimer, 1996)

In the context of adults with learning disabilities, this approach 'requires ... a move away from "developing services" and towards "providing appropriate personal supports for individuals"' (McIntosh and Whittaker, eds. 2000: p.5).

Paragraph 4.17 of the 2001 Learning Disability White Paper, *Valuing People*, states:

'A person-centred approach to planning means that planning should start with the individual (not with services), and take account of their wishes and aspirations. Person-centred planning is a mechanism for reflecting the needs and preferences of a person with a learning disability and covers such issues as housing, education, employment and leisure.'

Within the NSF for Older People, person-centred care has a slightly different emphasis. Paragraph 2.1 sets out that:

'Person-centred care requires managers and professionals to:

- listen to older people;
- respect their dignity and privacy;
- recognise individual differences and specific needs, including cultural and religious differences;
- enable older people to make informed choices, involving them in all decisions about their needs and care;
- provide co-ordinated and integrated service;
- involve and support responses whenever necessary.'

While the difference may appear slight, it is important to draw the distinction between the two approaches, not least in terms of understanding what may be meant by 'person-centred' in different contexts and with different client groups. For younger adults with learning disabilities, it is much more about their planning and controlling their lives, only part of which may involve care. For older people, it is more about the responses by statutory services to their care needs.

Involving housing agencies

As indicated on page 153, the development of SAP and other recent changes do not affect the duties on local authorities to assess individuals' needs for community care services – or their duty to invite relevant housing authorities to take part if the person appears to have housing needs.

Although SAP does not alter this requirement, it does represent an opportunity to make these arrangements more consistent. The domain of 'immediate environment and resources' is particularly suited to the involvement of housing professionals and organisations, as well as those from welfare advice and other agencies. This may include local Pension Service (formerly the Benefits Agency) offices. Occupational therapists will continue to assess individual's needs for adaptations under Disabled Facilities Grants (see Chapter 6). In addition, local authorities have been developing local access arrangements for the new models of financial support for older people living in sheltered or supported housing coming into effect in April 2003. These changes, called *Supporting People* (DSS, 1998) are described in Chapter 6.

Deciding about services

Once the assessment process has been completed, decisions need to be made about what services, treatment or other support should be offered – and about who should provide this.

The first step involves evaluating the assessment – for example, taking account of any prognosis of a person's conditions, or what the risks are to the older person or their family.

Ultimately, this evaluation must be translated into treatment, care and support. This is achieved by comparing individual's assessed needs with eligibility criteria for community and continuing health care services.

Unlike social services, the NHS operates eligibility criteria for one distinctive element of healthcare only – what are known as 'NHS continuing health care services' (see page 171). Social services are expected to operate eligibility criteria for all the care services they provide or arrange. However, although the NHS sets explicit criteria for this one element of health care, it can decide local priorities for other services (for example, particular operations or treatments), and can take the level of its resources into account when doing so.

Local authority eligibility criteria

As part of the 1993 community care reforms, for the first time local authorities had to publish eligibility criteria for the services they funded or provided. These criteria were meant to fit the financial resources available to them, with the intention that people's assessed needs would be met out of local budgets.

Originally, the then government planned to provide extra funds for local authorities in recognition of their extra responsibilities from April 1993. This involved a complex calculation over a period of three years, between 1993 and 1996. These extra, phased, funds were called Special Transitional Grants (STGs – see page 17).

Unexpectedly, the amount of these grants was changed during the first year following the community care reforms. Many local authorities found they would have fewer resources than originally expected. This meant, in many areas, that the authorities' eligibility criteria now appeared over-generous: the assessed need would exceed the budget.

As a result, several local authorities reduced or withdrew some of the services being received by users living in their own homes, including older people. One such authority was Gloucestershire County Council, which found itself subject to one of the earliest challenges to the community care legislation brought on behalf of a small group of service users. The case was heard by the High Court, Court of Appeal and the House of Lords, and it established some important legal precedents:

- local authorities can take the level of their own resources into account when setting criteria for care services, but this cannot be the only factor (otherwise, local authorities could legitimately provide no services at all if their resources were nil);
- once social services have assessed someone and agreed their needs meet the eligibility criteria, it cannot use a lack of resources as a reason for not meeting those needs;
- local authorities cannot use a lack of resources as the reason for providing some services (places in care homes) but not others (home help);
- services can only be changed following a reassessment of the person's needs.

Other cases have built on these precedents. A case in 1999, *R v Birmingham City Council ex parte Killigrew*, confirmed that if criteria are changed and someone's reassessed needs no longer meet the new criteria, the local authority must not withdraw or reduce someone's services if they would be left 'in serious physical risk'. Government guidance (LASSL (97) 13, *Responsibilities of Council Social Services Departments: implications of recent judgements*) set out the implications for social services departments of some of these cases.

These cases, and others, helped clarify some of the law about how local authorities set and use their criteria to decide whether someone 'qualified' for help. Problems over budgets led to serious concerns, in some areas, about whether older users were receiving sufficient services. There were also concerns because of the lengths of time some users and carers were waiting to receive either an assessment, or the subsequent care and support services. At the same time, local authorities were being told to target care on those most in need. Other concerns centred on the lack of nationally set criteria. Each local authority could – and did – set its own criteria for care. This resulted in significant differences around the country, and concerns about the development of a 'postcode lottery' of care: in short, that the services that users received depended on where they lived.

FAIR ACCESS TO CARE SERVICES (FACS)

In 2002, the Government published *Fair Access to Care Services* (LAC (2002) 13), containing guidance for local authorities on setting eligibility criteria for community care services. Although it fell short of explicit national criteria, it set out the framework that local authorities should implement by 7 April 2003.

One issue raised by this guidance concerns the short-term nature of local criteria. In many areas, social services eligibility criteria change each year. Sometimes criteria may change more than once in a year in response to budgetary pressures. This guidance asks councils to prioritise and meet individuals' assessed needs by taking a longer term, preventative view of individuals' difficulties and their circumstances. They are expected to consider the risks to people's independence (in both the long- and short-term) if they do not receive services.

From April 2003, local criteria must follow a framework based on four bands (Box 5.6).

Box 5.6 Four criteria bands for social services

[This list should be read with 'and/or' at the end of every bullet point]

1 Critical

- Life is, or will be, threatened
- Significant health problems have developed, or will develop
- There is, or will be, little or no choice and control over vital aspects of the immediate environment
- Serious forms of abuse or neglect have occurred or will occur
- There is, or will be, an inability to carry out vital personal care or domestic routines
- Vital involvement in work, education or learning cannot or will not be sustained
- Vital social support systems and relationships cannot or will not be sustained

---

- Vital family and other social roles and responsibilities cannot or will not be undertaken

2 Substantial

- There is, or will be, only partial choice and control over the immediate environment
- Abuse or neglect has occurred or will occur
- There is, or will be, an inability to carry out the majority of personal care or domestic routines
- Involvement in many aspects of work, education or learning cannot or will not be sustained
- The majority of social support systems and relationships cannot or will not be sustained
- The majority of family and other social roles and responsibilities cannot or will not be undertaken

3 Moderate

- There is, or will be, an inability to carry out several personal care or domestic routines. Involvement in several aspects of work, education or learning cannot or will not be sustained
- Several social support systems and relationships cannot or will not be sustained
- Several family and other social roles and responsibilities cannot or will not be undertaken.

4 Low

- There is, or will be, an inability to carry out one or two personal care or domestic routines
- Involvement in one or two aspects of work, education or learning cannot or will not be sustained
- One or two social support systems and relationships cannot or will not be sustained
- One or two family and other social roles and responsibilities cannot or will not be undertaken

(LAC (2002) 13, *Fair Access to Care Services: guidance on eligibility criteria for adult social care*)

These criteria bands apply across client groups. The Government claims that the framework is based on factors that are key to maintaining an individuals' independence over time, namely:

- autonomy;
- health and safety;
- the management of daily routines;
- involvement in family and wider community life.

No reference should be made in local criteria to an individual's age or gender, as these factors in themselves do not threaten independence. Social services departments must ensure that eligibility for services is not directly influenced by factors such as the person's age or living arrangements. Details of these criteria must be included in locally published *Better Care, Higher Standards* charters. Despite the setting of the four bands, however, councils are not required to make identical decisions about eligibility for care, nor to deliver similar sets of services to particular user groups.

Ensuring that decisions are not influenced by age also ties up with the NSF for Older People's requirement that social services departments review, by April 2002, their eligibility criteria to ensure they do not discriminate against older people. This is an important issue, especially in relation to maximum amounts of care provided to older people living in their own homes. A court case in Lancashire in 1996, concerning the care of an older woman, concluded that local authorities were not obliged to fund an intensive package of care at home, if a place in a nursing home was cheaper and would meet the woman's assessed needs (*R v Lancashire County Council ex parte Ingham, 1996*).

The gross cost of places in homes for older people tends to be less than in homes for younger adults – sometimes considerably less per week. When considering the cost of different types of care, local authorities need only look at the average net cost (i.e. the actual cost to the authority). Because of the impact of the means-test, whereby individuals contribute towards the cost through their income and savings, the average net cost to local authorities of a place in a home for older people may be relatively low. Local authorities, in some areas, have 'capped' – or put a ceiling, or maximum cost to – the amount they will pay for care to support someone living at home. These maximum amounts, where set and applied, can be lower for older users than for younger adult client groups. This issue of not discriminating by age may therefore need some further clarification.

Any maximum levels set by local councils usually determine the point at which an older person can still be supported at home or in sheltered housing. Care needed beyond this level generally results in an individual being assessed as needing care in a home. In effect, this draws a line between care at home, and care in a home. There is also a second dividing line, which determines eligibility to what are known as NHS continuing health care services (see page 171).

Importantly, the FACS guidance is also intended to provide a starting point for packages of continuing health and social care, and joint eligibility for services provided under the funding partnerships arrangements set out in Section 31 of the Health Act 1999.

'RATIONING' OF SOCIAL CARE

Earlier chapters have discussed how changes in local authority eligibility criteria meant some people faced the loss of services. Others have found difficulties in gaining access to either what they feel to be sufficient social care, or have been told they do not 'qualify' for any support. This issue continues to be raised, and is often closely linked with concerns that funding from central government to social services departments has failed to keep up with demand, expectation, or with central government targets.

In the summer of 2002, the Chancellor of the Exchequer published the *Spending Review* White Paper (HM Treasury, 2002). In a press release on 23 July, the Secretary of State for Health (DH, 2002) claimed this will release an additional £1 billion to be spent on care for older people, including more community equipment, and on supporting a greater number of older people to remain living in their own homes.

Eligibility criteria for NHS continuing health care services

As indicated above, these are the only services for which the NHS sets and publishes criteria. They are set by health authorities together with Primary Care Trusts (PCTs), and must be agreed with their counterpart local authority area. (Chapter 6 explains more of the background to these criteria, which were originally introduced in 1996.) A 1999 court case led to replacement guidance (HSC 2001/015; LAC(2001)18), *Continuing Care: NHS and local councils' responsibilities*), from which local and health authorities (and subsequently PCTs) have had to draw up more recent criteria. This guidance came into effect on 1 March 2002 and reflects changes in the funding responsibilities of the NHS and local authorities for registered nursing care in means-tested places in nursing homes, under the Health and Social Care Act 2001 (see Chapter 6). It further reflects the way in which PCTs are increasingly taking over many previous health authority funding responsibilities, including continuing health care. Health authorities' overall responsibilities for setting these local criteria have been subsumed by the Strategic Health Authorities established under the NHS Reform and Health Care Professions Act 2002. Over time, this change is likely to mean fewer local criteria covering the country.

The Department of Health defines continuing care as:

'... a general term that describes the care which people need over an extended period of time, as the result of disability, accident or illness, to address both physical and mental health needs.'

(HSC 2001/015; LAC(2001)18, *Continuing Care: NHS and local councils' responsibilities*; para. 5)

As such, it is distinct from intermediate care (which is time-limited), and any temporary or transitional form of care. Continuing health care services are those arranged or funded solely by the NHS. In drawing up local criteria, a number of issues must be reflected:

1 The eligibility criteria (or the application of rigid time limits) for NHS continuing health care services, should not mean that, in order for people to receive services, local councils have to go beyond the services they can legitimately provide under section 21 of the National Assistance Act 1948 – particularly in relation to means-tested care in nursing homes, where the NHS has some new funding responsibilities (see Chapter 6).

2 The nature *or* complexity *or* intensity *or* unpredictability of the person's health care needs (or any combination of these) means they need regular supervision by any member of the NHS multidisciplinary team, such as palliative care, therapy or supervision by a consultant, or other member of the NHS team.

3 The person needs routinely to use specialist health care equipment, under the supervision of NHS staff.

4 The person has a rapidly deteriorating or unstable medical, physical or mental health condition, and requires regular supervision by a member of the NHS multidisciplinary team, such as palliative care, therapy, the consultant, or other member of the team.

5 The person is in the final stages of a terminal illness and is likely to die in the near future.

6 The location of care should not be the only, or the main, determinant of eligibility. Continuing NHS health care may be provided in an NHS hospital, a nursing home, hospice, or in the person's own home.

7 Needing the care or supervision of a registered nurse and/or GP is not, by itself, sufficient reason to receive continuing NHA health care.

(HSC 2001/015; LAC (2001) 18, *Continuing Care: NHS and local councils' responsibilities*)

These issues build on the earlier 1995 guidance (HSG (95)8; LAC(95)5, *NHS Responsibilities for Meeting Continuing Health Care Needs*), which included criteria such as whether someone was considered 'likely to die in the near future'; and the needs of patients for relevant equipment, treatment or therapy to be supervised by NHS staff – especially in circumstances when patients' needs were complex or unpredictable.

Two aspects of the more recent (2001) guidance are particularly important. The first centres on the reminder to the NHS that its criteria should not be so narrow that, in order to ensure people receive services, local councils are forced to go beyond their legal responsibilities to fund care in homes (under Section 21 of the National Assistance Act 1948). This is particularly pertinent in the light of changes to the NHS's responsibilities to fund the nursing element of care in means-tested nursing homes (see Chapter 6). The guidance also further reiterates the need for local and health authorities to ensure there is no gap between their respective local criteria for community and continuing health care services. Following the implementation of continuing care criteria in April 1996, monitoring suggested that gaps did occur in some areas. In these instances, individual older people found their needs designated 'too high' for social services' criteria and provision, but not high enough for NHS continuing health care services or funding. Despite its illegality at the time, some local and health authorities acted together to fund places in nursing homes. Older people were means-tested for the social services' part of this arrangement, but not for the NHS element. Such arrangements have, at least to a degree, been both legitimised and superseded by changes to the funding of nursing care in nursing homes, under the Health and Social Care Act 2001, and the partnership arrangements under the Health Act 1999. Although both these provisions increase the ways in which individual's packages of care may be funded by _both_ the NHS _and_ social services, they do not preclude the NHS from funding the _entire_ costs of someone's care, should they meet the NHS criteria for fully funded continuing health care services. This could be provided in any setting – in the patient's own home, in hospital or in a nursing home. Under the 1995 guidance, this fully funded NHS care was referred to as 'NHS continuing inpatient care'. However, this term was deliberately removed from the 2001 guidance because of concerns that the word 'inpatient' suggested only hospital care.

The second issue arising from the 2001 guidance concerns the reiteration of the NHS's responsibility to provide _some_ continuing health care services for older people (and other patient groups) living in *all* settings. For example, those living in residential homes are entitled to the same NHS primary care and community services as if they were living in their own homes, or in sheltered housing. This encompasses:

- access to GP and other primary care services (including community nursing);
- district nursing and other nursing services, such as continence advice and stoma care;
- physiotherapy, speech and language therapy, occupational therapy, dietetics and podiatry;
- continence pads and equipment, and nursing aids;
- palliative care;
- access to hospital care.

The NHS's responsibilities, from April 2002, to fund the registered nursing element of otherwise means-tested care in nursing homes are discussed further in Chapter 6. Aside from this, the NHS is also responsible for providing the following to all nursing home residents:

- access to GP and other primary care services (including community nursing);
- the provision of other nursing advice, such as continence advice and stoma care;
- physiotherapy, occupational therapy, speech and language therapy, dietetics and podiatry;
- specialist medical and nursing equipment (such as specialist feeding equipment) normally only available through hospitals;
- palliative care;
- access to hospital care when required.

Since 1 October 2001, the NHS has been responsible for providing continence pads and other related equipment to people living in nursing homes. It also has responsibility for making available ambulances and other specialist transport on the basis of patients' needs for transport to and from hospital or hospice, for emergency admission to a residential home, and for non-emergency travel to and from health care facilities. Although it is expected that local authorities will provide or fund most respite care, the NHS may still need to provide some respite health care for people who could benefit from rehabilitation or intermediate care, or who have intensive or complex health care needs.

Care plans

Once assessed needs have been compared with eligibility criteria, and decisions taken as to whether services will be provided, a care plan should be drawn up. This should summarise the person's needs, and set out the objectives in providing support, and the anticipated outcome for users. It should detail which organisation will provide what service, and how frequently. It should also record any support from family carers, together with health, housing and social care services. Service users should be given a copy of their plan. Where users and/or carers disagree with service decisions, this should be recorded on the care plan. If users or carers do disagree with the care plan (perhaps disagreeing with the services being offered), they can use the local authority or NHS complaints system to raise their concerns (see Chapter 7). There is also a specific review procedure to use when people disagree with the decision about eligibility for NHS continuing health care services.

Disagreeing with NHS eligibility decisions

If people believe they should receive NHS continuing health care services, but have been told they do not meet the local criteria, they can ask for the decision to be reviewed. It is important to note that the original decision about such eligibility should not take place until the person's needs have been assessed under the comprehensive level of assessment outlined on pages 153–9, under the Single Assessment Process.

The aim of the review procedure is to check that decisions have been properly made, and local criteria consistently applied. However, people who believe that the criteria are wrong, or who have a complaint about the type, location or content of any NHS continuing health care services they have been offered, should pursue these through the NHS complaints procedure.

The NHS has been told to provide clear information to patients about the review procedure, and to provide advocacy support if needed. If an informal settlement cannot be reached, the case should be considered by an independent panel, which then advises the relevant NHS organisation. This should be completed within two weeks following the failure to resolve the case informally. The review panel should consist of an independent chair, and a representative from each of the health authority (the relevant Strategic Health Authority), local council and one of the PCTs in the health authority's area.

Although the health authority is not bound to accept the review panel's advice, the expectation is that it will do so in all but very exceptional circumstances. If a health authority rejects the review panel's advice, however, it must explain its reasons for doing so in writing to the patient and the review panel chair

Once this process has been exhausted, older people wishing to pursue the matter would most likely need to do so through the NHS complaints system. This could mean focusing the complaint on whether the review panel properly carried out its role, or complaining about the local criteria (see Chapter 7).

Box 5.7 Further information about NHS continuing health care

❋ **Age Concern England**
  Factsheet 20, *NHS continuing care, free nursing care and intermediate care*

Choices for older people

One of the reasons older people disagree with their care plan, or raise complaints about eligibility decisions, is because they are unhappy with the services being offered. This may be because they would prefer to stay at home but are being offered residential care, for example; or it may be because they do not feel they are being offered sufficient support. This raises issues both about how statutory agencies respond to people's choices, and about the choices older people are able to make.

Older people's right to choose the care home they move to live in was established under the community care reforms. Current guidance sets out that people can choose to enter their 'preferred accommodation' anywhere in England and Wales, and in Scotland by special arrangement (LAC(2001)25, LAC (2001)29, *Charging for Residential Accommodation Guide – CRAG changes nos. 15 and 16*). It is expected that this 'right to choose' a care home will be extended to Northern Ireland, the Isle of Man and the Channel Islands by the end of 2002, under the Health and Social Care Act 2001.

There are parameters to choosing the 'preferred accommodation', which apply particularly to people whose place in a home will be arranged by their local authority. These limits include that the home appears to the local authority to be suitable for the person's assessed needs, and that it has a vacancy. There are other parameters relating to the cost of the care in the home.

However, there is no comparable 'right to choose' domiciliary care agencies. Nor is there a right to insist that one type of care (such as support to stay at home) is provided over another (such as care in a nursing home). Despite this, there is nothing to stop older people asking their authority to work with them to find a solution that better meets their wishes. In practice, this can sometimes mean compromising on some areas of support in order to ensure the provision of help that all agree is a priority.

As part of its consultation on tackling delayed discharge, the Department of Health has said that it will provide guidance to health and social care agencies about providing patients with 'choices'. This includes intermediate care and short-term intensive care at home, which can be essential for people who need time to make decisions about their long-term future (*Implementing Reimbursement Around Discharge from Hospital – Consultation*, DH, 2002).

Within health care, *The NHS Plan* (DH, 2000) set out proposals to improve the choices available to patients. These tend to relate to matters such as enabling patients to choose the hospital and waiting time that is convenient to them (*Extending Choice for Patients*, DH, 2001).

Those who are able to pay privately for all the treatment, care and support services they require do have a wide choice. However, the vast majority of older people need some form of state assistance in order to pay for the care they need.

6 Paying for care

This chapter describes how different types of care are funded, and the implications for users and carers of different funding regimes. This includes the impact on state benefits of certain NHS services; charges for residential and domiciliary care; and charges for housing adaptations and aids. It further explores the recent history to the division between those NHS services that are 'free at the point of use', and social care provision for which there is a charge. It also reflects recent changes that identify specific services that will be free to individuals, irrespective of whether these are purchased or provided by the NHS or social services.

Who pays for residential care? The $64,000 question

Since 1948, there has been a dividing line between 'free' NHS long-stay care, and means-tested local authority and independent sector residential care. One of the main elements of the NHS and Community Care Act 1990 was that it formally recognised this dividing line had moved.

Much change had taken place by the time the community care reforms were fully implemented in April 1993 (see Chapter 1). NHS long-stay provision had reduced significantly during the 1970s and 1980s. This has been linked variously with the NHS's increasing desire to concentrate on acute care, and the realisation of the resources to be saved (and presumably invested elsewhere within the hospital system) by closing long-stay wards. As discussed in Chapter 1, the development during the 1980s of what became

n as the 'preserved rights' system of higher levels of Income
port led to a large increase in independent sector homes offering places for fee-paying residents, especially in nursing homes run
by the private sector. Although the state retirement pension and
some other state benefits are reduced once people become long-
stay NHS patients, other income and capital is untouched. In
contrast, residential and nursing home care not funded by the NHS
is subject to a means-test, in which individuals are asked to pay
towards their care from most sources of income and capital (or savings). A major impact of the decline in NHS provision, therefore,
and of the subsequent huge growth during the 1980s of independent sector nursing and residential homes, fell directly on older
people's finances.

Older people's initial perspective on 'preserved rights' to Income
Support is not particularly well known. Chapter 1 described, in
brief, how many NHS long-stay wards and hospitals had become
run down, and in poor condition. Some older people who opted
for means-tested care in the 1980s may have felt they would prefer
to pay for a more comfortable, homely care environment rather
than receive the often sparse and run-down, long-stay NHS geriatric provision of the 1970s and 1980s. Paying for a room of one's
own in a private home may well have seemed preferable to receiving 'free' care in an open, mixed-sex NHS ward. However, as time
went on, paying for this form of care became less of a choice.
Throughout the 1980s, more and more long-stay care for older
people was being provided through means-tested, private sector
nursing home care, and less and less was available via the NHS.

Local authorities, too, began to divest themselves of some of their
'Part III' residential homes during this time. In some areas, individual older people began to find there was little alternative to paying
for care in a residential or nursing home run by the private or voluntary sector. But not everyone was keen on Part III homes. Two
or three decades ago, some older people still held vivid memories of
such homes being used as workhouses prior to the pre-welfare state
Poor Law. For this group, entering a Part III home may have been
uncomfortably closely linked with fears about being a 'burden on

the parish'. Elsewhere, some older people discovered that the 'pre-served rights' means-test for independent sector residential homes was more generous than the national system that applied to local authority homes. One example concerned capital limits. Just prior to the community care reforms of 1993, the lower capital limit (the amount below which capital is not included in the means-test) under the 'preserved rights' system was £3,000. Under the local authority system, it was £1,250.

During this time, then, local authorities continued to apply a sep-arate national means-test for their own Part III homes, under the National Assistance Act 1948. This did not allow them to arrange, provide, or help to fund, nursing home care for older people. From the mid-1980s until April 1993, the means-test for independent sector nursing homes (as well as that for independent sector resi-dential homes) was administered by local offices of the then Department of Social Security.

The NHS and Community Care Act 1990 extended local authori-ties' powers and duties to fund long term care from 1 April 1993. It did so primarily by amending the National Assistance Act 1948, to give local authorities responsibilities and powers to administer a national, mandatory means-test for older people's nursing home care for the first time. As well as administering this means-test, local authorities were given new responsibilities (and new funding) to pay towards some of the costs of this care.

This change was one of the major elements of the community care reforms. Much has already been written explaining why and how this aspect of reform came into being. At its most basic, it was an attempt by the then government to contain the ever-growing costs to the state of care in homes, together with a desire to promote more care services at home, and so avoid unnecessary early admis-sions to residential care. The changes affected all residents in private and voluntary sector residential and nursing homes who first moved to live there on or after 1 April 1993; and all residents in local authorities' own residential homes, regardless of when they had moved to live there. However, although the reforms meant that the capital limits for Part III residents were raised to the same level as for independent sector residents, other differences remained (see page 192).

One of the main aspects to this change in the means-test arrangements was that it shifted the role of the state away from the 1980s approach of an individual's *entitlement to receive* (on the basis of their income and capital) state funding to pay towards their private and voluntary sector nursing home care. Instead, it became the state's *responsibility* to decide whether or not to release funding. This would happen if care was first – in the state's own view – *required*, and only subsequently given if the person qualified through a means-test, as explained in Chapter 5.

Some long-stay NHS provision did survive into the 1990s and, in a minority of cases, the NHS also made arrangements to purchase private sector nursing home places for patients. Arguments over the point at which people became the responsibility of the NHS, and therefore were not charged for their care, continued over many years. These funding controversies were not the only concerns. As Chapter 1 described, many older people felt strongly that the NHS had broken its contract with them to provide care from the 'cradle to the grave'. There were other concerns about the impact of the withdrawal by the NHS of long-term care on older people. For example, that means-tested residents in independent sector homes (particularly in nursing homes) were losing access to NHS medical and nursing supervision. Two cases in particular, had a major impact on arguments about the NHS's responsibilities and on the consequent 'dividing line' between free NHS care and means-tested social care. These, together with the 1999 Royal Commission Inquiry into the future funding of long-term care, which has also strongly influenced this debate, are explored in more detail, below.

The Leeds case

In 1994, the Health Service Commissioner for England (the NHS Ombudsman) published a report of a case that, perhaps more than any other, highlighted the extent and nature of the NHS's withdrawal from long-term nursing care. The report concerned the experience of a 55-year-old male patient. The man had been admitted to a Leeds hospital and received surgery for a brain haemorrhage. He survived the operation, but had severe neurological damage. This meant he was doubly incontinent, had no mobility, had to be fed and could not communicate. He also had a kidney tumour, cataracts in both eyes, occasional epileptic fits for which medication was required, and had had a heart attack.

Staff on the acute ward where he was receiving his care following the surgery, arranged with his wife for him to be discharged to a private nursing home. He was means-tested for the care he received in this home. There was no local NHS provision for long-term care for patients with his condition. He was deemed too young for the local NHS geriatric care, and not suitable for admission to a disability unit for younger people. In summary, the hospital (and subsequently Leeds Health Authority) determined that as they had no contract with any provider (whether NHS or private) for suitable care, there was no option but that he should pay for his own care in the private nursing home. The Health Authority's chief executive, in particular, argued that it was not possible to meet the needs of every patient because there was an overriding duty to:

> 'determine priorities within the financial resources available, and that consideration of clinical priority may mean that a particular patient needing inpatient nursing care may never have it provided.'
> (Health Service Commissioner 1994, para. 22).

The Health Service Commissioner concluded that:

> 'This patient was a highly dependent patient in hospital under a contract made with the Infirmary by Leeds Health Authority; and yet, when he no longer needed care in an acute ward but manifestly still needed what the National Health Service is there to provide, they regarded themselves as having no scope for continuing to discharge their responsibilities to him because

their policy was to make no provision for continuing care.' (Health Service Commissioner, 1994, para. 22).

In upholding the complaint, the Health Service Commissioner recommended that Leeds Health Authority reimburse the patient's wife for the costs of the nursing home care incurred, and take over provision of his care at their expense. This could be achieved through their contracting with the nursing home to pay for his care. The Health Authority agreed to implement the recommendations.

It is worth re-visiting this case in some detail, since its impact continues to resonate. The reaction of the then government was to issue new guidance to the NHS, to remind health authorities and other bodies of their responsibilities to provide NHS continuing health care services (HSG (95)8; LAC(95)5, *NHS responsibilities for meeting continuing health care needs*, 1995). This guidance set out a range of services for which the NHS had responsibility to provide or fund. It described the circumstances when the NHS would fund all of a person's care, because that person met the locally set NHS criteria for continuing inpatient care. Importantly, the guidance also gave patients a right to ask their health authority to review decisions not to provide them with NHS continuing inpatient care.

The guidance came into effect in April 1996, but itself became subject to further inquiry through the case brought by Pamela Coughlan against North and East Devon Health Authority.

The Coughlan case

In 1999, the Court of Appeal ruled in the case of *R v North and East Devon Health Authority ex parte Coughlan*. Pamela Coughlan had been severely injured following a traffic accident in 1971. Until 1993, she received NHS care in a hospital. When the then Exeter Health Authority decided to close this hospital, she and several other patients were moved to a new NHS facility, Mardon House. They were promised in writing that this would be their home for life. In late 1998, a successor Health Authority (North and East Devon) decided to close Mardon House and to transfer Miss Coughlan's care to social services. This would mean her 'free' care would now be means-tested. There were also concerns about whether or not any of the local homes offering care to fee-paying residents would be able to provide appropriate levels of care, although this aspect did not feature in the legal case.

Pamela Coughlan's case centred on two key points:

- **first,** that it was unlawful for the Health Authority to decide to transfer responsibility for her general (as opposed to specialist) nursing care to the local authority's social services department;
- **secondly,** that the Health Authority was in breach of the promise made to provide Miss Coughlan with a home for life.

The central policy issue rested on this matter of the NHS's responsibilities to provide *general* nursing care as opposed to *specialist* nursing care. The Court of Appeal ruled that whether the Health Authority's proposal to transfer responsibility for general nursing care to social services was lawful depended on (i) whether the nursing services in question were incidental or ancillary to the provision of the accommodation which a local authority is under a duty to provide and (ii) of a nature which it can be expected that an authority whose primary responsibility is to provide social services can be expected to provide. The Court ruled that Miss Coughlan needed services of a wholly different category (LAC(1999)30, *Ex parte Coughlan: follow up action Annex A*). Moreover, the Health Authority's eligibility criteria were unlawful as they were too restrictive, and depended on an approach to the services that the local authority had a duty to provide which was not lawful.

New guidance was therefore issued, although not until 2001 (HSC 2001/015; LAC (2001) 18, *Continuing Care: NHS and local councils' responsibilities*). This was discussed in detail in Chapter 5. The line between the responsibilities of the NHS and social services authorities for funding nursing care was further redefined under the Health and Social Care Act 2001. This amended section 21 of the National Assistance Act 1948 to give a more detailed definition of 'nursing care', and also reflected the Government's response to the Royal Commission's inquiry into long-term care funding for older people.

The Royal Commission

Aside from the cases outlined above, there was a growing concern about the post-1993 system of means-tested residential and nursing home care. Chief amongst these, and dominating newspaper headlines for some time during the 1990s, were concerns and fears about older people having to sell the family home in order to pay for care.

Those familiar with the means-test system will know that there are circumstances when the value of someone's former home is included in the means-test for their residential or nursing home care, and circumstances when it is ignored. For example, the value must be ignored if:

- the person's stay in a home is only temporary; or
- their house or flat is lived in by their spouse or partner; or
- another relative aged 60 or more (or a younger relative who is incapacitated) will remain living there after the person has moved permanently into a home (regardless of whether they have a financial interest in the flat or house).

Local authorities also have a discretionary power to ignore the value of property. They might choose to ignore the value if, for example, someone were to continue to live in the house or flat but did not fit into one of the categories above.

(As part of its response to the Royal Commission's Inquiry, the Government subsequently introduced a new disregard – see page 199.)

Even when the value of property is included in the means-test, this does not automatically mean the property must be sold. Although in practice many people do sell to release the funds, if there are other ways of meeting the fees (for example, by renting out property and using the rental income) then this approach can be adopted. This is not quite the same as 'having to sell your home to pay for care' – but it is this latter sentiment which tends to make for the better headline.

Arguably, people's fears about selling property to pay for care were exacerbated by the concern of the former Prime Minister John

Major, to ensure that wealth 'cascaded down the generations' (Age Concern England, 1995). For many people, wealth would only cascade if they inherited the family home from their older relatives. The growth in property prices during the later decades of the 20th century had resulted in some older people living in property worth increasingly significant sums – especially in comparison to the amounts they may have originally paid. The increase, since the Second World War, in home ownership amongst the general population, together with initiatives such as 'Right to Buy' council housing, introduced under the Conservative governments of the 1980s, also meant that the importance and relevance of home ownership issues had grown significantly amongst the electorate.

Recent trends in property prices, especially in London and much of the south of England, suggest that the value of some older people's property will exceed the likely cost of their care in a home by tens of thousands of pounds, if not more. For some (though by no means all) older homeowners, the prospect of using some of their housing capital to pay for care may, at present property values, care costs, and likely length of time living in a home, still leave significant sums in place for inheritance purposes. However, it is important to note that inheritance is not the only reason why older people may be reluctant to sell their homes to pay for care. Other factors include the extent to which some older people feel their own identities are bound up with their homes, and the positive feelings of independence and control that can come from living in their own homes (Askham *et al*, 1999).

An alternative future scenario, given the increase in property values over three decades, may mean that increasing numbers of this group of often 'asset-rich, income-poor' older people, seek to release some of the equity in their property, and use these funds to remain living at home for longer. However, property price increases do not apply equally to everyone across England, nor are all older people owner-occupiers. This raises issues about the continuing trend to – at least partially – rely on private housing assets, and the housing market, to fund elements of social care provision.

As discussed in Chapter 1, the Joseph Rowntree Foundation and the Health Select Committee explored other concerns about the system of funding long-term care in the mid-1990s. Both organisations held inquiries into the future funding of long-term care. They considered such aspects as the increasing numbers of older people as the UK's population ages during this century, and concerns about unequal access to services around the country (what became known as the 'postcode lottery of care'). At around the same time, the then Conservative government responded to these concerns by publishing its proposals, *A New Partnership for Care in Old Age* (DH, 1996), suggesting a solution based primarily in private insurance.

The Labour Party's contribution to the debate about the current and future arrangements for funding care was to promise, in its pre-1997 election manifesto, to set up a Royal Commission to investigate the matter, reach conclusions and make recommendations. This was established, following Labour's election earlier that year, in December 1997, and was chaired by Sir Stewart Sutherland (Box 6.1).

Box 6.1 Royal Commission on the Funding of Long-Term Care for the Elderly: Terms of reference for the Inquiry

'To examine the short and long term options for a sustainable system of funding of long term care for elderly people, both in their own homes and in other settings, and, within 12 months, to recommend how, and in what circumstances, the cost of such care should be apportioned between public funds and individuals, having regard to:

■ The number of people likely to require various kinds of long-term care both in the present and through the first half of the next century [sic], and their likely income and capital over their lifetime;

- The expectations of elderly people for dignity and security in the way in which their long-term care needs are met, taking account of the need for this to be secured in the most cost-effective manner;
- The strengths and weaknesses of the current arrangements;
- Fair and efficient ways for individuals to make any contribution required of them;
- Constraints on public funds; and
- Earlier work done by various bodies on this issue.

In carrying out its remit, the Royal Commission should also have regard to:

- The deliberations of the Government's comprehensive spending review, including the review of pensions;
- The implications of their recommendations for younger people who by reason of illness or disability have long-term care needs.

The Commission's recommendations should be costed.' (DH, 1998)

The report of the Royal Commission, *With Respect to Old Age* (DH, 1999), made a series of recommendations, including two key proposals:

1 The costs of care for those individuals who need it should be split between living costs, housing costs and personal care. Personal care should be available after an assessment, according to need and paid for from general taxation; living costs and housing costs should be subject to a means-test of residents' income and savings

2 The Government should establish a National Care Commission which would monitor longitudinal trends, including demography and spending, ensure transparency and accountability in the system, represent the interests of consumers, encourage innovation, keep under review the market for residential care, nursing care, and set national benchmarks, now and in the future.

Personal care was defined by the Commission as care which involves touching the person – for example, helping someone to bath or get dressed, as well as catheter care, or care for pressure sores, which might more traditionally be thought of as 'nursing care'. The Commission said it had deliberately not used the terms 'health care' or 'social care':

> 'because of the confusion which now surrounds those terms and their association with particular agencies or forms of funding.' (*With Respect to Old Age*, DH, 1999: para. 6.43)

Significantly, the Commission also made a series of other recommendations on funding long-term care which would be subsumed if the first of the two main recommendations, above, was adopted by government. These included:

- making the nursing element of care in nursing homes free to the resident;
- increasing the upper capital limit used in the means-test for residential and nursing home care to £60,000.

In terms of paying for care, the Commission also recommended:

- ignoring the value of the person's house for three months after they first move to live in a residential or nursing home;
- transferring the resources of the Residential Allowance means-tested state benefit (this was only payable to people who qualified on the grounds of income and capital, and who were paying towards their care in independent sector homes) from the Department for Work and Pensions to local authorities, to spend on care at home;
- considering whether to transfer responsibility for the funding of 'preserved rights' residents to local authorities;
- extending the direct payments system to those over the age of 65.

A number of other recommendations were made, relating to care standards, and types of services and care workers.

Not all the members of the Commission accepted all the recommendations. Two of the twelve Commissioners – Joel Joffe and David Lipsey – issued a note of dissent. They felt unable to support the first of the two main recommendations, to exempt personal care from charges. Their key concern was that standards of care for older people needed to be improved. Money could be spent making services free, or increasing their quality – but it was not possible to achieve both. (This view may become subject to renewed scrutiny in the light of the government's proposals, set out during the summer of 2002, to reconsider the application of some of the minimum quality standards to care homes.)

The Government's response

During the time when the Royal Commission was sitting, a variety of Government initiatives were announced and documents released. These included the 1998 White Paper, *Modernising Social Services*, and proposals to change the system of regulating care services, which culminated in the Care Standards Act 2000.

Some of the recommendations made by the Royal Commission had, in broad terms at least, already been addressed by these documents by the time the Commission's report was published. For example, plans to extend the provision of direct payments to those aged 65 or over were included in *Modernising Social Services* (DH, 1998), published five months before the Commission's report. The Government therefore felt able to say, in July 2000, that it had accepted (broadly or otherwise) 18 of the Commission's 24 recommendations (*The NHS Plan: the Government's response to the Royal Commission on long term care*, DH, 2000).

However, the Westminster Government rejected the Commission's main recommendation to make personal care free of charge. It opted instead for the smaller changes, such as making the nursing element of nursing home care exempt from the charge to residents, increasing the capital limits for the residential means-test (although not to the levels suggested by the Commission), and transferring responsibility for the remaining 'preserved rights' residents to local authorities. The cost of the nursing element of care in nursing homes would fall to the NHS, and would increasingly be administered by Primary Care Trusts (PCTs), as these developed. Costs associated with other changes fell to local authorities.

This distinction of the 'Westminster Government' is drawn because the Scottish Parliament opted separately to accept the Commission's findings, to make personal care free in all settings in Scotland, from July 2002. The Welsh Assembly, however, also opted only to make nursing care free, in line with the policy in England, although it has adopted a standard amount of £100 per week rather than the English banding system (see below). In Northern Ireland, nursing care is exempt from charges.

Paying for residential care – ending the anomalies

One of the main arguments adopted by the Government for removing the nursing element of care in nursing homes from the current means-test regime, is that this represented the only set of circumstances when people were obliged to pay for nursing care. Those living in their own homes, in sheltered housing or in residential homes were able to receive nursing care 'free at the point of use' from the NHS. The NHS should, therefore, take responsibility for funding the nursing element of care in nursing homes.

Other anomalies were also tackled. The Government decided to end the payment of the Residential Allowance, a means-tested benefit under the Income Support system. This could be paid to eligible residents in private and voluntary sector homes – but not to those living in local authority homes, or in their own homes. This benefit ceased to be paid to residents applying for Income Support for the first time after April 2002. Instead, additional funding has been provided to local authorities, transferred from the Income Support budget. This extra funding has a potential advantage in that it can be used to pay for care for people living at home as well as those in residential care. As such, it continues the now decade-long policy commitment of supporting people in their own homes for as long as possible.

Another anomaly concerned the continued payment of Attendance Allowance to people who funded their own care in private and voluntary sector homes, but not to those who funded their own care in local authority homes ('Part III' residents). The Government's response to the Royal Commission ended this anomaly, by making all self-funding residents eligible to receive Attendance Allowance, provided they meet the other eligibility tests for this benefit.

These changes, and the changes in the care regulatory system outlined in Chapter 4, make a significant difference to arguments about independent sector 'versus' local authority provision. This is because these changes create more of a 'level playing field' between the different providers. This should help make it easier to focus attention on the pattern, type, and quality – and overall cost – of residential services needed now and in the future, rather than on concerns about the differences in the means-test and regulatory arrangements between the sectors.

Free nursing care in nursing homes

Once the Government had decided to make nursing care free in all settings, an important step along the way to putting this into practice was agreement on the definition of 'nursing care'. For example, is 'nursing care' only the care carried out by trained nurses? This could pose problems in nursing homes, where only one qualified nurse may be on duty at any one time, leaving much of the care being carried out by care assistants. Our understanding of what 'nursing care' may be has also changed. In some parts of the country, the tasks carried out by qualified NHS nurses are significantly different from even a decade ago. For example, in some areas urinary catheters are no longer changed by district nurses, but by health care assistants – or even by care assistants paid for by social services. It has been suggested that a definition of 'nursing care' can be reached for funding purposes by calculating the cost of 'nursing care' in nursing homes as the difference in the average weekly charges between nursing home and residential home places. In the event, the Health and Social Care Act 2001 defined nursing care for which the NHS will pay in a nursing home as:

'Services provided by a registered nurse and involving:

(a) the provision of care, or
(b) the planning, supervision or delegation of the provision of care, other than services which, having regard to their

nature and circumstances in which they are provided, do not need to be provided by a registered nurse.'
(Section 49 (2), Health and Social Care Act 2001)

This definition means that the care provided by a registered nurse is included, together with the time the registered nurse spends monitoring and supervising the work they have delegated, when calculating the cost of the nursing care in a nursing home. However, the time spent by a non-registered nurse (such as a nursing or healthcare assistant) is not included.

One way to understand this change is that it removes local authorities' duties to fund (and to therefore apply the national, mandatory means-test) the costs of registered nursing time spent on providing, delegating or supervising care in nursing homes. In all settings, these tasks have formally become (or returned to) the responsibility of the NHS. Section 49 of the Health and Social Care Act 2001 changed the amendment to the National Assistance Act 1948 made by the NHS and Community Care Act 1990, outlined above, which had given local authorities their powers to fund means-tested nursing home care from April 1993.

Chapter 5 has described the different assessment stages leading up to decisions about services, including the ways in which the Registered Nursing Care Contribution (RNCC) is calculated. Nursing care in nursing homes is paid by the NHS from one of three bands, following assessment:

- **Low band (£35 per week).** This applies to people who are funding their own care in a nursing home, and who require only a minimal registered nurse input to their care. It is expected this level will usually be paid for people who have chosen to move into a nursing home, but whose care needs could have been met elsewhere (at home, or in a residential home, for example) with support from a district nurse.
- **Middle band (£70 per week).** This applies to nursing home residents whose multiple care needs require a registered nurse to intervene at least once a day; and where the resident may need

access to a nurse at any time. However, the resident's condition is stable and predictable, and likely to remain so.

- **High band (£110 per week)**. The highest band applies to nursing home residents with unstable or unpredictable and complex needs, which require frequent mechanical and/or therapeutic interventions from a registered nurse. These may include management of PEG feeding (a form of assisted feeding) or antidepressant therapy.

The Government has said these bands will remain unchanged until April 2003. Although there are three bands, the guidance allows for the possibility that someone's nursing needs may be greater than the High band, but still not meet the local criteria for fully-funded NHS continuing health care services. In these cases, the NHS has the power to fund at a higher level than £110 in order to meet the person's registered nursing costs, making such decisions on a case-by-case basis (HSC 2001/17, LAC(2001)26, *Guidance on Free Nursing Care in Nursing Homes*).

This change has been phased in over a period of time. Self-funding residents in nursing homes became eligible for free registered nursing care on 1 October 2001, and the NHS was asked to aim at completing all those determinations by the end of December 2001. However, health authorities did not receive the necessary detail for the calculations until just before the changes came into effect in October 2001, so there were some delays. Health authorities were told to allocate an appropriate band of nursing care to residents and pay at this rate from 1 October 2001, until such time as they could complete the assessment and make a decision for each individual resident. Payments should be made at the middle band for any self-funding resident who dies before the assessment has been carried out (unless there is evidence from the home's records that a resident would have been placed in the high band). Following the changes to health authorities (described in Chapter 2), these arrangements have become the responsibility of Primary Care Trusts (PCTs).

The provisions for free nursing care apply, from April 2003, to nursing home residents who receive state financial support from their local authority. This includes former 'preserved rights' residents (see page 197). Anyone who receives free NHS nursing care because they are self-funding, but who subsequently becomes eligible for state financial support from their local authority before April 2003, will continue to receive the NHS funding for their registered nursing care.

Aside from this element of care, however, residents in nursing homes continue to be means-tested for the care they receive or, in the case of self-funding residents, will be liable for the remainder of the home's fees. It is important to note that this funding from the NHS is passed to the home, not to the resident. In practice, the net result of this change should mean the amount residents are asked to pay each week will be reduced. In the early stages following implementation, there was some evidence to suggest that some nursing homes raised their fees for self-funding residents, some by the relevant band for each individual. Other homes were charging an extra amount based on the average of the bandings on which residents have been placed. In effect this meant that those residents were still paying the same amount each week for their care. It was suggested that this was the only way nursing homes could increase their total revenue, and was linked with concerns over what constitutes the 'real' cost of care, discussed in Chapter 3. However, these initial increases were applied to self-funding residents, not to those receiving state financial support towards the cost of their care. Research has shown that self-funding residents were already tending to pay more for their care than residents who receive state financial support (Laing, 1998), even before these additional NHS funds were being made available. Some concern has been expressed, therefore, about homes further raising the fees of self-funding residents.

In response to these concerns, in February 2002, the Government amended the care home regulations. Regulation 5 of the Care Homes Regulations 2001 requires homes to provide a breakdown of their fees, making clear to residents which aspects of fees relate to nursing care, and which to residential care. NHS bodies use a central core contract, which sets out how homes account for any

NHS nursing contribution they receive. Standard two of the National Minimum Standards for Care Homes for Older People states that any contribution to fees by the NHS or local authority must be recorded separately from contributions made by residents, relatives or other third parties.

Box 6.2 Further information on free nursing care

❋ **Age Concern England**
  Factsheet 20, *NHS continuing care, free nursing care and intermediate care*

Other changes

The 'preserved rights' system

Prior to the community care reforms, there were serious concerns that some residents in private and voluntary sector homes would not 'qualify' for state financial support under the new, post-1993, care assessment arrangements. These residents had been largely left to make their own arrangements to enter a home. There had been no question at that time about whether that care was 'needed' in the sense of meeting eligibility criteria on the basis of assessed need. The decision was made, therefore, to maintain the same system under which pre-1993 independent sector home residents had expected to claim state financial support.

However, 'preserved rights' residents faced a number of problems, mostly relating to the gap between the cost of their care and the amount of state support available through Income Support. Although there were provisions for local authorities to assist 'preserved rights' residents under the age of 65, they were specifically restricted from helping older residents, either with 'top-up' fees, or taking over the state financial support.

Another aspect to this is – put bluntly – that far more 'preserved rights' residents survived for far longer than initially anticipated. At the time the decision was taken to maintain the earlier system, it was expected that most residents would have died by the early years of the 21st century. The existence of two, separate systems (with slightly different rules) also caused considerable confusion at times in terms of both policy and information. In April 2002, as part of the Government's response to the Royal Commission, the 'preserved rights' system ended. Responsibility for those residents' care assessments and funding transferred to local authority social services departments (LAC (2002)7, *Guidance to Councils with Social Services Responsibilities on the Abolition of Preserved Rights*).

Changes to the local authority means-test

The national, mandatory means-test for places in residential and nursing homes is highly complex. It is so complex that Age Concern England produces four separate factsheets to explain all the details and cover all circumstances (see Box 6.3). These are not reproduced here, but it is worth reflecting on one or two of the more recent changes.

One of the ways in which the means-test has become more complex involves the minimum and maximum limits placed on people's savings (capital). These help determine the point at which older residents are eligible for financial support, as well as the amount of financial support available. In 1993, these limits were set at £3,000 and £8,000 – in line with the amounts for those claiming ordinary Income Support while still living at home. These ordinary Income Support amounts (or MIG) can still be claimed on entering a care home. This is important since local authorities calculate people's contribution as if they are receiving any of the other state benefits that they are entitled to claim.

In 1996, the capital limits applied by social services departments were raised to £10,000 and £16,000 – but the Income Support limits remained at £3,000 and £8,000. This meant someone might be eligible for financial support from the local authority butwould be eligible for Income Support (now called Minimum Income Guarantee, or MIG) at a later stage. Subsequently, levels were changed, and different capital limits now apply to MIG depending on whether someone is aged over 60, is living in their own home (rented or owned) or living permanently in residential care. For permanent residents over the age of 60, the relevant MIG levels are £10,000 and £16,000; for temporary residents over 60 years old (and those living in their own homes) the limits are £6,000 and £12,000. The capital limits applied by local authorities in the residential means-test were increased to £11,750 and £19,000 in April 2002. While such increases in the local authority and MIG capital limits have been welcomed, these diverse figures illustrate the complexity of calculating individual contributions.

A second change, introduced by the Government in its response to the Royal Commission, concerns the inclusion of the value of the resident's former property (the flat or house in which they lived before moving permanently to live in a care home). In circumstances when the value would otherwise be included in the means-test, the Government has told local authorities to ignore its value for the first 12 weeks in a home. This is intended to help ensure that the decision to move to live permanently in a home is the correct one. It is in addition to the other circumstances when the value of property must be ignored (or disregarded), set out on page 186.

The Government also extended local council's powers to create 'legal charges' on people's former homes. This is where the value of the property can legitimately be included in the means-test calculations, but the person does not wish to sell their home (or perhaps cannot sell their home quickly). Under the Health and Social Services and Social Security Adjudication Act 1983 (this Act is often referred to as 'HASSASSA'), local councils were given power to create a 'legal charge' on the property. This was a way of 'lending' the person the amount they would have to contribute if the property was sold and they had the cash. It was a way for the local authority to secure payment of the debt otherwise being run up by the person. It effectively acts as a mortgage in reverse, in that the amount owed to the council increases over time as the care fees mount up. Councils cannot charge interest on the legal charge until the day after the resident dies. In practice, it has not been much used, partly because it involves authorities tying up money they would otherwise expect to be able to use to purchase care services.

On 1 October 2001, another method – the 'deferred payment agreement' – was introduced under Section 55 of the Health and Social Care Act 2001. Local authorities have been given some extra funding to enter into these agreements (for example, through the Deferred Payments Grant Determination 2002–2003). Guidance from the Government sets out how the debt should accrue, and what happens when the remaining capital in the property reaches the means-test limits, set at £11,750 and £19,000 from April 2002 (LAC (2001)25, *Charges for Residential Accommodation*).

Box 6.3 Further information on the means-test for nursing or residential home care from Age Concern England

* Factsheet 10, *Local Authority charging procedures for residential and nursing home care*
* Factsheet 38, *Treatment of the former home as capital for people in residential homes*
* Factsheet 39, *Paying for care in a residential or nursing home if you have a partner*
* Factsheet 40, *Transfer of assets and paying for care in a residential or nursing home*

NHS continuing health care

Chapter 5 set out, in some detail, the NHS's responsibilities to provide continuing health care services. These, together with the new arrangements to fund the registered nursing element of nursing home care, are provided free to users.

Older people whose care is entirely funded by the NHS, however, may find their state benefits are affected if they are receiving this care in hospital, in an NHS nursing home or in an NHS-contracted bed in a private nursing home. Since March 2002, benefits such as the state retirement pension and Income Support are reduced after 13 weeks. They then reduce further after 52 weeks. (Before this date, benefits were initially reduced after six weeks.) Attendance Allowance is also affected by stays in hospital (although different periods of time apply), but other income (such as occupational pension) and any savings are not affected. The arrangement to reduce state benefits was introduced at the time the NHS was first set up, on the basis that people could receive one form of state support (NHS hospital care) or another (state retirement pension), but not both. However, this arrangement has been criticised, especially as the current state retirement pension is linked to the National Insurance contributions older people have paid over many years. People whose fully-funded NHS care is delivered to them in their own homes continue to receive their state benefits in full.

Paying for services at home, including sheltered housing

The ways in which individuals pay for their care at home (including sheltered housing) and in residential or nursing homes varies significantly. This section explains how older people are asked to pay towards a variety of services, including care services at home, aids to daily living, and adaptations to the home.

Charges for services at home

Section 17 of the Health and Social Services and Social Security Adjudication Act (HASSASSA) 1983 gave local authorities powers to charge for the community care services it arranges or provides to support people living in their own homes (sometimes collectively called day and domiciliary, or non-residential, services). This includes sheltered housing, and applies whether people are home-owners or tenants. Such charges must be 'reasonable' for the user to pay. As this was a power, not a duty, it was largely left to local authorities to decide whether – and how much – to charge for these non-residential services.

In practice, an increasing number of local authorities imposed charges for domiciliary and day care, in response to the expectations of successive governments that some element of their social services budget would be raised in this way. Social services' settlements from central government have reflected this expectation for some years. In short, authorities were left to either impose (or increase) charges and complete their budget, or leave charges low or at zero and face budget restrictions and likely reductions in services.

A key concern, and one considered by the Royal Commission among other bodies, was that this meant there were wide variations around the country in terms of whether or not – and how much – users paid for services. The Royal Commission suggested that a national system be introduced, following its overall recommendation that personal (or 'touching') care be free to users. Other concerns included whether charges on services provided to support family carers should be based on the financial resources of the user or of the carer. There have also been significant concerns about whether local charges have always been 'reasonable' for individuals to pay, especially for people with low incomes who may already have extra disability-related expenditure, because of extra heating or laundry requirements.

The White Paper, *Modernising Social Services* (DH, 1998) set out the Government's intention to issue guidance on charging for services at home. This guidance was published in November 2001. It left intact the discretionary power of councils to decide whether to charge. However, it set out a framework intended to help local councils to design consistent, reasonable and fair charging policies (LAC (2001) 32, *Fairer Charging Policies for Home Care and Other Non-residential Social Services*).

The guidance reiterates that some services are exempt from charges:

- aftercare services provided under s.117 of the Mental Health Act 1983 (this includes any residential services provided as aftercare);
- assessments by councils, including community care assessments or advice about the availability of services;
- time-limited, non-residential intermediate care.

It also sets out two groups of people who are exempt from charges for care at home:

- people using non-residential social services who have any form of Creuzfeldt Jacob Disease (CJD);
- people whose overall income equals the defined 'basic' Income Support levels plus a 25 per cent 'buffer'.

Services that can be charged for include:

- meals on wheels;
- day care;
- home care/home help;
- social services' support such as transport and equipment;
- housing adaptations not provided through Disabled Facilities Grants (see page 207).

The guidance recommends that charges for different services should be considered together – particularly when considering the collective impact on individual users. Flat-rate charges (where all users pay the same, regardless of their income or savings) are only acceptable in limited circumstances. Charges should not leave user's net income below a sum comprising basic Income Support (now the Minimum Income Guarantee, for older people) levels plus 25 per cent of this amount. Councils must take individual users' disability-related expenditure (for example, extra costs of special diets or laundry arising from disability) if they are taking disability benefits into account (Attendance Allowance or Disability Living Allowance). The guidance includes a comprehensive list of possible disability-related expenditure.

It also sets out expectations that the same savings limits as used by local authorities in the residential means-test should be applied as a minimum, although it also stresses that councils can operate more generous rules. They are reminded that the value of the property in which users live cannot be included when considering the amount of users' savings. Councils should ensure that welfare benefits advice is provided when a user's charges are being assessed. Carers can only be charged for services provided to them under the Carers and Disabled Children Act 2000.

Some concerns have been raised about how charges can or should be levied if health and social services have made funding arrangements under the Health Act 1999 partnerships. Neither the guidance nor the Health Act 1999 has changed local authorities' powers to charge for social care services provided in a partnership arrangement. However, the guidance does stress the need to clarify the difference between charged-for and non-charged-for services; and the need to be able to explain this difference to users. This will be essential where an NHS Trust (or a Care Trust) provides a service, part of which is charged for. Otherwise users might believe they are being charged for NHS care – especially if payments are made to NHS staff. This requirement may be helped, from April 2003, by proposed changes in charges for non-residential services. In the summer of 2002, the Secretary of State for Health announced plans to exempt from charges:

- community equipment;
- rehabilitation services;
- intermediate care services;

irrespective of whether these are provided or purchased by the NHS (including Care Trusts) or by social services. These changes will require new legislation, and are unlikely to be in place before April 2003 (DH, 2002).

This represents a significant move away from the more common current practice, where the distinction between 'free' and 'charged for' services is generally dependent on whether services are provided or purchased by the NHS ('free') or social services ('charged for').

The draft *Mental Health Bill* (2002) also sets out proposals for free care to be provided to anyone who receives services under compulsion. This would include aftercare provided following the period of compulsory treatment. Again, these services would be free regardless of whether these are provided or purchased by the NHS or social services, both of which currently share responsibilities in this respect.

The guidance on charges for non-residential services is being implemented in two stages. By 1 October 2002, councils should have individually assessed the disability-related expenditure of users receiving more than 10 hours of home care weekly, whose Attendance Allowance, Disability Living Allowance or other disability benefit is included in the calculation of their charge; and ensure that users whose overall income equals the defined 'basic' levels of Income Support plus the 25 per cent buffer are no longer charged from this date at the latest. From 1 April 2003, all charging policies should be in line with the full guidance.

Box 6.4 Further information on charges for non-residential services

* **Age Concern England**
  Factsheet 42, *Paying for help at home and local authority charges*
* **The Coalition on Charging**
  A consortium of charities concerned with local authority charges for domiciliary and day care

---

Adaptations

The system of state support for repairs, improvements and adaptations is undergoing a period of significant change between July 2002–July 2003. This section explains the pre-July 2002 system (which may continue in some areas until July 2003), and the new system that will be in place across England and Wales from July 2003, at the latest.

Until July 2003, local authorities can administer three grants for repairs and adaptations to housing, under the Housing Grants, Construction and Regeneration Act 1996. The first, a Renovation Grant, can be used for larger repair and improvement work. It can be awarded if, for example, housing is 'unfit for human habitation' (as defined in law); or has inadequate heating, or insulation. If someone receives a grant to repair or improve their home, and then moves within five years, the local authority will not require them to repay the grant if the person is moving to live permanently in a hospital, residential home or sheltered housing. Otherwise, people moving within five years would be expected to repay at least some of the grant funding they had received.

However, it has tended to be the two other grants that have been particularly relevant for older people needing treatment, care and support. These are Home Repair Assistance, and the Disabled Facilities Grant.

In July 2002, local authorities were given new powers to support the costs of renovation and repair work for individual homeowners. Under the Regulatory Reform (Housing Assistance) (England and Wales) Order 2002, local authorities are expected to design their own strategies for renewing private sector housing rather than being required to follow the 1996 Act. This Act, outlined above, set some obligations on councils to carry out certain repairs in particular circumstances. In its place, there is a new, general, power to provide financial assistance. From July 2002, local councils can provide financial assistance through grants, loans or equity release policies. The existing powers to provide Renovation Grants and Home Repair Assistance will cease in July 2003, although in practice, some councils have said they are no longer making these available to new applicants after July 2002.

HOME REPAIR ASSISTANCE

Until July 2003, this grant is available for older and disabled homeowners, or for others on low incomes. It is intended to pay for minor, but essential, repairs or adaptations. Work could include adding a downstairs toilet, improving door locks, or repairs to make the home weather-proof. This is the only grant available to those owning mobile homes or houseboats. The maximum that can be provided for each application is £5,000, and there are restrictions on the number of applications that can be made.

Generally, it is the council's housing or environmental health department that handles this grant. It is a discretionary grant, which means it is up to the council to decide whether to approve someone's application. Although there is no formal means-test, councils can decide to operate their own test if resources to fund this grant are limited, and they wish to prioritise those least able to afford to pay for the work privately.

As set out above, this form of support will cease in July 2003. Since July 2002, councils have been able to decide their own policies on offering individual homeowners grants, loans, or equity release options, to pay for small repairs. It is up to each council what type of support it makes available, and to whom. After July 2003, local councils will still be able to assist on a discretionary basis, but from their own resources rather than through the grants system (which attracted specific government reimbursement).

DISABLED FACILITIES GRANT

To be eligible for a Disabled Facilities Grant, the older person must meet the definition of disability under the Housing Grants, Construction and Regeneration Act 1996, which includes people who:

- have substantially impaired sight, hearing or speech;
- have a mental disorder or impairment of any kind;
- are substantially physically disabled by illness, injury or impairment (whether or not since their birth).

People whose condition meets the definition of disability under the National Assistance Act 1948 are also eligible to apply for this grant. Councils must award this grant if someone who is disabled does not have access to their home and to the basic amenities within it – for example, if the person cannot use their bathroom, or operate their heating or lighting controls, or easily get in and out of the house. In addition, discretionary grants can be made for other work to make the home suitable for the person with a disability.

Disabled Facilities Grants are available from the local authority's housing department, although the social services department may also be involved. This is because the person's needs have to be assessed, usually by occupational therapists who tend to be employed by social services departments.

In some areas there have been difficulties, as people have had to wait for the occupational therapist's assessment. In some cases, they have had to wait more than 12 months for this. The delay is largely attributed to the shortage in occupational therapists, which has existed for several years. There are also concerns that hold-ups have been caused by local authorities running short of funds for this grant. In addition, there have been delays in approving completed applications for Disabled Facilities Grants, although the law says that people should not have to wait for more than six months after applying for such grants to hear whether their application has been successful. However, the completed application involves submitting builders' estimates, which can only be done if the council has drawn up the specification of works. In practice, this usually depends on the occupational therapist having first carried out an assessment. Once a completed application has been made, however, a court case has confirmed that a council cannot refuse to approve the application on the grounds that it has insufficient resources (*R v Birmingham City Council ex parte Mohammed, June 1998*).

Disabled Facilities Grants (DFGs) are means-tested on the basis of income and savings but, in the case of owner-occupiers, the value of their house or flat is ignored. It is calculated using different figures from those used in the mandatory residential care means-test, and recommended for discretionary charges for care at home. For DFGs, savings up to £6,000 are ignored. There is a maximum to the overall cost of the works, above which local councils are not obliged to pay. In England, as at April 2002, this maximum is £25,000. Until July 2003, local authorities can pay additional discretionary grants for adaptations works, which cost more than this. Social services departments may also provide some funding under the Chronically Sick and Disabled Persons Act 1970. However, since July 2002, councils have had the power to decide new strategies for supporting these additional costs. In some areas, local councils may expect costs that are greater than £25,000 to be met through the individual seeking a housing-related loan, under the Regulatory Reform (Housing Assistance) (England and Wales) Order 2002. Alternatively, councils can decide to supplement these statutory DFGs from their own resources.

This Order does not otherwise affect the statutory nature of the DFG, except that it can now be claimed by people needing adaptations who live in mobile homes or houseboats.

Box 6.5 Further information on grants for home improvements

❊ **Age Concern England**
Factsheet 13, *Older home owners – financial help with repairs and adaptations*
Factsheet 35, *Rights for council and housing association tenants*
Factsheet 36, *Private tenants' rights*

❊ More information may be available from **RADAR**, and from **foundations** – the National Co-ordinating body for Home Improvement Agencies. See Useful Contacts on page 249.

AIDS TO DAILY LIVING

The Chronically Sick and Disabled Persons Act 1970 states that, aside from assistance with adaptations to the home, local authorities have responsibilities to meet the needs of people with disabilities for aids and equipment. Local authorities can operate a charge for these, as part of non-residential service charges (see pages 201–2). The NHS also has some responsibilities, but any equipment it provides must be free at the point of use. The type of equipment both organisations can provide was considered in Chapter 3.

By 2004, health and social services are expected to have integrated their equipment provision under a Community Equipment Service (HSC 2001/008, LAC (2001)13, *Community Equipment Services*). Councils were originally expected to be able to charge for providing disability equipment, but in the summer of 2002 the Secretary of State for Health set out the Government's intention to exempt community equipment from charges from April 2003 (DH, 2002). This will be subject to the necessary legislation being passed.

Box 6.6 Further information on community equipment

* **Age Concern England**
  Factsheet 42, *Disability equipment and how to get it*
* **Help the Aged**
  Information Sheet 15, *Disability living equipment*
* **Disabled Living Foundation**
  Provides information on disability equipment and other services

---

The *Supporting People* reforms

In 1998, the Government published inter-departmental proposals to deal with the overriding question of how to fund personal support in supported housing settings. The proposals, *Supporting People* (DSS, 1998), set out plans to bring together several streams of funding, including Housing Benefit, the Housing Corporation Grant, the Home Improvement Agency Grants, the Supported Housing Revenue Grant in Wales, and the Special Needs Allowance Package in Scotland. These will form a single budget, from which authorities can fund housing-related support services such as:

- warden services to help tenants to fill out forms, or pay bills;
- community alarms;
- advocacy services;
- funding for home improvement agencies (which act locally to help co-ordinate the grants for repairs and adaptations, outlined on page 205).

However, this new fund, or grant, will not replace existing funding mechanisms for social care services (such as home help/home care services, or meals on wheels).

These reforms began as a response to inconsistencies in the funding of support services for older people living in sheltered housing, as well as other client groups, during the 1990s. In many areas, local councils were seeking to fund some support elements of these housing arrangements (such as some warden services in sheltered housing, for example), by including these costs in rental charges. Such costs were then often being met through Housing Benefit claims made by individual tenants to pay their rent. A 1997 Divisional Court judgement confirmed that Housing Benefit should only cover service charges for personal support in limited circumstances. Many tenants, including older people in sheltered housing, therefore faced the possibility of either having to pay charges for warden services (for which they would not receive any state financial support), or the withdrawal by housing providers of some of the warden services. Interim regulations were therefore issued to protect most tenants in existing supported accommodation.

Separately, an Audit Commission report (*The Way to Go Home*, 2000) had drawn attention to the lack of co-ordination between housing and social services departments in terms of funding a range of housing-related support services. *Supporting People* aims to increase older people's choices; provide better information on the choices available; and to develop new services that avoid or delay moves to institutional care.

The *Supporting People* changes come into effect in full from April 2003, under the Office of the Deputy Prime Minister (ODPM). They apply to people from the following groups:

- older people who live in sheltered housing, or who want to carry on living in their own home but need some help to do so;
- people with learning disabilities who can move out of institutional care and into the community, if given appropriate help and support;
- people with mental health problems who can move out of hospital if regular help is available to support their living independently.

Other client groups are also included in the changes, which will limit Housing Benefit to the rent for tenants' accommodation from April 2003. Some housing management work can be included in the rent, however. Although local authorities will be expected to operate some kind of gate-keeping system for access to sheltered housing (for example, applying a minimum age), existing tenants will not be reconsidered for their eligibility to live in rented sheltered housing. The Government has said it does not require local authorities to carry out a community care assessment of someone's need for support if individuals are only seeking a place in a sheltered housing scheme.

The changes mean that some individuals may have to pay for some housing-related services that were previously included in their rent and paid via Housing Benefit. However, some support services – such as 'short-term' support – are expected to be free of charge; some tenants, such as those receiving Housing Benefit, should also receive free services. There are also some transitional protection measures for tenants who will no longer be eligible for Housing Benefit after April 2003 because their eligible rent has been reduced. Those who do pay towards support services will do so through a means-test that will be set locally and jointly with the social services' means-test for non-residential social care. There are other changes for older, sheltered leaseholders who may have been receiving additional financial support for some housing costs from the Department of Work and Pensions. The changes are likely to mean differences in the amounts individual older people pay, depending on whether they were already living in sheltered housing before April 2003. There are also concerns that the new arrangements will be administratively complex, and difficult to understand.

Importantly, the *Supporting People* reforms are expected to provide the strategic framework for older people's housing services (including sheltered provision) and its preventative role within health and social services' overall programmes. It is also a part of an overall approach to improving options for older people to remain in their own homes for as long as possible. This reflects the aims of many older people, whose views are increasingly being sought by central government and other bodies.

Box 6.7 Further information on *Supporting People*

❋ **The Office of the Deputy Prime Minister (OPDM)**
   Has a special website dedicated to *Supporting People* – www.spkweb.gov.uk
❋ **National Housing Federation**
   Publishes a variety of information materials. See Useful Contacts list on page 249

---

7 Communicating with users and carers

The emphasis placed by successive governments on involving users and carers has continued since the implementation of the community care reforms. This is particularly the case in terms of seeking their views through consultation. Users and carers also have expectations – sometimes rights – to receive information about their care plan, and about criteria for services, for example. This involves users and carers in giving information about their health and care needs, alongside other personal details, which is then recorded and, potentially, shared with a range of commissioners and providers of services. This chapter reflects on these varied aspects of communicating with users and carers:

- initiatives that involve the general public, including users and carers;
- initiatives specifically for users and carers;
- information needs of users and carers;
- raising concerns and making complaints;
- ways of involving, and seeking the views of, users and carers.

Listening to the general public

One of the overarching themes in central government since 1997 has been the need for public services to involve, seek the views of, and respond to, the general public. Such schemes do not exclude users and carers of community and continuing care services, but nor are they necessarily exclusive to this group.

The Cabinet Office has tended to lead the way in recent years on work for government (locally and centrally) to seek the views of a wider general public. It has been responsible for setting up initiatives such as the People's Panel, as well as producing good practice guidelines for government departments to adopt when issuing documents for consultation.

The NHS Plan (DH, 2000), together with some of the changes already enacted under the Care Standards Act 2000 and the Health Act 1999, further developed this theme. For example:

• PCG and PCT Boards must include one lay member;
• Lay assessors (first introduced in 1994) will continue to be involved in the inspection of care homes;
• CHI, NICE, the General Medical Council (and its proposed successor organisation) and the NHS Modernisation Board are also expected to include (or increase) lay and citizen membership.

Within social services, local authority Overview and Scrutiny Committees (OCS) are developing to include membership from Patients' Forum representatives (see below), and from voluntary organisations that represent particular client groups.

The emphasis on responding to individuals is also reflected in the language being employed, particularly the many references to 'patient-centred' and 'person-centred' aspects of treatment, care and support – for example, in *The NHS Plan* (DH, 2000), in the NSF for Older People (DH, 2001) and the Single Assessment Process (SAP – see Chapter 5).

Initiatives for users and carers

As might be expected, a significant number of other initiatives and proposals are explicitly targeted at patients, users and carers. Key among these are:

• 'expert patients', and patient-focused benchmarking;
• consent to treatment;
• patients' forums;
• NHS and social services surveys.

Expert patients and 'patient-focused benchmarking'

In 2001, the Department of Health published *The Expert Patient*. This set out plans for those with chronic long-term conditions, such as asthma and arthritis, to take far greater control over their own care.

Between 2001 and 2004, pilot user-led groups are being run at selected Primary Care Trust sites. These groups pool and share their knowledge with other users, in order to manage their conditions better. It is expected that the programme will be expanded to the whole of the NHS between 2004 and 2007. It builds on the North American model of self-managed programmes of care, which have been found to improve patients' confidence, enhance their relationship with health care professionals, and improve clinical outcomes.

The Expert Patient plans also set out the establishment of a National Co-ordinating and Training Research Centre, to provide training and up-to-date information for health, social services and voluntary sector professionals about self-managed care, including the ways in which these groups may need to change their working practices with users.

Separately in 2001, the Department of Health also published *The Essence of Care*. This sets out ways in which NHS health care practitioners can develop, with patients, what is being called 'patient-focused benchmarking'. This considers how to draw up a series of outcomes (or results) based on what patients and carers want to happen, and then measuring the extent to which this has been reached. Possible outcomes cover personal and oral hygiene, and food and nutrition.

Consent to treatment

Guidelines were published in 2001 relating to consent by patients for examination or treatment within the NHS (HSC 2001/023, *Good Practice in Consent*). This was partly in response to concerns about possible ageism within some 'do not resuscitate' hospital policies for patients, and partly as a result of the 2001

Kennedy Report into Bristol Royal Infirmary (see Chapter 4). It also follows the commitment, within *The NHS Plan*, to produce practice guidelines on patient-centred consent.

Aside from the circular outlined above, which covers all adults, separate good practice guidelines were published by the Department of Health for different patient groups, including older people (*Seeking Consent: working with older people*, DH, 2001). This good practice guidance considers issues such as when the patient has the capacity to accept or refuse treatment or care; circumstances where this capacity is lacking; and decisions about the withdrawal or withholding of life-prolonging treatment. The guide emphasises that health care professionals and others should never assume that people cannot make their own decisions simply because of their age or frailty. The Government has also published, in its draft *Mental Health Bill* (Home Office, 2002), proposals for a new legal framework for adults who are unable to give consent for themselves.

Patients' Forums

During 2001, the Government carried out consultation on plans to implement what it described in *The NHS Plan* (2000) as the 'patient-centred NHS'. This process includes establishing Patients' Forums in all NHS Trusts and PCTs. The key role of Patients' Forums will be to monitor and review each Trust's services, and provide feedback to the Trust on patients' and local people's views of the services. Patients' Forums also have the power to inspect any premises where patients receive NHS services. They are expected to produce an annual report to the local Trust, the Secretary of State for Health and the Commission for Patient and Public Involvement in Health (see below). Patients' Forums will be able to elect a non-executive Director to sit on their local NHS Trust or PCT Board, and monitor the effectiveness of two new bodies – PALS and ICAS (see page 222) – being introduced to improve the handling of complaints about NHS services (see below). The legislative framework covering Patients' Forums is set out in the NHS Reform and Health Care Professions Act 2002. It is expected that the first Patients' Forums will commence in early 2003.

National and local NHS and social services surveys

The first national NHS survey of patients' views was carried out in 1998–1999, and concerned primary care. The second survey concentrated on experiences of patients with coronary heart disease. This alternating of survey years between general views, and the experiences of those with a specific condition, will form the likely pattern for future surveys, which are intended to cover both primary care and specific conditions.

The first annual social services survey of user's views was published in 2001. As with the NHS surveys on patients' views, older users and patients tend to record greater satisfaction with services, treatment and care than younger adult users. There are mixed views as to whether this reflects lower expectations amongst an older generation, a higher propensity to complain amongst younger generations (although whether all such complaints are always believed to be justified is unclear), or something entirely different.

Both of these national surveys also provide some of the information for the elements of the annual Performance Assessment Framework (PAF) indicators for the NHS and social services that relate to patient and user views and experiences. In addition, since 2001, all NHS Trusts have been required to undertake their own annual patients' survey. The Government has said it will make a link between survey results and the availability of additional funds, in order to create a financial incentive on NHS organisations to act on patients' views.

As part of the development of the long-term care charter, *Better Care, Higher Standards* (DETR/DH, 2000), local authorities have been told to ensure that users' and carers' experiences of existing local charter standards (for housing, health and social care) help to determine the following year's charter standards (HSC 2001/06; LAC (2001)06, *Better Care, Higher Standards – guidance for 2001/2002*). There should also be an annual survey of users and carers (jointly across services), which should be published either as part of an annual report on the charter standards, or as part of the annual charter.

Information needs of users and carers

Guidance issued in 1999 on the development of *Better Care, Higher Standards* local charters set out the requirement for everyone with long-term care needs to be provided with, at least, a summary of their local charter. This should be accessible, in a range of languages and formats (including Braille, video tape or audio tape). In addition, guidance for the 2001–2002 charter standards sets out the need for health, housing and social services to agree a strategy for providing information about long-term care services. This should include:

- training front-line staff in basic information-giving, including where to refer enquirers for more detail;
- using the views of users and carers to improve the accessibility of information, including how documents are worded, as well as the places from which they should be available;
- 'one stop shops' providing comprehensive information about long-term health, housing and social care services, and welfare benefits.

The previous charter for general NHS services, *The Patient's Charter*, was replaced by the Department of Health in 2001 by *Your Guide to the NHS*. This sets out information about local NHS services.

From April 2003, each NHS Trust and care home (residential and nursing homes) must publish an annual prospectus, describing the range of services available (for the NHS, this is being called the 'Patients' Prospectus'). In homes, the prospectus must set out the aims of the care home; how the home meets the services it says are available (for example, how the needs of people with dementia are actually met); and the terms and conditions of the home. This is a requirement of regulation under the Care Standards Act 2000, as is the requirement that every resident has a written contract (or statement of terms and conditions) with the home for the care they receive.

Copies of care plans, drawn up following care assessment under the Single Assessment Process, should also be available to users.

Carers should have a copy of any care plan drawn up for services they are to receive; and should also have sight of any care they agree to provide in the plan of the cared-for person.

Information held on record by the NHS and social services is also available to users and patients. Plans to develop electronically recorded patient and user records are being put into place. It is intended that this will help with the sharing of an individual's details between agencies and will lead to Electronic Social Care Records (ESCR), and its equivalent within the NHS, Electronic Patient Records (HSC 1998/168, *Information for Health: an information strategy for the modern NHS*). These developments raise questions about how information is recorded and input into any system, as well as issues of controlling access to personal details. Under the Data Protection Act 1998, people can be charged for access to their medical records. In 2002, this was a maximum of £10 for records held on computer and £50 for paper records (and other media).

Concerns over the way patients' personal information can be used, expressed during a 1997 Review of patient information (the Caldicott Review), led to the development of what are known as 'Caldicott guardians'. A Caldicott guardian should be in place in each NHS and social services organisation (the latter from April 2002), and forms part of an overall framework to govern the sharing of confidential information about individuals within and between NHS and social services organisations (HSC 2002/003; LAC (2002)2, *Implementing the Caldicott Standard in Social Care*).

Raising concerns and making complaints

A number of the ways in which users, patients, their relatives and carers may seek to raise concerns and make complaints have been subject to recent change. Further change is also anticipated.

One recent change concerns the regulatory system in place since April 2002. Homes and care agencies regulated under the Care Standards Act 2000 must have, and publish details of, their own complaints systems. Once complainants have exhausted the homes' and agencies' systems, complaints about the quality of care can be taken to the National Care Standards Commission (NCSC). However, complaints about local authorities' purchasing decisions should be made through the local authority complaints system, which ultimately leads to the Local Government Ombudsman. People who are unhappy with how the Local Government Ombudsman or the NCSC have conducted a complaint, can take this matter to the Parliamentary Commissioner (sometimes called the Parliamentary Ombudsman).

This role of the NCSC in this respect should help ease a situation that has, in the past, caused some confusion. It has not always been clear how individuals should pursue complaints about the quality of services in independent sector homes that have been purchased on their behalf by their local authority. There have also been difficulties for privately-funded residents in homes, who have sometimes lacked access to an obvious complaints route. The NCSC arrangements, from April 2002, give people who are privately paying for their care (whether at home or in care homes), a clear and – importantly – a statutory route for the investigation of complaints about the standard of care they receive.

Local authority complaints procedures

Established under the NHS and Community Care Act 1990, there are three stages to the complaints procedures that must be offered by each local authority. Originally called 'Complaints and Compliments', it is the former that has been much more widely used, and for which the system is best known. Information about the complaints system must be available locally, and there should be a designated person (sometimes called the Complaints Officer) working in the local authority who deals with the system, and can provide information and suggestions about advocacy – a service where someone else helps put over the complaint, or point of view.

The first stage of the complaints procedure is informal. It is hoped most complaints can be resolved at this stage – especially where these concern misunderstandings, for example. This stage tends to involve the person (or their advocate) making the complaint, being in contact with the person they usually deal with at social services (or their manager), to see whether an acceptable solution can be found.

A second, formal, stage can be used if there is no acceptable solution, or if the person does not want to pursue this first stage. This involves submitting a written complaint to the Complaints Officer, who should investigate and reply with their findings within 28 days of receiving the complaint. Alternatively, they must write within 28 days to let the person know the complaint will be investigated and reported within three months.

If the matter is still unresolved from the complainant's point of view, they can ask for a review panel to consider the complaint. This request must be made within 28 days of receiving the Complaints Officer's findings. The review panel consists of at least three people, with the chair being independent from the local authority. The panel must re-examine the decision about the complaint within 28 days of receiving the request. This is likely to be carried out at a meeting, which the complainant should be invited to attend, and be given at least 10 days' notice of the date. The complainant can take someone with them to speak on their behalf, but not a lawyer who is acting in their professional capacity.

If the complainant is still unhappy at the end of this process, they can ask the Local Government Ombudsman to investigate, although there is no absolute right to insist on the Ombudsman doing so.

NHS complaints

Significant change is anticipated from 2003 in the context of complaints and concerns about NHS services. The introduction of Patients' Forums (see page 216) is one element of the Department of Health's plans to increase the involvement of patients and the public in the NHS's services (*Involving Patients and the Public in Healthcare*, DH, 2001). While Patients' Forums will work in each Trust to influence the day-to-day management of NHS services, three further bodies will support people making complaints.

PATIENT ADVICE AND LIAISON SERVICE (PALS)

This is the service that was referred to as the Patient Advocacy and Liaison Service in government documents published before November 2001 (including *The NHS Plan*). This body had to be in place in every NHS Trust and PCT from April 2002. In practice, in some areas recruitment of PALS staff continued throughout the summer of 2002. PALS staff are employed by Trusts, and are intended to provide immediate support for patients. This role involves providing information for patients, carers and others about local health services, and putting people in touch with relevant support groups. Importantly, PALS are intended to help people resolve problems and concerns at an early stage but, where this is not possible, to inform them of the NHS complaints procedure, and put them in touch with specialist independent advocacy services, if patients (or others on their behalf) choose to complain formally.

The Department of Health has published a resource pack to help the NHS develop this service (*Supporting the Implementation of Patient Advice and Liaison Services*, DH, 2002).

INDEPENDENT COMPLAINTS ADVOCACY SERVICES (ICAS)

This second body will be independent of the NHS and will complement any existing advocacy services (for example, mental health advocacy services). Such services provide support for patients, their families and others, in pursuing complaints formally. In some cases, this may involve someone from the advocacy service speaking on behalf of a patient, or their family, through part, or all, of the complaints process.

COMMISSION FOR PATIENT AND PUBLIC INVOLVEMENT IN HEALTH (CPPIH)

The third new body, the Commission for Patient and Public Involvement in Health (CPPIH), will monitor ICAS, PALS and Patients' Forums. In some government documents, CPPIH is also referred to as 'Voice', not to be confused with 'VOICES', an entirely separate voluntary sector 'umbrella' group. CPPIH is also expected to work nationally, setting standards and providing training for PALS, Patients' Forums and ICAS; and acting to co-ordinate and develop the involvement of both patients and the wider public in the NHS across each PCT area. It will also commission the ICAS service, and will be an independent statutory body.

It is expected that the CPPIH will come into being in January 2003. In the meantime, an overall Transition Advisory Board (TAB) has been established to oversee these changes. TAB is an independent body that advises the Department of Health.

These arrangements bring to an end Community Health Councils (CHCs), first formed during the 1974 health and local government reorganisation. The proposed abolition of CHCs has been the subject of much political debate in recent years. Various proposals have been put forward to ensure some CHC roles continue in the future. For example, where the NHS locally is proposing substantial changes to services, and the Overview and Scrutiny Committee (OSC) has concerns that consultation has been inadequate, OSC will take on the previous CHC role of referring the matter to the Secretary of State for Health.

At present, the final layer of complaints about the health services is the Health Service Ombudsman (also sometimes still called by the previous title of Health Service Commissioner). It is anticipated that further change to the Ombudsman's role will be announced during 2003. This may require further legislative change.

Until all these changes are in place, complaints about the NHS will continue to be handled under the existing scheme. This broadly mirrors the local authority system, in that there are informal, formal and review stages to the complaint. From April 2002, PALS in each NHS body have the role to try to resolve complaints informally. If this is unsuccessful, or where patients and anyone acting on their behalf choose to side-step this informal first stage, a formal complaint can be made.

The draft *Mental Health Bill* (Home Office, 2002) sets out proposals for a new independent, specialist, mental health advocacy service in England and Wales. This change would require new legislation.

Ways of involving users and carers

As set out at the beginning of this chapter, the overall theme of involving users and carers has continued to grow over the past decade. A number of good practice guidelines have been published, highlighting the ways in which users and carers can best be enabled to take part.

Consultation has a cost – in terms of both money and time spent on the consultation process, by staff, users, carers, families and friends. Sometimes there is confusion over the meaning and purpose of user involvement, or there may be a limited commitment of resources to make further participation possible. People may need transport, have interpretative or other communication needs, or – in the case of carers – may also need appropriate services for the person being cared for whilst the carer takes part in consultation. People taking part in consultation may also, as citizens, need access to the same resources as paid staff, such as photocopying, office space and other working facilities (Joseph Rowntree Foundation, 1995).

One of the ways the financial cost is beginning to be recognised is through the Government specifically allocating public funds for consultation, albeit in a relatively modest way. One example was the 2000–2001 Carers Grant allocated by the Department of Health. This specifically required each local authority to spend 5 per cent of its grant allocation on consultation with carers – in this case, to consult over the services to be provided by the grant.

Other concerns have focused on the demands made on users and carers, both in terms of their time and energy. This can cause particular problems, if only a handful of users and carers are actively involved in most of the consultation processes locally. There may also be other barriers to people taking part: older people may lack confidence, fear recrimination from services providers, or be faced with staff who do not believe they are able to comprehend issues or share responsibility for decisions taken during (or following) the consultation process (Gilchrist, 2000; Duncan, 2001). Good practice has been developed for councils and other organisations to identify and involve as many people as possible, including what are sometimes called 'hard to reach groups'. These are people who tend, for a variety of reasons, not to be represented or to take part in consultation exercises. This can include people who live alone and are isolated from mainstream and specialist services; people who live in care homes; people who are terminally ill; and people who find communicating difficult, for whatever reason.

There are ways to include these groups, however, as research on consulting and communicating with older people with dementia, carried out in 2001, shows:

- there are various ways of communicating with people with dementia, including staff changing activities or routines in response to people's non-verbal reactions;
- communication may not always happen at 'prescribed' times, but may occur as a brief verbal exchange whilst watching televisions, walking outdoors, or getting dressed;
- consultation needs to be developed on an individual basis. Staff should take each person's background and interests into account when finding the right starting point, and concentrate on helping people express themselves rather than sticking to particular techniques;
- people with dementia respond to different approaches in different ways and at different times. Indirect approaches can be effective – for example, showing the person a photograph of someone the person can identify, and asking what they think the person in the photograph might think or feel about a service;
- staff confidence in their skills and knowledge often needs to be increased. Staff need time during their daily work to talk to each other about their experiences of communication work.

(Allan, 2001)

Many of the local projects set up under the *Better Government for Older People* initiative (BGOP – see Chapter 2) involved some aspect of consulting with older people. Some projects chose to carry out consultation with older people who had little to do with health, housing or social care services. In these projects, small groups of older people acted as external readers, checking local authorities' pamphlets and leaflets before printing, to ensure the language used was as jargon-free as possible. It was felt this could be best achieved by involving older people with no prior knowledge of these services or support systems. Other areas developed the role of older people to monitor services, reporting on public transport, or seeking the views of other older people, including consultation through telephone discussion groups. Many of these different ways of involving older people locally are set out in the Cabinet Office's 1998 guide to consultation for the public sector.

It is important to be aware that consultation in itself may, from the viewpoint of users and carers, be irrelevant (Joseph Rowntree Foundation, 1995). Users and carers need to believe that consultation makes a difference. At the very least, older people who have taken part in consultation should receive some feedback. Where decisions are taken following consultation, older people should receive information about the outcome, and the reasons why certain decisions have been made. This may be particularly critical in circumstances where decisions follow more closely the views of other consulted parties or organisations, rather than those of users or carers; or where decisions have been taken to reduce services or change service arrangements. In the case of the latter, the involvement of users and carers may be more important, in order to ensure that the best use is made of the remaining resources from the point of view of users and carers (Joseph Rowntree Foundation, 1995). Creating carer-centred and user-centred services may need to involve greater power sharing along these lines, including users and carers taking increased co-responsibility for difficult decisions.

Epilogue –
Where next?

There are any numbers of ways in which to end this book; however, there are two important issues that should not be overlooked.

The first concerns the simple – yet complicated – matter of keeping up-to-date with change. As is apparent throughout this text, we are effectively in the middle of a 20-year period of change, from the community care reforms of the 1990s to the full implementation of *The NHS Plan* by 2010. A great deal has changed already, much is currently in a state of flux, and more change will come. While this book may have given you a solid grasp of the background to this explosion of change and some understanding of how we have arrived at where we are now, readers will need to ensure they find ways of keeping abreast of the changes. In today's climate, you cannot maintain a sufficiently accurate and detailed knowledge and understanding of health, housing and social care for older people, unless you continue to follow the relevant legal, social and policy developments.

Increasing amounts of central government proposals, guidance, legislation, initiatives and other material are now available on the Internet. There are some useful government websites, as well as those of organisations such as the Audit Commission, the Commission for Health Improvement, and the Social Care Institute for Excellence, which are all listed in the 'Useful Contacts' on page 249. Many of the major charities, housing associations, and other service providers and campaigning bodies will also have websites.

However, this may be of little use for people for whom website access is restricted, or simply not an option. For this group – as well as for those with Internet access – there are a range of journals that should help with keeping informed: for example, *Community Care* magazine; *The Health Service Journal*; *British Medical Journal*; *Inside Housing*; *Health Matters*; *Working with Older People*; and Age Concern England's monthly *Information Bulletin*. Broadsheet newspapers also often cover relevant stories in some detail. Staff working in appropriate organisations may find their employers provide newsletters, or other documents which summarise changes and developments in an easily digestible form. Many charities send regular written material to their members and supporters, as do trade unions and professional associations. Some specialist libraries, for example the one at the King's Fund, may also be able to help with enquiries. Academic libraries are often helpful too. Obtaining copies of *The NHS Plan*, and *The National Service Framework for Older People* would also be useful, especially in terms of keeping in mind the timetable for some of the future, planned change. Inevitably, however, the onus will lay upon you the reader to seek out new information yourself, in an active manner.

The second issue concerns identifying those groups of older people for whom treatment, care and support services are being provided and planned. What might their life experiences be? How different might these be from those of older people now? Or of older people in 1993, at the time of the community care reforms? A simple way to think this through is to work out when they might have been born.

One example can be drawn by considering which group of older people might be receiving the services as envisaged at the completion of the NHS Plan, in 2010. People aged 80 in 2010 will have been born in 1930; people aged 70, in 1940. This provides a neat symmetry – this book began with a brief consideration of London's older evacuees during the Second World War, and some of the 2010 service users will also have been evacuated, but as children.

It is those born in 1945 who will be 65 by the time the changes in *The NHS Plan* are completed in 2010 – the first of the two post-Second World War 'baby boomer' generations. This raises two immediate issues. At present, old age tends to be synonymous with retirement. However, it is possible that this may begin to change, and that the work-based distinction between 'working age' adults and 'older people' may need to be rethought. Secondly, we should not overlook, in our haste to assert how older generations are changing, the issue of who will be planning and providing these services from 2010 onwards. It is likely that the younger, 1960s, baby boomer generation will hold much of the responsibility – at least for some of the time – for its older, 1940s, counterpart. Anyone involved in older people's care might wish to ponder the implications of this change a little further.

Glossary

This glossary brings together some of the terms used in the book, but is not a complete list of all the words used in the text. There is also a list of abbreviations used in government guidance (as part of the Bibliography, see page 235) and an index.

Care homes: under the Care Standards Act 2000, which came into effect in April 2002, all types of homes are called 'care homes'. The Act distinguishes those offering nursing care, where necessary, as 'care homes with nursing'. Unless that distinction needs to be drawn, 'care homes' is used to mean both 'residential' and 'nursing' homes.

Care homes with nursing: under the Care Standards Act 2000, which came into effect in April 2002, all nursing homes are called **'care homes with nursing'**.

Care Trusts: these are NHS bodies that combine either a PCT or an NHS Trust with local authority services, using the powers to delegate functions set out in Section 31 of the Health Act 1999. The first Care Trusts were established in April 2002.

CPA: Care Programme Approach (CPA) describes the ways adult patients of consultant psychiatrists should be assessed and reassessed if they either live in the community or are being discharged from psychiatric hospital. The current Government is also using CPA to denote Comprehensive Performance Assessments for social services and health bodies.

Delayed discharge/delayed transfer of care: used (instead of 'bed-blocking') to describe NHS patients whose hospital care has been completed and who are ready to be discharged, but who cannot leave before arrangements are made for post-hospital care. Typically used to describe older people waiting for funding or services from social services departments.

Duties (and powers): in government guidance and legislation, attention is often drawn to the 'duties' and 'powers' of organisations (usually statutory or public bodies, such as the NHS or local authorities). A **'duty'** means that the organisation is bound by law to do something – such as provide a service, or assess someone's needs. A **'power'** means the law leaves it up to the organisation whether or not to do something. However, this does not mean that an organisation can always refuse to exercise that power – that is, always refuse to do the action that the power allows. Case law has established that organisations must act reasonably when deciding whether to exercise their powers. Refusing to do so at all times, and in all circumstances, would be considered unreasonable by the courts.

FACS: Social services departments in England and Wales must use FACS (Fair Access to Care Services) as the basis for their eligibility criteria for social care services.

Income Support: a means-tested benefit intended to cover general living costs – renamed the Minimum Income Guarantee (MIG, see below) for older people.

Independent sector: together, the private and voluntary sectors are often referred to as the 'independent sector'.

Intermediate care: a broad term describing a range of services intended to ensure people (especially older people) do not enter hospitals or residential homes unnecessarily, and to speed up their discharge from hospital to their own homes.

Local authorities: local councils (also sometimes called 'local government').

Local councils: see 'local authorities'.

Minimum Income Guarantee (MIG): a means-tested benefit for older people to cover general living costs, previously known as Supplementary Benefit or Income Support.

NHS: the range of bodies and organisations that make up the National Health Service – this includes Primary Care Groups and Trusts, as well as health authorities.

NSF: National Service Frameworks are intended to set national standards and define services for a specific service area (e.g. cancer) or care group (e.g. older people).

Nursing homes: care homes that provide nursing care (generally, because there is at least one registered nurse on duty at any one time). Under the Care Standards Act 2000, which came into effect in April 2002, nursing homes are called 'care homes with nursing'.

PCG/PCT: Primary Care Groups and Primary Care Trusts replaced GP Fundholding practices. PCTs have greater purchasing powers than PCGs, and have taken over some of the powers previously held by health authorities.

Powers: see Duties (and powers).

Private sector: consists of individual proprietors and organisations that own and run services for a profit – these include care homes for older people, clinics and hospitals, nursing agencies and domiciliary care services. Some of the larger private organisations (for example, some of those running care homes) have been 'floated' on the Stock Market.

Provider: broad term used to denote individuals or organisations that supply services received by different client groups, including older people

Purchaser: sometimes also called a commissioner, used to describe those parts of the statutory sector that contract with external organisations and individuals to provide services to patients or users on the purchaser's behalf

Residential homes: homes that do not provide nursing care. The Care Standards Act 2000, which came into effect in April 2002, defines all homes, including residential homes as 'care homes'.

SAP: the Single Assessment Process (SAP) sets out how older people (and their carers) should have their needs assessed by social services and the NHS.

Social services departments (also 'social services', and 'social services authorities'): part of local authorities (sometimes also called local councils), and are run by County Councils, Metropolitan and London Boroughs and, in some areas, Unitary Authorities. Responsible for providing and funding a wide range of what are often called social care services, for older people and other user groups.

Statutory sector: an umbrella term often used to denote both the NHS and local government, whose responsibilities are set out in law by the state.

Supplementary Benefit: the name by which Income Support was previously known.

Voluntary sector: a term covering a range of organisations set up on a 'not-for-profit' basis. This includes registered charities, as well as housing associations and many religious organisations.

Bibliography

Abbreviations used in government guidance

CI Chief Inspector

Cm Command papers. Technically, Green and White Papers, and sometimes special reports, are presented by Parliament under the command of HM The Queen – hence the name.

HC Health Circular (also used to denote House of Commons Papers, such as Select Committee Reports)

HSC Health Service Circular

HSG Health Service Guidelines

LAC Local Authority Circular

LASSL Local Authority Social Services Letter

s.1 This refers to the number of a particular section (sometimes also called a 'clause') in an Act of Parliament – for example, s.1 of the Health Act 1999 refers to section 1 of this Act.

Acheson, Sir D. (Chair) (1998). *Independent Inquiry into Inequalities in Health*. London: Stationery Office.

Age Concern England (1995). *Cascade or Care? Implications for the future of the transfer of assets* (Briefing Paper). London: Age Concern England.

Age Concern England (1998). *Equal Access to Cardiac Rehabilitation: age discrimination in the NHS: cardiac rehabilitation services* (Policy Paper). London: Age Concern England.

Age Concern England (1998a). *The Age of Individuals: factors in the receipt of social care. Submission to the Royal Commission's Inquiry into the future of long-term care funding for older people* (Briefing Paper 1298). London: Age Concern England.

Age Concern England/Association of Charity Officers (1996). *Preserved Rights to Income Support*. London: Age Concern England.

Allan, K. (2001). *Communication and Consultation: exploring ways for staff to involve people with dementia in developing services.* Bristol: Policy Press.

Askham, J., Nelson, H., Tinker, A., Hancock, R. (1999). *To Have and to Hold: the bond between older people and the homes they own.* York: York Publishing Services.

Audit Commission (1986). *Making a Reality of Community Care.* London: HMSO.

Audit Commission (1995). *United They Stand: co-ordinating care for elderly patients with hip fracture.* London: Audit Commission.

Audit Commission (1997). *The Coming of Age.* London: Audit Commission.

Audit Commission (2000). *Forget-me-not.* London: Audit Commission.

Audit Commission (2000). *Fully Equipped.* London: Audit Commission.

Audit Commission (2000). *Home Alone: the role of housing in community care.* London: Audit Commission.

Audit Commission (2000). *The Way to Go Home: rehabilitation and remedial services for older people.* London: Audit Commission.

Audit Commission (2001). *Day Surgery Report.* London: Audit Commission.

Audit Commission (2002). *Forget-me-not 2002.* London: Audit Commission.

Audit Commission (2002). *Fully Equipped 2002: assisting independence.* London: Audit Commission.

Better Government for Older People Steering Committee (2000). *All Our Futures.* Warwick: Better Government for Older People.

Black, Sir D. (Chair) (1988). *Inequalities in Health: report of a research working group chaired by Sir Douglas Black.* London: Department of Health and Social Security.

Bowling, A., Grundy, E. (1997). *Living Well in Old Age*. London: Age Concern Books.

British Geriatrics Society (1998). *Compendium of Standards and Guidelines for the Care of Older People*. London: British Geriatrics Society.

Burgner, T. (Chair) (1996). *Moving Forward: the regulation and inspection of social services*. London: Department of Health/Welsh Office.

Cabinet Office (1998). *An Introductory Guide: how to consult your users*. London: Stationery Office.

Cabinet Office (1998). *Reforming the Mental Health Act* (White Paper Cm 4480). London: Stationery Office.

Cabinet Office (1999). *Modernising Government* (White Paper CM 4310). London: Stationery Office.

Cabinet Office (2002). *The Government's Response to the House of Commons Health Committee's First Report on the role of the private sector in the NHS* (Cm 5567). London: Stationery Office.

Centre for Policy on Ageing (1984). *Home Life: A code of good practice*. London: Centre for Policy on Ageing.

Centre for Policy on Ageing (1996). *A Better Home Life: A code of good practice for residential and nursing home care*. London: Centre for Policy on Ageing.

Centre for Policy on Ageing (1999). *Fit for the Future? National Required Standards for residential and nursing homes for older people*. London: Centre for Policy on Ageing.

Clark, H., Dyer, S., Horwood, J. (1998). *'That Bit of Help': The high value of low-level preventative services for older people*. Bristol/York: Policy Press/Joseph Rowntree Foundation.

Department of Health (1989). *Caring for People: community care in the next decade and beyond* (White Paper Cm 849). London: HMSO.

Department of Health (1991). *Care Management and Assessment. Summary of Practice Guidance.* London: HMSO.

Department of Health (1993). *Approvals and Directions for Arrangements from 1 April 1993 made under schedule 8 to the National Health Service Act 1977 and sections 21 and 29 of the National Assistance Act 1948* (LAC (93) 10). London, DH.

Department of Health (1994). *The Hospital Discharge Workbook.* London: HMSO.

Department of Health (1995). *NHS Responsibilities for Meeting Continuing Health Care Needs* (HSG (95)8; LAC(95)5). London: DH.

Department of Health (1996). *A New Partnership for Care in Old Age.* London: HMSO.

Department of Health (1997). *Achievement and Challenge.* London: Stationery Office.

Department of Health (1997). (Press release, 4 December) *Royal Commission into Long-term Care Announced by Frank Dobson.* London: DH.

Department of Health (1997). *Social Services – Achievement and Challenge* (White Paper). London: Stationery Office.

Department of Health (1997). *The Caldicott Committee Report on the Review of Patient-identifiable Information.* London: DH.

Department of Health (1997). *The New NHS: modern, dependable* (White Paper Cm 3807). London: Stationery Office.

Department of Health (1998). *A First Class Service – consultation document* (HSC 1998/113). London: DH.

Department of Health (1998). *Information for Health: an information strategy for the Modern NHS 1998–2005* (HSC 1998/168). London: DH.

Department of Health (1998). *Modernising Social Services* (White Paper Cm 4169). London: Stationery Office.

Department of Health (1998). *Royal Commission on the Funding of Long-Term Care for the Elderly: terms of reference.* London: DH.

Department of Health (1998). *The transfer of frail older patients to other long stay settings* (HSC 1998/048). London: DH.

Department of Health (1999). *Caring for Carers: a national strategy for carers.* London: DH.

Department of Health (1999). *Effective Care Co-ordination in Mental Health Services.* London: Stationery Office.

Department of Health (1999). *Ex parte Coughlan: follow up action Annex A* (LAC (1999)30). London: DH.

Department of Health (1999). *Implementing Section 21 of the Disability Discrimination Act 1995 across the NHS* (HSC 1999/156). London: DH.

Department of Health (1999). *National Priorities Guidance 2000/01–2002/03* (HSC 1999/242, LAC (99) 39). London: DH.

Department of Health (1999). *Royal Commission on Long-term Care: with respect to old age* (Cm 4192-I). London: Stationery Office.

Department of Health (1999). *Saving Lives: Our Healthier Nation* (White Paper Cm 4386). London: Stationery Office.

Department of Health (2000). *A Quality Strategy for Social Care.* London: Stationery Office.

Department of Health (2000). *Building a Safer NHS for Patients.* London: Stationery Office.

Department of Health (2000). *Implementation of Health Act Partnership Arrangements* (HSC 2000/10, LAC (2000)09). London: DH.

Department of Health (2000). *Intermediate Care* (HS 2000/001; LAC 2000/001). London: DH.

Department of Health (2000). *Resuscitation Policy* (HSC 2000/028). London: DH.

Department of Health (2000). *Shaping the Future NHS: long-term planning for hospitals and related services. Consultation document on the findings of the National Beds Inquiry* (HS 2000/004). London: DH.

Department of Health (2000). *The NHS Plan* (Cm 4818–1). London: Stationery Office.

Department of Health (2000). *The NHS Plan: The Government's response to the Royal Commission on Long Term Care* (Cm 4818–11). London: Stationery Office.

Department of Health (2001). *A Guide to Contracting for Intermediate Care Services.* London: DH.

Department of Health (2001). *Better Care, Higher Standards – guidance for 2001/2002* (HSC 2001/06; LAC (2001)06). London: DH.

Department of Health (2001). *Care Homes for Older People, National Minimum Standards.* London: Stationery Office.

Department of Health (2001). *Charging for Residential Accommodation Guide: CRAG changes no. 15* (LAC (2001) 25). London: DH.

Department of Health (2001). *Charging for Residential Accommodation Guide: CRAG changes no. 16* (LAC (2001) 29). London: DH.

Department of Health (2001). *Community Care Statistics 2001: home care services, England.* London: DH.

Department of Health (2001). *Community Equipment Services* (HSC 2001/008, LAC(2001)13). London: DH.

Department of Health (2001). *Continuing Care: NHS and local councils' responsibilities* (HSC 2001/015, LAC (2001) 18). London: DH.

Department of Health (2001). *Extending Choice for Patients: a discussion document.* London: DH.

Department of Health (2001). *Fairer charging policies for home care and other non-residential social services* (LAC (2001) 32). London: DH.

Department of Health (2001). *Free Nursing Care: guide to managers on GP services for residents.* London: DH.

Department of Health (2001). *Good Practice in Consent: achieving the NHS Plan commitment to patient-centred consent practice* (HSC 2001/023). London: DH.

Department of Health (2001). *Guidance on Free Nursing Care in Nursing Homes* (HSC 2001/17, LAC (2001)26) London: DH.

Department of Health (2001). *Guidance on the Single Assessment Process for Older People* (HSC 2002/001, LAC (2002) 01). London: DH.

Department of Health (2001). *Health and Social Care Planning, 2001–2002* (CI (2001)5). London: DH.

Department of Health (2001). *Involving Patients and the Public in Healthcare.* London: Stationery Office.

Department of Health (2001). *National Service Framework for Older People.* London: Stationery Office.

Department of Health (2001). *Regulation of Domiciliary Care* (LASSL (2001)10). London: DH.

Department of Health (2001). *Seeking Consent: working with older people.* London: DH.

Department of Health (2001). *The Essence of Care. Patient-focused benchmarking for health Care practitioners.* London: DH.

Department of Health (2001). *The Expert Patient – a new approach to chronic disease management for the 21st century.* London: DH.

Department of Health (2001). *Valuing People: a new strategy for learning disability for the 21st century* (White Paper Cm 5086). London: Stationery Office.

Department of Health (2001). *Your guide to the NHS: the Patient's Charter.* London: Stationery Office.

Department of Health (2002). *Charging for Residential Accommodation Guide: CRAG changes no. 17* (LAC (2002) 11). London: DH.

Department of Health (2002). *Community Care (Direct Payments) Act 1996: draft policy and guidance consultation paper*. London: Stationery Office.

Department of Health (2002). *Community Care Plans (Directions)*. London: Stationery Office.

Department of Health (2002). *Day Surgery – Operational Guide*. London: Department of Health.

Department of Health (2002). *Delivering the NHS Plan* (White Paper Cm 5503). London: Stationery Office.

Department of Health (2002). (Press release, 23 July) *Expanded Services and Increased Choices for Older People*. London: DH.

Department of Health (2002). *Fair Access to Care Services: guidance on eligibility criteria for adult social care* (LAC (2002) 13). London: DH.

Department of Health (2002). *Growing Capacity: a new role for external healthcare providers in England*. London: DH.

Department of Health (2002). *Guidance to Councils with Social Services Responsibilities on the Abolition of Preserved Rights* (LAC (2002) 7). London: DH.

Department of Health (2002). *Implementing Reimbursement around Discharge from Hospital* (Consultation Paper). London: Stationery Office.

Department of Health (2002). *Implementing the Caldicott Standard in Social Care* (HSC 2002/003, LAC (2002) 02). London: DH.

Department of Health (2002). *Letter from Jacqui Smith MP to Anne Parker, Chair of the National Care Standards Commission*. London: DH.

Department of Health (2002). *Mental Health Bill: a consultation document*. London: DH.

Department of Health (2002). *Supporting the Implementation of Patient Advice and Liaison Services – a resource pack*. London: DH.

Department of Health (2002). *The Single Assessment Process: assessment tools and scales*. London: DH.

Department of Health (2002). *Treating More Patients and Extending Choice: draft guidance*. London: DH.

Department of Health/Home Office (2000). *No Secrets: guidance on developing and implementing multi-agency policies and procedures to protect vulnerable adults from abuse*. London: Stationery Office.

Department of Health and Social Security (1968). *Report of the Committee on Local Authority and Allied Personal Social Services* (the Seebohm Report). London: DHSS.

Department of Social Security (1998). *Supporting People – Inter Departmental Review of Funding for Supported Accommodation*. London: DSS.

Department of the Environment, Transport and the Regions (1998). *Walking in Great Britain*. London: HMSO.

Department of the Environment, Transport and the Regions (2001). *Supporting People: policy into practice*. London: Stationery Office.

Department of the Environment, Transport and the Regions (2002). *Quality and Choice: a decent home for all*. (The Housing Green Paper). London: Stationery Office.

Department of the Environment, Transport and the Regions/Department of Health (2000). *Better Care, Higher Standards: a charter for long-term care*. London: DETR/DH.

Department of Trade and Industry (1999). *Time Off for Dependants: a short guide*. London: DTI.

Department of Transport, Local Government and the Regions (2001). *Best Value in Housing Care and Support: guidance and good practice*. London: DTLR.

Department of Transport, Local Government and the Regions (2001). *Strong Local Leadership, Quality Public Services* (White Paper Cm 5327). London: Stationery Office.

Department of Transport, Local Government and the Regions (2002). *Your Region, Your Choice* (Cm 5511). London: Stationery Office.

Department of Transport, Local Government and the Regions/ Department of Health (2001). *Quality and Choice for Older People's Housing: a strategic framework*. London: Stationery Office.

Duncan, L. (2000). *Voice and Choice Training Pack*. London: Age Concern England.

Easterbrook, L. (2001). *'Friday is Pay Day': a study of the personal expenses allowance in residential and nursing homes*. London: Help the Aged.

Gilchrist, C. (2000). *Speaking Out: older people and complaints against the NHS*. London: Age Concern England.

Glendinning, C., Jacobs, S., Alborz, A., Hann, M. (2002). A survey of access to medical services in nursing and residential homes in England. *British Journal of General Practice*, 52 (480).

Griffiths, Sir R. (Chair) (1988). *Community Care – Agenda for Action. A report to the Secretary of State for Social Services*. London: HMSO.

Health Advisory Service 2000 (1998). *Not Because They are Old*. London: HAS 2000.

Health Advisory Service (1999). *Standards for Health and Social Care of Older People*. London: HAS.

Health Select Committee (1996). *Long-term Care: future provision and funding: third report* (HC59-1). London: House of Commons.

Health Select Committee (1998). *First Report on the Relationship between Health and Social Services* (HC 74–1) London: Stationery Office.

Health Select Committee (2002). *Delayed Discharges*. Third Report of Session 2001–2002 (HC 617–1) London: Stationery Office.

Health Select Committee (2002). *First Report on the Role of the Private Sector in the NHS* (HC 308–1) London: Stationery Office.

Health Service Commissioner (1994). *Second Report for Session 1993–94: failure to provide long-term NHS care for a brain-damaged patient* (HC 197). London: HMSO.

Help the Aged (2002). *Age Discrimination in Public Policy*. London: Help the Aged.

HM Treasury (2002). *Opportunity and Security for All: the 2002 Spending Review White Paper*. London: Stationery Office.

Home Office (1998). *Getting it Right Together*. London: Stationery Office.

Joseph Rowntree Foundation (1995). *From Margin to Mainstream: developing user- and carer-centred community care*. York: Joseph Rowntree Foundation.

Joseph Rowntree Foundation (1997). *Inquiry into Meeting the Costs of Continuing Care*. York: York Publishing Services.

Kennedy, Sir I. (Chair) (2001). *Learning from Bristol: the report of the public inquiry into children's heart surgery at the Bristol Royal Infirmary* (Cm 5207). London: Stationery Office.

Kelly, S., Bunting, J. (1998). Trends in suicide in England and Wales 1982–1996. *Population Trends* 92. London: Office of National Statistics.

Killick, J., Allan, K. (2001). *Communication and the Care of People with Dementia*. Buckingham: Open University Press.

King's Fund (2000). *Rehabilitation and Intermediate Care for Older People* (Briefing Paper No 6). London: King's Fund.

Laing and Buisson. *Care of the Elderly Market Survey*. London: Laing and Buisson: 11 ed, 1998; 14 ed, 2001; 15 ed, 2002.

Laing, W. (1998). *A Fair Price for Care? Disparities between market rates and state funding of residential care*. York: York Publishing Service.

Levenson, R. (1998). *Drugs and Dementia: a guide to good practice in the use of neuroleptic drugs in care homes for older people*. London: Age Concern England.

Lewis, H., Fletcher, P., Hardy, B., Milne, A., Waddington, E. (1999). Promoting *Well-being: developing a preventative approach with older people*. Oxford: Anchor Trust.

Lord Chancellor's Office (2002). *Mental Health Bill* (Draft). London: Stationery Office.

Lowdell, C., Evandrou, M., Bardsley, M., Morgan, D., Soljak, M. (2000). *Health of Ethnic Minority Elders in London*. London: The Health of Londoners Project.

McIntosh, B., Whittaker, A. (2000). *Unlocking the Future: developing new lifestyles with people who have complex disabilities*. London: King's Fund.

Means, R., Smith, R. (1998). *From Poor Law to Community Care*. Bristol: Policy Press.

National Association of Health Authorities and Trusts (1985). *Registration and Inspection of Nursing Homes. a handbook for health authorities*. Birmingham: NAHAT.

National Council for Voluntary Organisations (Deakin Commission) (1996). *Meeting the Challenge of Change: voluntary action into the 21st century. Report of the Commission on the Future of the Voluntary Sector*. London: NCVO.

Office for Fair Trading (1998). *Choosing a Care Home*. London: Office for Fair Trading.

Office for National Statistics (2001). *Social Trends* (2001). London: Stationery Office.

Office for National Statistics (2002). *Population Trends* 108. London: Stationery Office.

Office of the Deputy Prime Minister (2002). *Best Value in Housing Framework*. London: The Stationery Office.

Phillips, J., Bernard, M., Chittenden, M. (2002). *Juggling Work and Care: the experiences of working carers of older adults*. Bristol: Policy Press.

Public Accounts Select Committee (2002). *NHS Direct in England* (Report). London: Stationery Office.

Rowlands, O. (1998). *Informal Carers: results of an independent study carried out on behalf of the Department of Health as part of the 1995 General Household Survey.* London: Stationery Office.

Salisbury, C., Chalder, M., Manku-Scott, T., Pope, C., Moore, L. (2002). What is the role of walk-in centres in the NHS? *British Medical Journal*, 324: 399–402.

Scally, G., Donaldson, L. J. (1998). Clinical governance and the drive for quality improvement in the new NHS in England. *British Medical Journal*, (4 July): 61–65.

Social Services Inspectorate (1989). *Homes Are For Living In.* London: Department of Health Social Services Inspectorate.

Social Services Inspectorate (1998). *They Look After Their Own, Don't They?* London: Department of Health Social Services Inspectorate.

Social Services Inspectorate (2002). *From Lip Service to Real Service – audit tool.* London: Department of Health.

Statutory Instrument 2000, No. 617 (2000). *NHS Bodies and Local Authorities Partnership Arrangements Regulations 2000.* London: Stationery Office.

Statutory Instrument (2001). *Private and Voluntary Health Care (England) Regulations 2001.* London: Stationery Office.

Statutory Instrument (2001). *The National Care Standards Commission (Fees and Frequency of Inspections) Regulations 2001.* London: Stationery Office.

Statutory Instrument 2002, No. 305 (2002). *The Local Government (Best Value) Performance Plans and Reviews Amendment and Specified Dates Order 2002.* London: Stationery Office.

The Guardian (2002). Advertisement for Chair of CHAI. 24 July.

Townsend, P. (1962). *The Last Refuge*. London: Routledge and Kegan Paul.

Wagner, G. (Chair) (1988). *Residential Care: A positive choice*. London: HMSO.

Wanless, D. (2001). *Securing our Future Health: taking a long-term view. Interim report*. London: HM Treasury.

Wanless, D. (2002). *Securing our Future Health: taking a long-term view. Final report*. London: HM Treasury.

Wertheimer, A. (ed) (1996). *Changing Days*. London: King's Fund.

Useful contacts

Age Concern England
1268 London Road
London SW16 4ER
Tel: 020 8765 7200
www.ageconcern.org.uk

Alzheimer's Society
Gordon House
10 Greencoat Place
London SW1P 1PH
Tel: 020 7306 0606

Audit Commission
1 Vincent Square
London SW1P 2PN
Tel: 020 7828 1212
www.audit-commission.gov.uk

Carers UK (formerly the Carers' National Association)
20–25 Glasshouse Yard
London EC1A 4JT
Tel: 020 7490 8818
Helpline 0808 808 7777
www.carersonline.org.uk

Carers Scotland
91 Mitchell Street
Glasgow G1 3LN
Tel: 0141 221 9141

Helpline 0808 808 7777

Coalition on Charging
c/o Disability Alliance
Universal House
88–94 Wentworth Street
London E1 7SA
Tel: 020 7247 8776
www.mencap.org.uk/coc

Commission for Health Improvement
First Floor
Finsbury Tower
103–105 Bunhill Row
London EC1Y 8TG
Tel: 020 7448 9200

Counsel and Care
Twyman House
16 Bonny Street
London NW1 9PG
Tel: 020 7241 8555
www.counselandcare.org.uk

Department of Health
Richmond House
79 Whitehall
London SW1A 2NS
Tel: 020 7210 4850

www.doh.gov.uk
(www.nhs.gov.uk – the site for
NHS information)

**Department for Work and
Pensions**
Olympic House
Olympic Way
Wembley
Middlesex HA9 0DL
Tel: 020 8795 8400
Helpline 0800 88 22 00
www.dwp.gov.uk

Disability Rights Commission
Freepost
MID 02164
Stratford-upon-Avon
CV37 9HY
Helpline 08457 622 633
www.drc-gb.org

**Elderly Accommodation
Counsel (EAC)**
Third Floor
89 Albert Embankment
London SE1 7PT
Tel: 020 7820 1343
www.housingcare.org.uk

**foundations (the National
Co-ordinating Body for Home
Improvement Agencies)**
Bleaklow House
Howard Town Mill
Glossop
Derbyshire SK13 8HT
Tel: 01457 891 909
www.foundations.uk.com

Help the Aged
207–221 Pentonville Road
London N1 9UZ
Tel: 020 7278 1114
Seniorline (free welfare advice)
0808 800 6565
www.helptheaged.org.uk

**Independent Healthcare
Association**
Westminster Tower
3 Albert Embankment
London SE1 7SP
Tel: 020 7793 4620
www.iha.org.uk

Joseph Rowntree Foundation
The Homestead
40 Water End
York YO3 6WP
Tel: 01904 629241
www.jrf.org.uk

King's Fund
11–13 Cavendish Square
London W1NG 0AN
Tel: 020 7307 2400
www.kingsfund.org.uk

NHS Direct
Tel: 0845 4647
www.nhsdirect.nhs.uk

**National Centre for
Independent Living**
250 Kennington Lane
London SE11 5RD
Tel: 020 7587 1663
www.ncil.org.uk

National Housing Federation
175 Gray's Inn Road
London WC1X 8UP
Tel: 020 7278 6571
www.housing.org.uk

National Institute for Clinical Excellence (NICE)
11 The Strand
London WC2N 5HR
Tel: 020 7766 9191
www.nice.org.uk

Office of the Deputy Prime Minister
26 Whitehall
London SW1A 2WH
Tel: 020 7944 4400
www.odpm.gov.uk

Patients' Association
PO Box 935
Harrow
Middlesex
HA1 3YJ
Tel: 020 8423 9111
Helpline 0845 608 4455
www.patients-association.com

RADAR
12 City Forum
250 City Road
London EC1V 8AF
Tel: 020 7250 3222
www.radar.org.uk

Social Care Institute for Excellence (SCIE)
First Floor
Goldings House
2 Hay's Lane
London SE1 2HB
Tel: 020 7089 6840
www.scie.org.uk

The Stationery Office
51 Nine Elms Lane
London SW8 5DR
Tel: 020 7873 8787
www.tso.co.uk

About Age Concern

Moving on from Community Care is one of a wide range of publications produced by Age Concern England, the National Council on Ageing. Age Concern works on behalf of all older people and believes later life should be fulfilling and enjoyable. For too many this is impossible. As the leading charitable movement in the UK concerned with ageing and older people, Age Concern finds effective ways to change that situation.

Where possible, we enable older people to solve problems themselves, providing as much or as little support as they need. A network of local Age Concerns, supported by many thousands of volunteers, provides community-based services such as lunch clubs, day centres and home visiting.

Nationally, we take a lead role in campaigning, parliamentary work, policy analysis, research, specialist information and advice provision, and publishing. Innovative programmes promote healthier lifestyles and provide older people with opportunities to give the experience of a lifetime back to their communities.

Age Concern is dependent on donations, covenants and legacies.

Age Concern England
1268 London Road
London SW16 4ER
Tel: 020 8765 7200
Fax: 020 8765 7211

Age Concern Scotland
113 Rose Street
Edinburgh EH2 3DT
Tel: 0131 220 3345
Fax: 0131 220 2779

Age Concern Cymru
4th Floor
1 Cathedral Road
Cardiff CF1 9SD
Tel: 029 2037 1566
Fax: 029 2039 9562

Age Concern Northern Ireland
3 Lower Crescent
Belfast BT7 1NR
Tel: 028 9024 5729
Fax: 028 9023 5497

Publications from Age Concern Books

An Introductory Guide to Community Care
Alan Goodenough

This book is a useful starting point for new or inexperienced carers, particularly paid carers, who are unsure of what services are available or who they can turn to for support or advice. It guides them through the basics of care plans, relevant legislation and regulations, useful contacts, and the roles of other professionals they will encounter. The book encourages the carer to feel part of a team, offers self-assessment opportunities, and encourages them to seek further training opportunities.

£6.99   0-86242-340-6

Culture, Religion and Patient Care in a Multi-ethnic Society: A handbook for professionals
Alix Henley and Judith Schott

A multi-disciplinary handbook which aims to guide health professionals towards identifying and meeting the needs of different religious and cultural groups. It promotes the need for a framework of knowledge and ideas as well as increased self-awareness. It will enable everyone involved in patient care to:

- explore aspects of patient care that may be affected by culture and religion;
- develop skills and awareness needed to communicate across cultural and language barriers;
- examine their own personal attitudes and working practices;
- fully understand the concepts of culture and 'race' and inequalities in health and healthcare provision;
- have a better understanding of the influence of culture and religion on everyday life, major events, and people's needs and reactions.

£19.99   0-86242-231-0

Residents' Money: A guide to good practice in care homes

Residents' Money is a guide for people who work in residential and nursing homes who may be involved in handling residents' money or in helping them to manage their financial affairs. It includes detailed advice for care managers and staff on how to design and put into practice policies that reflect the very best in good practice.

£7.99   0-86242-205-1

Dementia Care: A handbook for residential and day care
2nd edition
Alan Chapman, Donna Gilmour and Iain McIntosh

This revised edition of a successful book stresses a more holistic approach to the support of people with dementia: in essence, dementia, as an illness, does not rob the person of the influence of their past life. Topics include:

- the individual and their previous lifestyle
- staff teamwork
- approaches to the person
- issues for day care
- what is dementia and what is not?
- health matters
- behaviour as a response to the living environment
- behaviour as a response to the daily routine and staff actions
- dilemmas and challenges
- feelings of loss, pain and palliative care

A comprehensive, practical guide to the delivery of care to people with dementia, this book has been designed for use by those working in both residential and day care settings, providing sound advice on good practice and offering reassurance and support.

£14.99   0-86242-313-9

If you would like to order any of these titles, please write to the address below, enclosing a cheque or money order for the appropriate amount (plus £1.95 p&p) made payable to Age Concern England. Credit card orders may be made on 0870 44 22 044 (individuals) or 0870 44 22 120 (Age Concern and organisations).

Age Concern Books,
PO Box 232, Newton Abbot, Devon TQ12 4XQ

Factsheets subscription/Information Line

Age Concern produces 46 comprehensive factsheets designed to answer many of the questions older people (or those advising them) may have. These include money and benefits, health, community care, leisure and education, and housing. For up to five free factsheets, telephone: 0800 00 99 66 (7am–7pm, seven days a week, every day of the year). Alternatively you may prefer to write to Age Concern, FREEPOST (SWB 30375), ASHBURTON, Devon TQ13 7ZZ.

For professionals working with older people, the factsheets are available on an annual subscription service, which includes updates throughout the year. For further details and costs of the subscription, please write to Age Concern at the above Freepost address.

Index